Philosophy of SOCIAL WORK

Philosophy of SOCIAL WORK

K. Narendra Mohan

CENTRUM PRESS
NEW DELHI-110002 (INDIA)

CENTRUM PRESS
H.O.: 4360/4, Ansari Road, Daryaganj,
New Delhi-110002 (India)
Tel: 23278000, 23261597, 23255577, 23286875
B.O.: No. 1015, Ist Main Road, BSK IIIrd Stage,
IIIrd Phase, IIIrd Block, Bengaluru-560085 (INDIA)
Tel: 080-41723429
Email: centrumpress@gmail.com
Visit us at: www.centrumpress.com

Philosophy of Social Work

First Edition, 2012

ISBN 978-93-81293-69-0

PRINTED IN INDIA

Printed at Tarun Offset, Delhi

Contents

Preface (*vii*)

1. Basic Principles in Social Work 1
2. Evaluation and Ethics of Social Work 45
3. Philosophy and Ideology of Social Work 77
4. Origin and Development of Social Work in India 105
5. Social Reform Movements 135
6. Social Work Education in India 203
7. Fields of Social Work 249

Bibliography 291

Index 293

Preface

The basic principles of social work, and the ethics of a social worker. It gives a clear view of how a social worker is expected to carry out his duties. It also specifies the demands made by social work, and provides important reminders for the social worker.

Social work is not about providing solutions to problems, but it provides an arena in which clients can review their concerns, and sec how they can manage them best and live an effective life. Social work links clients with services, resources and opportunities, which might provide them with the help they need. This contributes to problem-solving for clients. It is important to recognize in social work the fact that it is an adaptable service, and one which is more responsive and accountable to a particular locality and its people. Social work is concerned with the provision of welfare services, when people's capacity for responding to the demands of life is strained, when capacity growth seems unattainable, and when important decisions elude resolution. Social work should assist clients to deal with life, engage in growth-producing activities, and make effective decisions. Naturally when people have a problem, they look for help. Usually, they think they have no capacity to solve their problem unless someone helps them to do so. And even when help comes, they expect the helper to produce the magic which will solve their problems. Social workers must make the role of their work clear when they are approached by a client. Their role is to assist the client to know why they need help and where they can get it.

Social Work is a discipline involving the application of social theory and research methods to study and improve the lives of people, groups, and societies. It incorporates and uses other social sciences as a means to improve the human condition and positively change society's response to chronic problems. It is a profession committed to the pursuit of social justice, to the enhancement of the quality of life, and to the development of the full potential of each individual, group and community in the society. It seeks to simultaneously address and resolve social issues at every level of society and economic status, but especially among the poor and sick. Social workers are concerned with social problems, their causes, their solutions and their human impacts. They work with individuals, families, groups. In the developed countries, only professionally qualified persons with social work education can intervene with the psycho-social problems of individuals and practitioners must obtain a license or be professionally registered. Unfortunately in India, in spite of the fact that the number of social work schools, institutes and departments of colleges and universities have been growing slowly but steadily during the initial six decades and growing rapidly over the last one decade or so, the quality of professional social work education and training and professional standards of practice have been declining and as a result, there is a serious damage to the 'professional status and image' of social work. With innumerable departments of social work mushrooming each day, professional social work education is being commercialized and issues of quality, credibility and ethical standards are compromised by the different stakeholders.

This concise and legible book will provide key text to all students of Social Work.

—*Editor*

1

Basic Principles of Social Work

INTRODUCTION

Social work is a profession committed to the pursuit of social justice, to quality of life, and to the development of the full potential of each individual, group and community in a society. Social workers draw on the social sciences and on clinical expertise to solve social problems. They may work in research, practice, or both. Practitioners will usually possess a degree or registered license in the discipline, dependent on national law. Social work research is often focused in areas such as individual and family therapy, social policy, public administration and development. Social workers are organized into local, national, and international professional bodies to further the aims of the profession.

Social work is a professional and academic discipline committed to the pursuit of social welfare, social change and social justice. The field works towards research and practice to improve the quality of life and to the development of the potential of each individual, group and community of a society. Social workers perform interventions through research, policy, community organizing, direct practice and teaching. Research is often focused on areas such as human development, social policy, public administration, program evaluation and international and community development. Social workers are organized into local, national, continental and international professional bodies. Social work, an interdisciplinary field, includes theories from economics, education, sociology, medicine, philosophy, politics, psychology, and as well as anti-oppressive and anti-racist discourse. Many times social workers handle clients who have been abused or molested many times and/or use drugs habitually.

History of Social Work

Social work has its roots in the struggle of society to deal with poverty and the resultant problems. Therefore, social work is intricately linked with the idea of charity work; but must be understood in broader terms. The concept of charity goes back to ancient times, and the practice of providing for the poor has roots in many major ancient civilizations and world religions.

Contemporary professional development

The International Federation of Social Workers states, of social work today, that, "social work bases its methodology on a systematic body of evidence-based knowledge derived from research and practice evaluation, including local and indigenous knowledge specific to its context. It recognizes the complexity of interactions between human beings and their environment, and the capacity of people both to be affected by and to alter the multiple influences upon them including bio-psychosocial factors. The social work profession draws on theories of human development, social theory and social systems to analyse complex situations and to facilitate individual, organizational, social and cultural changes."

A hopeful development for bridging this gap is the compilation of collections of "best practices" which attempt to distill research findings and the experience of respected social work practitioners, educators and researchers into effective interventions. Another important contemporary development in the profession is overcoming suspicion of technology and taking advantage of the potential of information technology.

Qualifications

Professional social workers are generally considered those who hold a degree in social work. Often these practitioners must also obtain a license or be professionally registered. The education of social workers begins with a Bachelor's degree

(BA, BSc, BSSW, BSW, etc.) or diploma in Social Work. Some countries offer Postgraduate degrees in Social Work like Master's (such as MSW, MA, MSc, MRes, MPhil etc.) or PhD (doctoral studies). More and more graduates of social work continue to post-doctoral studies. It has been argued that social work education is supposed to be a lifelong process.

In a number of countries and jurisdictions, registration or licensure of people working as social workers is required and there are mandated qualifications. In other places, a professional association sets academic and experiential requirements for admission to membership. The success of these professional bodies' efforts is demonstrated in the fact that these same requirements are recognized by employers as necessary for employment.

Professional Associations

There are a number of associations for social workers, which exist to provide ethical guidance and other forms of support for their members and social work in general. These associations/organizations are distinguished in international, continental or semi-continental, national and regional. The main international ones are the International Federation of Social Workers (IFSW) and International Association of Schools of Social Work (IASSW).

ROLE OF THE PROFESSIONAL

The main tasks of professional social workers can include a variety of services such as case management (linking users/ clients with agencies and programs that will meet their psychosocial needs - mainly common in US and UK), counseling (psychotherapy), human services management, social welfare policy analysis, policy and practice development, community organizing, international, social and community development, advocacy, teaching (in schools of social work), and social and political research.

PRINCIPLES OF SOCIAL WORK

Ethical awareness is a necessary part of the professional practice of any social worker. His or her ability to act ethically is an essential aspect of the quality of the service offered to clients. The purpose of IFSW's work on ethics is to promote ethical debate and reflection in the member associations and among the providers of social work in member countries.

The basis for the further development of IFSW:s work on ethics is to be found in "Ethics of Social Work-Principles and Standards" which consists of two documents, International Declaration of Ethical Principles of Social Work, and International Ethical Standards for Social Workers. These documents present the basic ethical principles of the social work profession, recommend procedure when the work presents ethical dilemmas, and deal with the profession's and the individual social worker's relation to clients, colleagues, and others in the field. The documents are components in a continuing process of use, review and revision.

The basic principles of social work, and the ethics of a social worker. It gives a clear view of how a social worker is expected to carry out his duties. It also specifies the demands made by social work, and provides important reminders for the social worker.

GUIDELINES FOR SOCIAL WORKERS

These are guidelines on how social workers operate.

Establishment of a counselling relationship. The relationship as a process of giving the client an opportunity to grow, develop, and ultimately to understand and discover himself, and make appropriate choices.

Acceptance: Recognize the worth of the individual regardless of his/her circumstances, status, religion, race, politics, behaviour, and wish to foster human dignity and self-respect.

Self-determination: Encourage self-help as a means of growing in self-confidence, and the ability to take on more responsibility for one's own affairs.

Freedom to choose: The client must be able to make appropriate choices, and consider how his/her choice may affect others. Be able to respect and care for clients as individuals without ridicule.

Confidentiality: The relationship is based on trust. You must recognize that what passes between you and your client is confidential. Assume that all information is given in trust, and therefore confidential, unless permission is given to use it in another context.

Being empathetic: You must be sensitive to the client's feelings. Put yourself in the client's position. It helps if you understand your strengths and weaknesses. If you accept yourself as you are, you may be able to accept others.

Genuineness: You must be genuine and not defensive. Be open, real and honest. Studies indicate that positive outcomes can be achieved if the client sees in you empathy, genuineness and a positive regard.

ETHICS OF A SOCIAL WORKER

The following are the ethics of a social worker:

1. Respect the dignity of the individual as the basis for all social relationships.
2. Have faith in the capacity of the client to advance towards his/her goals.
3. Base your relations with others on their qualities as individuals, without distinction as to race, creed, colour, or economic or social status.
4. Recognize that your greatest gift to another person may be to give an opportunity for him/her to develop and exercise his/her own capacities.
5. Do not invade the personal affairs of another individual without his/her consent, except in an emergency, where you must act to prevent injury to him/her or to others.
6. Believe and accept the differences and individuality of others, and endeavour to build a useful relationship on them.
7. Base your opinion of another person on a genuine attempt to understand the whole person, his/her situation, and what it means.
8. Constantly try to seek understanding and control yourself, your attitudes, and the prejudices which may affect your relationships.

DEMANDS ON SOCIAL WORK

It is common to find clients who expect much from you. Usually they expect immediate material assistance. For

are assisted. The person in need of case work may be physically, mentally, or socially handicapped. Among those regarded as socially handicapped are: the unemployed, the homeless, members of broken families, alcoholics, drug addicts, and neglected or problem children. To determine the cause of maladjustment, the social worker must understand individual psychology as well as the sociology of the community. Physicians, psychiatrists, and other specialists may be required to help diagnose the difficulty.

Social group work is exemplified by the social settlement, the supervised playground and gymnasium, and the classroom, where handicrafts may be learned. The community may be called upon to provide the buildings and grounds for such activities; often the services of volunteers and of public groups are utilized; in recent years people living in poverty areas have been employed to work in and direct poverty projects in their own communities.

Through community organization the welfare work of single agencies as well as of whole communities is directed, cooperation between public and private agencies is secured, and funds are raised and administered. The funds required by private agencies are often pooled in a community chest community chest, cooperative organization of citizens and social welfare agencies in a city. Also known as a united fund, it has two purposes: to raise funds through an annual campaign for its member agencies and to budget the funds raised.

The Development of Social Work

Social work emerged as a profession out of the early efforts of churches and philanthropic groups to relieve the effects of poverty, to bring the comforts of religion to the poor, to promote temperance and encourage thrift, to care for children, the sick, and the aged, and to correct the delinquent. Orphanages and homes for the elderly were typical results of these activities. The word *charity* best describes the early activities, which were aimed at the piecemeal alleviation of particular maladjustments. In such charitable work the principal criterion in determining aid to families was worthiness, while the emphasis in later social work was on restoring individuals to normal life both for their own sake and for the sake of the community.

The first attempts to solve the problem of poverty in a modern scientific way was made by P. G. F. Le Play, who in the 1850s made a detailed study of the budgets of hundreds of French workers' families. Forty years later Charles Booth investigated wages and prices, working conditions, housing and health, standards of living, and leisure activities among the poor of London and revealed the extreme poverty of a third of the population. Booth's social survey became a method for determining the extent of social maladjustment, and through surveys in other cities in Europe and the United States a vast number of facts were accumulated, and methods were developed that provided the basis for modern social work.

Social work has its roots in the struggle of society to deal with poverty and the resultant problems. Therefore, social work is intricately linked with the idea of charity work; but must be understood in broader terms. The concept of charity goes back to ancient times, and the practice of providing for the poor has roots in all major world religions.

Pre-Modern History

In the West, when Constantine I legalized the Christian Church, the newly legitimised church set up poorhouses, homes for the aged, hospitals, and orphanages. These were often funded, at least in part, from grants from the Empire.

By 590 the church had a system for circulating the consumables to the poor: associated with each parish was a *diaconium* or office of the deacon. As there was no effective bureaucracy below city government that was capable of charitable activities, the clergy served this role in the west up through the 18th century. During the Middle Ages, the Christian church had vast influence on European society and charity was considered to be a responsibility and a sign of one's piety. This charity was in the form of direct relief (for example, giving money, food, or other material goods to alleviate a particular need), as opposed to trying to change the root causes of poverty. The practice and profession of social work has a relatively modern (19th century) and scientific origin.

Modern History

Social work, as a profession, originated in the 19th century.

The movement began primarily in the United States and England. After the end of feudalism, the poor were seen as a more direct threat to the social order, and so the state formed an organized system to care for them. In England, the Poor Law served this purpose. This system of laws sorted the poor into different categories, such as the able bodied poor, the impotent poor, and the idle poor. This system developed different responses to these different groups.

The 19th century ushered in the Industrial Revolution. There was a great leap in technological and scientific achievement, but there was also a great migration to urban areas throughout the Western world. This led to many social problems, which in turn led to an increase in social activism. Also with the dawn of the 19th century came a great "missionary" push from many Protestant denominations. Some of these mission efforts (urban missions), attempted to resolve the problems inherent in large cities like poverty, prostitution, disease, and other afflictions. In the United States workers known as "friendly visitors", stipended by church and other charitable bodies, worked through direct relief, prayer, and evangelism to alleviate these problems. In Europe, chaplains or almoners were appointed to administrate the church's mission to the poor.

During this time, rescue societies were initiated to find more appropriate means of self-support for women involved in prostitution. Mental asylums grew to assist in taking care of the mentally ill. A new philosophy of "scientific charity" emerged, which stated charity should be "secular, rational and empirical as opposed to sectarian, sentimental, and dogmatic. " In the late 1880s, a new system to provide aid for social ills came in to being, which became known as the settlement movement. The settlement movement focused on the causes of poverty through the "three Rs"-Research, Reform, and Residence. They provided a variety of services including educational, legal, and health services. These programs also advocated changes in social policy. Workers in the settlement movement immersed themselves in the culture of those they were helping.

In America, the various approaches to social work led to a fundamental question – is social work a profession? This debate can be traced back to the early 20th century debate between Mary Richmond's Charity Organization Society (COS) and Jane Addams's Settlement House Movement. The essence of this debate was whether the problem should be approached from COS' traditional, scientific method focused on efficiency and prevention or the Settlement House Movement's immersion into the problem, blurring the lines of practitioner and client. Even as many schools of social work opened and formalized processes for social work began to be developed, the question lingered. In 1915, at the National Conference of Charities and Corrections, Dr. Abraham Flexner spoke on the topic "Is Social Work a Profession?" He contended that it was not because it lacked specialized knowledge and specific application of theoretical and intellectual knowledge to solve human and social problems. This led to the professionalization of social work, concentrating on case work and the scientific method.

SOCIAL WORK IN INDIA

Starting with one institute offering a programme in Social Work in 1946, we have today a hoard of such institutes functioning from all across the country. But in India, social work as a profession has failed to take roots.

Starting with one institute offering a programme in Social Work in 1946, we have today a hoard of such institutes functioning from all across the country. The earliest graduates in Social Work migrated to the United States of America or Europe because Social Work is a recognised profession there. A degree in Social Work offered good employment opportunities as well as scope for private practice.

In India Social Work never got established as an independent profession. The government social welfare departments, hospitals largely employed trained social workers against lower middle rung posts. When Indian labour laws made it compulsory to appoint welfare officers in the factories, Social Work degree became a passport to appointment against these posts. With time, welfare officers saw themselves becoming personnel officers and later human resource development (HRD) managers. People with Social Work background thus got higher status in society.

When management education came to India (also from the USA), HRD became a preferred area of specialisation and management graduates soon replaced Social Work graduates from HRD jobs. A new attractive field opened for the Social Work graduates when some non-government organisations (NGOs) adopted corporate culture under the influence of its foreign donors. But these employment opportunities were limited in numbers because how many NGOs in India would find foreign funds? High profile jobs for Social Work graduates were therefore ruled out.

The scope for practicing Social Work as private profession in India is next to nil. Petty political party workers who also call themselves social workers appear to be doing better. The image of a social worker amongst the general public is such that if a trained social worker were to introduce himself/herself the response coming from the opposite person most likely is to be: I am a social worker too.

It is difficult for the Indian people to conceive that there could be professionals around called social workers to be approached when facing personal or family problems. The reason is not far to see. Helping each other in the Indian traditions is a noble cause. Every body therefore shows eagerness to help every body else. Why in that case someone pay a social worker? Since the very concept of professional social work is missing from the Indian minds, trained social workers are going to find it very difficult to establish roots in this country. It is also to remember that profession wise it is the clients who approach the professionals and not the other way round.

If we look at the methods of professional social work, they talk of (1) helping people individually (Social Case Work Method) (2) helping people in groups (Social Group Work Method) and (3) helping people's communities (Community Development Method). It may be seen that of these, the last two methods can not be practiced by trained social workers in private practice since these require a larger setting. Only organised bodies such government, corporate houses, NGOs can afford it. Trained social workers therefore have to be necessarily employed to be able to practice these two methods. This leaves Social Case Work method as the only method that can be employed by trained social workers to earn an independent living.

In Social Case Work method, the trained social worker interviews his/her client, in private and takes down the personal history. Through this he/she makes an assessment of the likely cause for the problem faced by the client. The process of interviewing is simple chit-chatting. The client may not even know if he/she is being helped or having a street corner talk. One interview with the client is not sufficient; more have to be arranged. Some clients may not be prepared for repeat visits. Even if the cause is discovered successfully, the solution that is offered to the client may not be out of the ordinary. It consists of plain suggestions and motivational talks. Unlike doctors and psychiatrists who prescribe medicines, professional social workers prescribe no such thing. This leaves the clients a bit disappointed. In fact, many people (the household social workers) have been giving advises to them.

Experience shows that people in India are happier discussing their personal problems with astrologers, tantrics, priests and saddhus for they offer mantras, tabeej (locket), bhasma (ashes), flowers, etc. said to be containing charismatic powers or ask to perform certain rituals such as feeding the fish, donating mustard oil, performing puja etc. that heal all the problems. People have no hesitation in paying them; sometimes even paying big money. It appears that people are more interested in purchasing hope than getting rid of the problem.

From the discussion so far it is clear that professional Social Work is a big failure in India; it can neither provide you decent employment nor earn an independent living. Students of Social Work at the universities, colleges and departments are therefore heading for a disaster. The government should take steps to weed out such unnecessary disciplines from our education system or consider modifying these to suit our conditions. Employing trained social workers in rural areas where community organisation is a big challenge also appears to be an attractive option. Is any body listening?

WHAT IS SOCIAL WORK?

According to the National Association of Social Workers (NASW), " Social work is the professional activity of helping individuals, groups, or communities enhance or restore their capacity for social functioning and creating societal conditions favourable to this goal. The profession of social work is based on the values of service, social and economic justice, dignity and worth of the person, importance of human relationships, and integrity and competence in practice. With these values as defining principles, the purposes of social work are:

- To enhance human well-being and alleviate poverty, oppression, and other forms of social injustice.
- To enhance the social functioning and interactions of individuals, families, groups, organizations, and communities by involving them in accomplishing goals, developing resources, and preventing and alleviating distress.
- To formulate and implement social policies, service, and programs that meet basic human needs and support the development of human capacities.
- To pursue policies, services, and resources through advocacy and social or political actions that promote social and economic justice.
- To develop and use research, knowledge, and skills that advance social work practice.
- To develop and apply practice in the context of diverse cultures.

What are the requirements for becoming a social worker?

If you are thinking about a career in social work, you want to work with people and you want a career that makes a difference. There are certain personal attributes that a social worker must have. First, a social worker must like working with people. As a social worker, you will be involved with people from all walks of life. These people, who come from diverse backgrounds, can have ideas, values and expectations very different from the social worker. Being aware of and sensitive to the beliefs of others is not always an easy task. In dealing with different people, a social worker must really want to understand the troubles that others face. So first of all, a good social must genuinely like working with diverse individuals.

Second, a social worker must want to help people. A social worker will encounter all types of problems ranging from abuse and neglect, to mental health issues to community-based substance abuse problems. A good social worker wants to help his client in their efforts to figure out what is going on and how best to resolve their problems. Social workers value working in partnerships with both their clients and their colleagues. Social work practice involves facilitating change: Working with others, not doing something to them or for them.

Third, social workers want the community to be a better place for all people. Through his or her professional activities, a social worker help a client and at the same time he or she tries to better the community for all people.

Where are Social Workers Employed?

Social Workers help people deal with complex problems such as poverty, homelessness, substance abuse, domestic violence, and so forth. Settings that employ social workers include schools, hospitals, mental health clinics, crisis intervention programs, child welfare services, hospices, correctional institutions, business and industry and community organizations. Social workers can be found in federal and state government as lobbyists, policy makers and elected officials. They are employed as researchers and professors in colleges, and private and public foundations that are created for studying social issues such as domestic violence, AIDS, child welfare, poverty and so forth.

What is the Employment outlook for Social Workers?

The professional ranks of social workers are expanding. Occupational outlook estimates that the workforce of social workers will increase by over 36 percent by the year 2008 (Bureau of Labour Statistics, 2000a). Recent trends in service delivery reveal an increasing number of social work positions in home health, mental health, criminal justice, school-linked services and neighbourhood based, multidisciplinary service centres.

FUTURE OF SOCIAL WORK

Social work is continually adapting to demographic and cultural changes in Canadian society. In this respect, an AGING population, the increasing diversity of society, and the social needs of NATIVE PEOPLE are emerging priorities in social services and social work education. The profession is also concerned about the preservation of quality programs and the nature of practice in a time of fiscal restraint and cutbacks. The profession continues to be engaged in reform movements to change negative societal attitudes toward people in need and to advocate for HUMAN RIGHTS, social justice and gender equality. In spite of these professional commitments, however, the future role of social work within the public sector remains uncertain. On the one hand, social work and social services have become an integral part of PUBLIC SERVICE provision in Canada as a result of the growth of the welfare state. On the other hand, the current retrenchment of the welfare state means that social services, like other public services, are restrained by cutbacks in social expenditures as governments adapt to a changing economic environment in a global era. Like other professional fields in the public sector, social work is being shaped by globalization. While the impact of globalization remains unclear, it is likely that social work will have to think beyond the public services of the welfare state, to develop new concepts of social entitlement, and to identify new ways of meeting human need.

SOCIAL INSTITUTIONS

A social institution is a complex, integrated set of social norms organized around the preservation of a basic societal value. Obviously, the sociologist does not define institutions in the same way as does the person on the street. Lay persons are likely to use the term "institution" very loosely, for churches, hospitals, jails, and many other things as institutions.

Sociologists often reserve the term "institution" to describe normative systems that operate in five basic areas of life, which may be designated as the primary institutions. (1) In determining Kinship; (2) in providing for the legitimate use of power; (3) in regulating the distribution of goods and services; (4) in transmitting knowledge from one generation to the next; and (5) in regulating our relation to the supernatural. In shorthand form, or as concepts, these five basic institutions are called the family, government, economy, education and religion.

The five primary institutions are found among all human groups. They are not always as highly elaborated or as distinct from one another as into the United States, but, in rudimentary form at last, they exist everywhere. Their universality indicates that they are deeply rooted in human nature and that they are essential in the development and maintenance of orders. Sociologists operating in terms of the functionalist model society have provided the clearest explanation of the functions served by social institutions.

Apparently there are certain minimum tasks that must be performed in all human groups. Unless these tasks are performed adequately, the group will cease to exist. An analogy may help to make the point. We might hypothesize that cost accounting department is essential to the operation of a large corporation. A company might procure a superior product and distribute it then at the price which is assigned to it, the company will soon go out of business. Perhaps the only way to avoid this is to have a careful accounting of the cost of each step in the production and distribution process.

TYPES OF SOCIAL MOVEMENTS

Reform Movements

Reform movements are organized to carry out reforms in some specific areas. The reformers endeavour to change elements of the system for better. For example: Civil Rights Movement, Women's Liberation Movement, Arya Samaj Movement, Brahmo Samaj Movement etc.

Revolutionary Movements

The revolutionary movements deny that the system will even work. These movements are deeply dissatisfied with the social order and work for radical change. They advocate replacing the entire existing structure. Their objective is the reorganization of society in accordance with their own ideological blueprint. Revolutionary movements generally become violent as they progress. Example: The Protestant Reformation Movement, the Socialist Movement, the Communist Revolution of China.

Reactionary or Revivalist Movement

Some movements are known as reactionary or regressive movements. These aims to reverse the social change. They highlight the importance and greatness of traditional values, ideologies and institutional arrangements. They strongly criticize the fast moving changes of the present.

Resistance Movement

These movements are formed to resist a change that is already taking place in society. These can be directed against social and cultural changes which are already happening in the country.

Utopian Movement

These are attempts to take the society or a section of it towards a state of perfection. These are loosely structured collectivities that envision a radically changed and blissful state, either on a large scale at some time in the future or on a smaller scale in the present. The Utopian ideal and the means of it are often vague, but many utopian movements have quite specific programmes for social change. The Hare Krishna Movement of the seventies, the movement towards the establishment of Ram Rajya and the Sangh Parivar, the Communists and Socialists pronouncement of a movement towards the classless, casteless society free from all kinds of exploitation etc.

Peasant Movement

Peasant movement is defined by Kathleen Gough as an attempt of a group to effect change in the face of resistance and the peasant are people who are engaged in an agricultural or related production with primitive means who surrender part of their or its equivalent to landlords or to agents of change. The history of peasant movements can be traced to colonial period when repressive economic policies, the new land revenue system, the colonial administrative and judicial system and the ruin of handicrafts leading to the overcrowding of land transformed the agrarian structure and impoverished the peasantry. In the zamindari system peasants were left to the mercies of the Zamindars who exploited them in form of illegal dues. The British government levied heavy land revenue in the Ryotwari areas. Peasants were forced to borrow money from the moneylenders and they were reduced to the status of tenants at will, share croppers and landless labourers while their lands, crops and cattle passed into the hands to landlords, trader moneylenders and such peasants. When the peasants could take it no longer they resisted against the oppression and exploitation through uprisings. Peasant Movements occupy an important place in the history of social unrest in India though the aims and objectives of these movements differ in nature and degree from region to region. It is in this sense that these movements also aimed at the unification of the peasants of a region, development of leadership, ideology and a peasant elite. Through these movements emerged a new power structure and peasant alliance. The genesis of peasant movements rest in the relationship patterns of different social categories existing within the framework of feudal and semi feudal structure of our society. In the post Independence period the nature and objectives of the peasant movement have changed to getting remunerative prices for agricultural produce, to increase agricultural production, to establish parity between prices of agricultural produce and industrial goods and to get minimum wages for the agricultural labourers.

Some of the important peasant uprising:

1770- Sanyasi rebellion

1831- Wahabi uprising

1855- Santhal uprising

1859- Indigo revolt

1890-1900- Punjab Kisan struggle

1917-18- Champaran satyagraha

1921- Moplah rebellion

1928- Bardoli satyagarya

1946- Telangana movement

1957- Naxalbai movement.

Women's Movement

The women's movement in India is a rich and vibrant movement which has taken different forms in different parts of the country. Fifty years ago when India became independent, it was widely acknowledged that the battle for freedom had been fought as much by women as by men. One of the methods M K Gandhi chose to undermine the authority of the British was for Indians to defy the law which made it illegal for them to make salt. At the time, salt-making was a monopoly and earned considerable revenues for the British. Gandhi began his campaign by going on a march - the salt march - through many villages, leading finally to the sea, where he and others broke the law by making salt. No woman had been included by Gandhi in his chosen number of marchers. But nationalist women protested, and they forced him to allow them to participate.

The first to join was Sarojini Naidu, who went on to become the first woman President of the Indian National Congress in 1925. Her presence was a signal for hundreds of other women to join, and eventually the salt protest was made successful by the many women who not only made salt, but also sat openly in marketplaces selling, and indeed, buying it. The trajectory of this movement is usually traced from the social reform movements of the 19th century when campaigns for the betterment of the conditions of women's lives were taken up, initially by men.

By the end of the century women had begun to organize themselves and gradually they took up a number of causes such as education, the conditions of women's work and so on. It was in the early part of the 20th century that women's organizations were set up, and many of the women who were active in these later became involved in the freedom movement. Independence brought many promises and dreams for women in India - the dream of an egalitarian, just, democratic society in which both men and women would have a voice. The reality was, however, somewhat different.

For all that had happened was that, despite some improvements in the status of women, patriarchy had simply taken on new and different forms. By the 1960s it was clear that many of the promises of Independence were still unfulfilled. It was thus that the 1960s and 1970s saw a spate of movements in which women took part: campaigns against rising prices, movements for land rights, peasant movements. Women from different parts of the country came together to form groups both inside and outside political parties. Everywhere, in the different movements that were sweeping the country, women participated in large numbers. Everywhere, their participation resulted in transforming the movements from within. One of the first issues to receive countrywide attention from women's groups was violence against women, specifically in the form of rape, and 'dowry deaths'. This was also the beginning of a process of learning for women: most protests were directed at the State. Because women were able to mobilize support, the State responded, seemingly positively, by changing the law on rape and dowry, making both more stringent.

In the early campaigns, groups learnt from day to day that targeting the State was not enough and that victims also needed support. So a further level of work was needed: awareness raising so that violence against women could be prevented, rather than only dealt with after it had happened. Legal aid and counseling centres were set up, and attempts were made to establish women's shelters. Knowledge was also recognized as an important need.

The women's activity was geared towards improving the conditions of women's lives. In recent years, the euphoria of the 1970s and early 1980s, symbolized by street-level protests, campaigns in which groups mobilized at a national level, has been replaced by a more considered and complex response to issues. In many parts of India, women are no longer to be seen out on the streets protesting about this or that form of injustice. This apparent lack of a visible movement has led to the accusation that the women's movement is dead or dying. While the participation of urban, middle class women is undeniable, it is not they who make up the backbone of the movement, or of the many, different campaigns that are generally seen as comprising the movement.

The anti-alcohol agitation in Andhra Pradesh and similar campaigns in other parts of India were started and sustained by poor, low-caste, often working-class women. The movement to protect the environment was begun by poor women in a village called Reni in the northern hill regions of India, and only after that did it spread to other parts of the country. One of the biggest challenges women have had to face in recent years is the growing influence of the religious right in India. Right-wing groups have built much of their support on the involvement of women: offering to help them with domestic problems, enabling them to enter the public space in a limited way, and all the while ensuring that the overall ideology within which they operate remains firmly patriarchal. For activists too, this has posed major problems. It has forced them to confront the fact that they cannot assume solidarity as women that cuts across class, religion, caste, ethnic difference. It is important to recognize that for a country of India's magnitude, change in male-female relations and the kinds of issues the women's movement is focusing on will not come easy. For every step the movement takes forward, there will be a possible backlash, a possible regression. And it is this that makes for the contradictions, this that makes it possible for there to be women who can aspire to, and attain, the highest political office in the country, and for women to continue to have to confront patriarchy within the home, in the workplace, throughout their lives.

Backward Caste Movement

The Backward castes have been deprived of many social, economic, political and religious privileges. These people provided manual labour and the untouchables occupied the lowest position among the caste hierarchy. They were subjected to extreme form of exploitation. The colonial power accentuated the disparities in the distribution of economic power. The atrocities united the lower castes against the upper castes. Some of the important backward caste movement which came up was Satyashodak Samaj and Nadar Movement which consolidated the masses along the castelines.E.V Ramaswamy started Self-Respect movement against the Brahmins in South India. The SNDP movement in Kerala was more of a reformist movement. In 1950s there was a widespread desire among the non-Brahmin castes to be categorized as Backward.Subsequently Backward Class commission was set up to look into the conditions and requirements of these classes. Mandal Commission submitted its report in 1980 recommending reservations for backward castes in educational institutions and government offices. However this move resulted in anti-Mandal Commission movement which resulted in large scale violence and many students lost their lives.

Dalit Movement

Dalits are the suppressed people at the lost rung of the cast-based hierarchy. Their inferior occupations and low levels of ascriptive status make them vulnerable for attacks at the hands of upper-caste people. The organizational efforts made by Dalit leadership for uplifting their status are known as Dalit movement. It is a protest against untouchability,casteism and discrimination faced by the dalits. Dalit movement indicates some trends of protest ideologies which entail the following - withdrawal and self organization, high varna status and extolling of non-Aryan culture's virtues, abandoning of Hinduism and embracing other religions like Buddhism and Islam. Mahatma Gandhi in 1923 founded the All India Harijan Sevak Sangh to start education and schools for the dalits. Another most important dalit leader Dr.Ambedkar struggled to secure the basic human dignity to the dalits. The Mahad Satyagarh for the right of water led by him was one of the outstanding movements of the dalits to win equal social rights. The role of All India Depressed Classes Association and All India Depressed Classes Federation were the principal organizations which initiated a movement to improve the conditions of the dalits.These organizations aimed at improving their miserable conditions and to spread education among them. They worked to secure rights of admission to school, drawing water from the public wells, entering the temples and to use the roads.

GANDHI'S CONCEPT OF SOCIAL WELFARE

With Gandhi's advent on the Indian scene in 1915, things began to change all round. Gandhi looked at social welfare in his own unique way. His ways, indeed, were unique, so much so that even as early as 1894 i.e. when he was just 25 years old, he wanted to help his compatriots in South Africa by saving them from blatant and crushing racial discrimination. This shows Gandhi's consideration of his fellow men even at that young age. Gandhi never equated happiness with economic prosperity and physical pleasure alone. His concept of the welfare of society was totally opposed to the utilitarian concept, viz. the greatest good of the greatest number. Gandhi said, "A votary of Ahimsa would strive for the greatest good of *all* and die in the attempt to realise this ideal. He would be willing to die so that others might live. He would serve the rest by dying himself. The greatest good of all, inevitably included the good of the greatest number, and, therefore, he and the utilitarian would converge on many points. But ultimately they would have to part company and even work in opposite directions. The utilitarian to be logical will never sacrifice himself. The absolutist will even sacrifice himself'. It is Gandhi's deep-rooted conviction that individual happiness lies in the happiness of society and vice-versa; and this is constantly seen in almost all his pronouncements regarding social welfare. He considered man superior to the system he propounded, and so he was against the system which brought about moral degradation of Indian society. Gandhi never drew a sharp distinction between economics and ethics. For him, economic policies which were harmful to the moral well-being of an individual, community, society, country or a nation were immoral and therefore, sinful. For him happiness meant the happiness of the society as a whole and was indicated primarily, by its moral standard and secondarily, by its physical and economic well-being.

'Sarvodaya' the greatest good of all through truth and non-violence became the ultimate goal of Gandhi in social welfare. His methods of working towards this goal were different from those of many other leaders and social reformers. He took an integrated view of life and disapproved of dividing an individual's life into different compartments. Also the individual was looked upon by him not as a separate entity but as a constituent unit of society.

On his return from South Africa, he perceived after a year of extensive travel all over India, that if his mother-land wanted to get out of the grinding poverty, political freedom was the foremost requirement. This could come only through the awakening of society. His ideas of social reconstruction had already started forming in the last few years of his stay in South Africa. He believed firmly that the individual and the society were contributory to each other's happiness.

Truth & Non-violence

To Gandhi, nothing was more sacred than truth and non-violence. Originally he believed that God is Truth. Later he changed this a little and maintained that Truth is God. "Generally speaking", Gandhi said, "observation of the law of truth is understood merely to mean that we must speak the truth but we...should understand the word 'satya' or truth in a much wider sense. There should be truth in thought, truth in speech and truth in action". For seeking as well as for finding truth, Ahimsa - non-violence - love for all beings - was a necessity. Although Ahimsa - non-violence - is a negative word, Gandhi certainly did not consider it as a negative force. His concept of Ahimsa is not confined to human beings but includes the entire creation. He says, "In spite of the negative particle 'non', it is no negative force. Superficially we are surrounded in life by strife and blood- shed, life living upon life. But some seer, who ages ago penetrated the centre of truth, said, 'It is not through strife and violence that man can fulfil his destiny and his duty to his fellow creatures'. It is a force which is more positive than electricity and more powerful than even ether". It is essential to under- stand the implications of non-violence as Gandhi understood them as it was the creed to which he rendered life-long service.

1. Non-violence is the law of human race and is infinitely greater than and superior to brute force.
2. In the last resort it is of no avail to those who do not posses a living faith in the God of love.
3. Non-violence affords the fullest protection to one's self-respect and sense of honour, but not always to possession of land or money, though its habitual practice does prove a better bulwark than the possession of armed men to defend them.
4. Non-violence is a power which can be wielded equally by all - children, young men and women or grown-up people, provided they have a living faith in the God of love and have therefore equal love for all mankind...
5. It is a profound error to suppose that whilst the law is good enough for individuals, it is not for the masses of mankind.

According to Gandhi, Ahimsa is a necessity for seeking, as well as, for finding Truth. To him both are so intertwined that it is almost impossible to disentangle them. He calls Truth and Ahimsa two sides of' a smooth unstamped metallic disc', nevertheless, to Gandhi ahimsa is the means and Truth the end. Gandhi's non-violence was not a weapon of the weak and cowardly. It was meant for the fearless and the brave.

It was on these two rock-like pillars of truth and non-violence that Gandhi strove all his life to build the edifice of social reconstruction for *'Sarvodaya'*. Of course, he believed that it was only by individual reformation through his famous eleven vows that an ideal society could be built.

Individual and Society

To Gandhi, the individual was as important, if not more, than the society, as he firmly believed that the happiness of the individual formed the constituent part of the happiness of the society. So, for him, social welfare meant the conscious submission of the individual and a voluntary contribution of one's possession to the society, which consisted of *all,* not a majority and, in return, the social system, built upon the principles of non-violence and democracy, was to give a complete guarantee for the maximum development of the individual's personality.

As early as 1915, on his return to India from South Africa, Gandhi's concept of an individual's development had completely formed as is evident from the following: "Truthfulness, Brahmacharya, non-violence, non-stealing and non-hoarding, these five rules of life are obligatory on all aspirants. Every one should be an aspirant. A man's character, therefore, is to be built on the foundation' of these disciplines. Beyond doubt, they are to be observed by everyone in the world. Though a businessman, one must never utter or practice untruth; though married, one must remain celibate; though keeping oneself alive, one can practise non-violence".

After the establishment of the Sabarmati Ashram, Gandhi added the following vows of physical work, control of palate, fearlessness, acceptance of all faiths, Swadeshi and the removal of untouchability to those already mentioned, as an Ashram rule 'to enable an individual to lead a disciplined life.

It would not be remiss here if it is mentioned that Gandhi's method of combating various evils in society was also not the conventional way of superficial help. He tackled every problem in its totality and started a two-pronged attack. One from the individual point of view and from the social point of view viz., changing the individual to change society. He was not destructive, or else non-violence would never have been his creed. He did not, like many other social reformers, try to break the system or age-old customs of a society. He tried to give those age-old customs a rational interpretation and apply them in the changed context of modem times. In short, he tried to bring about a synthesis between the good points of both the old customs and the modem ways to bring about real social welfare.

State and Individual

Like the Anarchists, Gandhi also has a stateless society as his ideal. He is opposed to the State because the State, according to him, is an instrument of violence. He says, "The State represents violence in a concentrated and organised form. The individual has a soul, but as the State is a soul-less machine, it can never be weaned from the violence to which it owes its very existence".

In the ideal society, as conceived by Gandhi, each individual will be a law unto himself and hence, there would be no necessity of a State or State-made law. He, however, was realist enough to realise that it would take a long time for this ideal to be attained, maintaining that, "A government cannot succeed in becoming entirely non-violent because it represents all the people. I do not to-day conceive of such a golden age. But I do believe in the possibility of a predominantly non-violent society. And I am working for it."

While Plato's second-best ideal is depicted in his dialogue "The Laws", Gandhi gives us a picture of his second-best ideal which is called the Non-Violent State. This State will not be able to completely eliminate violence.

Though as a general rule, Gandhi does not believe in the State encroaching upon the liberty of the individual, he, at the same time, realizes that so long as the State exists, it will have to try to create conditions which will enable an individual to realise his best self.

The main characteristics of the Non-Violent State are:

1. There would be minimum use of coercion in it. Police force, with arms; cannot be eliminitated. But the police will be servants, not masters of the people. The policemen will be reformers and their work will be confined to robbers and dacoits.

   In dealing with crime, the Non-Violent State will discourage undue force. The object of the State will be neither retribution nor deterrence. Punishment becomes necessary in some cases of crime. But it will be corrective and reformative and not vindictive.

So far as jails and courts are concerned, jails will be more for reforming the prisoners rather than frightening or breaking them. Prisoners will be treated as defectives and not as criminals to be looked down upon. The jail officials will be their mends and instructors. Judicial work will be done by the Panchayats.

2. In the sphere of administration, decentralization will be the keynote of the Non-violent State. It will be a decentralized society with equality pervading every sphere of life. Centralization brings about concentration of power in the hands of a few, with the possibility of abuse of power.
3. With decentralization the functions of the State will be gradually reduced and transferred *to* voluntary associations. In performing its functions, the object of the State will be *to* serve the masses, and the voluntary organizations will be more effective in this as their aim is more 'service of the people' than acquisition and retention of power.

So far as institutional changes are concerned, some of the main suggestions made by Gandhi regarding different institutions are:

Family

Family, one of the many social institutions, was sacred *to* him. He considered family as a 'God-ordained institution'. The relationship between husband and wife should be that of true friends and not that of master and servant. He certainly did not approve of the relationship of husband and wife -one superior and the other inferior -as was the case in majority of Indian families. Both must hold the other's body and soul as sacred as one's own. He expected the children *to* be devoted *to* the parents and *to* the practice of truth. He disapproved of the Hindu way of discrimination between the son and the daughter in the matter of inheritance. He wanted sons and daughters *to* be treated with absolute equality. *Just* as children should be devoted *to* parents, so also the parents must mould the character of the children and provide education *to* enable them to become self-reliant and *to* earn an "honest livelihood by the sweat of the brow" instead of, "making them slaves of ancestral property which kills enterprise and feeds the passions which accompany idleness and luxury".

Child-Marriage

Gandhi was totally opposed to child-marriage. He considered the custom of child-marriage indicative of physical and moral degeneration. He said, "This custom of child-marriage is both a moral as well as a physical evil. For, it undermines our morals and induces physical degeneration. By countenancing such customs, we recede from God as well as Swaraj. A man who has no thought of the tender age of a girl has none of God. And under-grown men have no capacity for fighting battles of freedom, or having gained it, of retaining it... Legislation is being promoted to raise the age of consent. It may be good for bringing a minority to book... But it is *not legislation that will cure a popular evil,* it is enlightened public opinion that can do it. I am not opposed to legislation in such matters, but I do lay greater stress on cultivation of public opinion... Ordinarily, a girl under 18 years should never be given in marriage". He gave enthusiastic support to the Child Marriage Restraint Bill (1929) passed by the then assembly. This bill legally forbade marriages between boys under eighteen and girls under fourteen years of age, while the Hindus and Muslims were very much against it and opposed it bitterly.

Gandhi also abhorred any measure or condition like widowhood, divorce, the dowry system, which smacked of victimization in any form of the weaker section of society. Gandhi had specific ideas about widowhood and he said, have repeatedly said that every widow has as much right to remarry as every widower. Voluntary widowhood is a priceless boon in Hinduism; enforced widowhood is a curse".

Women

One of the main problems of society and more so in India, which drew Gandhi's attention was the social status of women. "His attitude to women's rights was uncompromising under all conditions". "He could visualize woman only as man's companion, gifted with equal mental capacities, possessing 'the right to participate in every minute detail in the activities of man' and an equal right of freedom and liberty". It would be relevant to state that Gandhi's *'Satyagraha'* movement was instrumental in releasing the countless inhibitions, social, emotional, political and physical, of the woman in India from the villages as well as from the cities, from the highest caste and class to the lowest. It was as if the flood-gates of suppression were lifted, and out flowed the unbreakable force of the strength that was latent in the so called weaker sex.

Gandhi wanted the enlightened women of India to seek relentlessly the repeal of all legal disqualifications and removal of social discrimination against women in India. He considered legislation to remove the inequalities of women as essential... But at the same time, he did not favour women competing with men in -all vocations. He advocated selective education for women, not with any sense of women being inferior to men, but he did believe that they were not identical and that their fields of work were different.

Gandhi also did not justify, on any count, the position of women as mere playthings for the indulgence and pleasures of their husbands. Gandhi saw the mother in every woman. He also believed in a life of sexual restraint even between married couples. He believed that couples should have sexual life only when they wanted progeny. This was his ideal. But he believed in restraint only when it was both mental and physical and not mere outward suppression in the case of married couples.

In the matter of family planning, Gandhi firmly believed that self-restraint was the only method of family planning. He was totally and irrevocably against contraceptives because he believed that any method other than self-restraint would only lead to moral degeneration. He did not at all agree with the view that abstinence was harmful to men and women, as it was a denial of a natural urge. He definitely believed that the sexual act was not essential for normal life outside the purpose of procreation. He has said, "Self-indulgence with contraceptives may prevent the coming of children, but will sap the vitality of both men and women". He also believed that for self-restraint not only sex, but all the senses of sight, hearing, taste and touch should be under restraint. He said, "If self-control be an interference with nature precisely in the same sense as contraceptives, be it so. I would still maintain that the one interference is lawful and desirable because it promotes the well-being of the individuals as well as society, whereas the other degrades both and is therefore unlawful. Self-control is the surest and the only method regulating the birth-rate. Birth-control by contraceptives is race-suicide".

Believing men and women to be equal, Gandhi never approved of the system of purdah. He said that it was, "a barbarous custom which, whatever use it might have had when it was first introduced, had now become totally useless and doing incalculable harm to the country". He further said, "Chastity is not a hot-house growth. It cannot be superimposed. It cannot be protected by the surrounding wall of the purdah. It must grow from within, and to be worth anything, it must be capable of withstanding every unsought temptation... It must be a very poor thing that cannot stand the gaze of men. Men, to be men, must be able to trust their womenfolk, even as the latter are compelled to trust them... By seeking to-day to interfere with the free growth of womanhood of India, we are interfering with the growth of free and independent-spirited men... It partly accounts for our weakness, indecision, narrowness and helplessness".

Devadasis & Prostitutes

As said earlier, Gandhi considered a situation in all its aspects and so when he was keen to raise the status of women in India to its rightful place, he took into account the question of the prostitutes and Devadasis. He felt very pained at the problem of Devadas is, because he felt that it was deceiving God to use young girls for the priests' carnal pleasures under the guise of service to God. Similarly, he considered the existence of the institution of prostitutes a shame on society and more so a shame on men. In connection with the problem of Devadas is, Gandhi considered the name 'Devadasi' a euphemism for prostitutes. He considered it in the same light as that of prostitution. And to him this crime of man against woman was much more serious than that of a hungry man stealing a banana or that of a needy youngster picking a pocket. Gandhi believed that this vice was prevalent in cities and the majority of villages were more or less free of it.

Thus, in the question of uplifting the status of women, as in other questions, Gandhi looked at it from the totality and believed that the change should start at the root of social thinking. He held that was the only way to bring about a meaningful improvement in any situation. Gandhi's method of combating an evil in society did not vary in its fundamental principle of social reconstruction from within and synthesis of the old and the new.

Untouchability

Another question that shook Gandhi to the innermost core of his being was that of untouchability in Hinduism. He believed in 'varnashrama', which meant division according to one's profession, but he certainly did not accept the rigid caste system which had taken the place of the original 'varnashrama'. Untouchability, he maintained, was no part of Hinduism. He wrote, "Untouchability is not only not a part and parcel of Hinduism, but a plague, which is the bounden duty of every Hindu to combat". According to Gandhi, the deviation from the 'varnashrama dharma' was largely responsible for the economic and spiritual ruin of India. Gandhi believed that there was a lot of sense in the law of 'varna' as discovered by Rishis of old and it was a simple precept in Hinduism. But he certainly did not accept the claims of superiority by any 'varna'. The superiority in the type of service did not give the right of superiority to one 'varna' over the other. It was the violation of the spirit of the 'vamashramadharma' which led to the degeneration of Hindu society; and untouchability was the lowest point touched by this violation. It made Gandhi shudder to think of and see the conditions, the untouchables were made to stay in. They were treated as social lepers. The higher castes did not touch them and gave the poor creatures a terrible beating if by accident they touched a higher caste person. The untouchables had literally to beg for water, because they were not allowed to draw it from the village wells. They were denied entry to the temples, forgetting that the All-Merciful God did not make any distinction between man and man. Gandhi firmly believed that Indians were treated as pariahs in South Africa, because of the treatment they meted out to the untouchables in India. Removal of untouchability became one of the major missions of his life. He called the untouchables, 'Harijans', which meant people of God. He went and stayed in Bhangi colonies, undertook a fast for getting them temple entry, undertook an all-India tour for removal of untouchability and fought relentlessly for them throughout his life, by creating the Harijan Sevak Sangh, to help them remove evil habits nom their lives with the help of a batch of devoted workers.

The abject poverty in which the majority of his countrymen lived, prompted him to be active in public life. He blamed the rich for the condition of starvation and poverty and considered it immoral to keep such vast numbers under those conditions. He said,: it is the fundamental law of nature, without exception, that nature produces enough for our wants nom day to day; and if only everybody took enough for himself, and nothing more, there would be no pauperism in this world, there would be no man dying of starvation". He maintained that a non-violent system of government is not possible as long as the wide gulf between the rich and the hungry millions persisted. Therefore, he suggested, "leveling down of a few rich in whose hands is concentrated the bulk of the nation's wealth on the one hand and the levelling up of the semi-starved, naked millions on the other". But this result had to be accomplished by a non-violent process.

To achieve the above for maintaining some equality and stability, he propagated his doctrine of Trusteeship. Trusteeship meant that "the rich man will be left in possession of his wealth, of which he will use what he reasonably requires for his personal needs and will act as a trustee for the remainder to be used for the rest of the society".

Urban & Rural Labour

The other major aspect of social welfare which drew Gandhi's attention was that of urban labour as well as that of the landless farmers, constituting rural labour. He was appalled at the living conditions of the factory workers in the city and of the landless farm-labourers in the village. He believed that the spinning wheel was the answer to many of India's problems. By the spinning wheel, he no doubt meant Khadi, but he also meant the revival of village industries. He was of the opinion that India was a country of villages. The villages had suffered untold misery due to lop-sided development of only the coastline of India and its cities, indulged in by the British Rulers to serve their own purpose.

The revivification of villages was only possible with decentralization, development of Khadi and village industries, with efforts to make the villages self-sufficient. The self-sufficiency of villages would then gradually eradicate the need to migrate to the over-crowded cities for work and employment to earn their daily bread. Gandhi was completely conscious of the miseries of the urban labourer and believed that the urban labourer must have a minimum living wage, adequate living conditions and ideally, every concern should have a scheme for sharing of profits with all the workers. On the other hand, the workers also must put in their best in whatever work. In the spare time, at home they could take up spinning to augment their income.

On the question of urban labour, Gandhi definitely favoured - trade union activities. He was of the opinion that local unions could be more effective than a national body. Nevertheless, he was responsible for establishing the Indian National Trade Union Congress (INTUC) in 1947 which had evolved from Hindoostan Mazdoor Seva Sangh started in 1938. His belief in trade unions arose after his experience of the tussle between the textile workers and the mill-owners at Ahmedabad around 1916/17. He felt that it was necessary for labour to be united. But he firmly believed that the trade union should only take up issues that were correct from the ethical point of view; that negotiations were the best way to resolve issues; and that confrontation and strikes should be resorted to only in extreme cases of injustice. Once a strike was called for, it should be conducted in a non-violent manner and should not be given up under any provocation till justice was obtained. But it was essential that the union leaders did not resort to a strike unless the issue was thoroughly examined from all sides and its moral justification was fully established. He was of the opinion that if the cause was right and non- violence adhered to, labour would ultimately win.

Evaluation

Thus Gandhi's concept of social welfare was 'Sarvodaya' based on a healthy give and take between the individual and society; each contributing to the other's moral, spiritual, economic arid social progress, prosperity and happiness, based on the firm foundation of truth and non-violence. Examined from all angles, this concept enveloped the field of social welfare in its entirety, unlike the modem western concept. Even the modem institutional concept of citizen-right is concentrated on the different needs, of an individual or a group like physical, mental or economic.

The Gandhian concept takes a total perspective and focuses on the development of the moral and spiritual aspects with truth and non-violence as its base; with all the other aspects, such as physical, mental and economic, to enhance the individual's social sense, thereby creating a society of healthy individuals. "One important aspect of Gandhi's social thought was his tendency not only to bridge the gap between individual and social ethics but also" to regard social reality as a counterpart of man's inner reality". In the western concept of social welfare there lies a sense of giver and receiver even in today's institutional and citizen-right concept. This may be due to the fact that the present concept has developed from the initial residual concept of charity.

In the Gandhian concept there is no giving or receiving. As said earlier, it is a total perspective, not divided into areas, i.e. the total individual or society has to "reform and thus build up the society on a moral concept of happiness which covers all other aspects. The individual contributes to the society and the society helps the individual. The modem concept of social welfare developed in the West with the onset of industrialization and hence into that of citizen- right.

The Gandhian concept has been built up in India, where social welfare was woven in the fabric of its society since time immemorial. Help to the needy was enjoined by 'dharma' for the joint families, communities and kings. Gandhi went a step further and for him, rights and duties Went hand-in-hand. Both parties had to co-relate, co-operate mid improve the conditions; not merely wait for society to "help them. In the modern concept, the welfare services consist of help in one form or another and the emphasis is on help in the form of money or material or services obtained through them.

In the Gandhian concept the emphasis is on the human aspect and the dependence to contribute to social welfare is not on money or materials alone. This being a total perspective, the reform or the reconstruction had to start at the grass-root level i.e. the village level, gradually reaching the seat of the government. Not only India, but the world came under its purview. "Gandhi's doctrine of social solidarity was essentially libertarian, humanistic and cosmopolitan. He said, 'As with the individual so with the society. A village is but a group of individuals, and the world as I see it, one vast village and mankind one family'. Here there is a resemblance to Kropotkin's social philosophy, as one of its main ingredients was his elaborate analysis of the part played in history by people's constructive agencies of 'mutual aid' rather than 'competition' in the Darwinian sense - a point stressed also by Gandhi in every aspect, but emphatically so in human welfare."

The government and the law took a secondary place, unlike in the modem concept and the responsibility of 'Sarvodaya' rested solely on human effort and on developing the individual along natural and ethical lines to create a better society. For this Gandhi had already formed the eleven vows for the individual. These eleven vows and the items of Gandhi's programme of constructive work, touched every aspect of an individual's and a society's life in every minor and major field.

In the case of women welfare too, Gandhi wanted the change in social thinking about the status of women. He did not say that women have to be given their rights. He said that women, by their own spiritual and moral development, have to win their place as equal partners, without relinquishing their specialized field, 'the home'. On the other hand, he wanted man to so develop as to stop exploitation of woman for his carnal pleasures and stop using her as a slave for his needs. "Gandhi was a critic of society, both Eastern and Western. He judged a social structure in terms of his own valuation of what the social process is or could be... He had a clear awareness of the 'imperfect state' of society, irrespective of whether it was Eastern or Western. Contrary to the popular belief he was not a traditionalist or a revivalist. Nor could he be a revolutionary who would tear up the foundation of a social structure without even trying to transform it by peaceful means".

He did not believe that traditions should be adhered to if they become a constraint on the development of new social processes demanded by changing values of the modem world; but neither did he favour, "uncontrolled operation of blind economic forces released by the contemporary technological and industrial civilization, undermining the social foundation in both overt and insidious ways".

It is difficult to determine Gandhi's concept of social welfare, because, he dealt with all problems from the point of view of a social revolutionary without violence. His humanism and relentless efforts to wipe off injustice in any form, to any person or group such as women, Harijans, landless farmers, makes him a pioneer of social welfare through social change with a base of truth and non-violence leading to 'Sarvodaya'. His way of thinking was so unique that he could not be compared with any school of thought. "Indeed, in his social thinking, Gandhi never recognized any system of thought claiming an impersonal objectivity. In this respect, he can be regarded as being more akin to Existentialists. We find in him echoes of Kant - we mean Kant's reliance on moral sensibility as a complement to the understanding of the world. Bred in the Indian philosophical traditions, Gandhi believed in the penetration of self and personality as a prelude to the development of moral sensibility which, he thought was an important factor in individual and social life, and in terms of which man could judge the validity of his social ideals and of his own social institutions".

Ralph Templin, a champion of coloured peoples' cause and an American missionary of Indian Methodist Church said in 1930s, "What is Gandhi's meaning for us? The world social revolution is long overdue. Time presses us to bring our social arrangements up to the level of our technological achievements. Many urge the use of the age's favourite weapon, the 'coup d'etat', which would reform politics from the top down and from outside in. Some of these with the usual impatience of immediatists in all ages, reveal contempt for morality as a support of their reform. They are indifferent to the violence which drenches the world in blood. Their futility has been demonstrated by every Western revolution, beginning with the French. Gandhi offers an alternative way of revolution. In this lies his great gift to the world. He begins with a basic philosophy of eminent soundness which combines all the power of personal integrity - 'Satyagrahi' or soul-force with the pooled strength of the co-operative means to mastery of nature and human nature - 'Swadeshism' or the economics of group self-help. This way of revolution turns its followers back from the political instrument - the mutual application of labour to natural resources in the production and distribution of all that is needed by the human family. Machinery is to be opposed only when it magnifies the power of the political instrument in the hands of those who would attempt to thwart the people's mastery of their own destiny. Without disrupting all at once the structure of a society that has evolved through generations, this way of revolution begins its reformation within each life by stripping away all the psychological elements that divide and disorganize people, such as the desire for power over others, the desire to exploit or regiment others, and violent attitudes and methods in conflict. Simultaneously, it attacks both the inner and outer citadels of resistance to reform. On the positive side, it engages people at once and in even wider areas in the mutual conquest of power within and without".

Thus Gandhi did not visualize social reconstruction and welfare as a field for helping the needy as charity, but as the emergence of people through individual and social discipline, towards a healthy and happy society.

Major Social Development Strategies

A grasp of the parameters, styles, and the concept of social strategy is useful for identifying different strategies for social development. The major strategies for social development are identified as income distribution, popular participation, human development, and social integration. These are identified as separate strategies for analytical purposes. In a specific situation, one could find a dominant strategy or a mix of selective strategies that were adopted to achieve social development goals. The following section will analyse these strategies according to their tasks, roles, instruments and outcomes.

Distributive Strategy

The distributive strategy is geared toward achieving social equity in the process of national development. It includes equitable distribution of income, resources, and wealth. It may also include equal access to employment opportunities, consumption goods, and social services. Any such strategic approach might require more or less simultaneous changes at three levels: the distribution pattern of current income, the structure of wealth resources, and the distribution of future benefits accruing from development programmes. However, the development setting, level, and experiences of a particular country might make one action more feasible and acceptable than another. A distributional diagnosis should specify the expected impact of different component measures of a strategy on different population groups. It might probe such basic questions as 'who pay? Who distributes? who benefits? on what conditions? and in what ways?' Such diagnosis could also establish the minima or norms of distribution and determine the extent to which they might be realised in any specific contexts.

There are several factors that influence the trends and outcome of a distributive strategy. They include the characteristics and distribution of power in society, the political commitment to social development, the structure of the economy including control over the means of production, and consumers' demands for goods and services. Each factor plays a critical role in shaping the strategic measure. For example, the question of income distribution is most closely associated with the distribution of power. In Latin America, and that also applies to other developing regions, policies adopted are effective in redistributing income within the middle strata and contribute to improving the relative position of some organised urban groups, but have little effect on the general distinctions between upper, middle and lower strata. A distributive strategy may comprise a variety of institutional measures to achieve the goals of social development. These are generally identified under three broad categories: fiscal, occupational, and social welfare. Fiscal measures used as instruments of the distributive strategy are geared toward raising public revenue and distributing the burden of taxation more equitably among broad income groups. Different taxation measures are recommended as appropriate to different social strata. The occupational measures are related to wage payments and different kinds of benefits that are associated with the work input of an individual.

Both fiscal and occupational measures, according to Titmus, 'can have major redistributive effects in terms of command-over-resources-through-time by certain social groups in the population.' The social welfare measures are designed to redistribute social resources for meeting those basic human needs which could not otherwise be met even at the minimal level through the institutions of the family and the private market.

Thus a distributive strategy requires social analysis and simultaneous action in several directions: income, wealth, goods and services; social classes and institutions; and instruments and measures. Distributive strategies at the international level are generally geared toward the poorer strata of society, access to consumption goods and social services, broadening the base of public social action, progressive financing within the public sector, and productivity. These are some general strategic issues that must be analysed in the process of social development planning. However, one might also observe considerable variations in different national contexts.

Participative Strategy

One of the major goals of social development is to effect structural and institutional reforms in order to involve all sections of the population in the development process, leaving none outside the scope of change and development. There are three distinct but closely related aspects of this process: mass sharing of the benefits; mass contribution; and mass involvement in the decision making process. While the two-way relationship between mass contribution to development and mass sharing of its benefits has long been recognised, popular participation in decision making is a relatively new concept. Recent national experiences suggest that various social development goals require broad participation of the masses in the decision making process. Here a link is considered essential between the 'development through whom' and the 'development for whom' concepts at all levels of decision making: local, regional, state, and national.

A participative strategy may address itself to such specific questions as: who is to participate? why? through what channels? and in what kinds of programmes? It may focus attention on the potential role of the large population strata characterised by low income, low educational levels, and restricted or nonexistent opportunities. In the case of less developed countries, the participation of youth and women is most critical in the process of social development.

The primary focus of participative strategy is on changing the role and character of the government in relation to social development. In almost all countries, the government has already assumed responsibility for social and economic change but is under the influence of elite classes. In these situations, a participative strategy might be directed toward changing the administration's elite class character into a government of and by the masses. This means broadening the scope of public social action and infusing it with citizens' input. The process involves recognition of conflicting interests, but it stresses their constructive handling with a view to achieving some sort of consensus. Thus, the strategy demands continual interplay of initiatives from above and below, along with an interplay of conflict and consensus at many levels of the social order.

Lack of adequate institutional support is a constraint on effective participation in social development. Many countries have developed a network of popular institutions at the local level, but they do not provide for any institutional channels for citizens' input at higher level policy making and planning. Frequently people have been mobilised around certain development issues and activities, but they have been unable to sustain their efforts. Sometimes their energies are misdirected to certain channels that might be dysfunctional to the process of social development. Hence, it is widely held that mass mobilisation in order to sustain development requires popular institutions at different levels.

Human Development Strategy

The people are involved in social development in several capacities: as resources, agents, and beneficiaries. Development planners have for a long time viewed the people merely as a resource. Their thinking was based on a false distinction between capital investments which promote economic growth and social expenditures which divert resources from economic growth. The human resource approach, on the other hand, lays stress on the enhancement of productivity and on the income generating capacity of the labour force. Human beings play the roles of agent and beneficiary, not merely of resource. They contribute values and preferences, participate in the implementation of policies and programmes, and share the benefits of national development. This broad perspective has led to the redefining of social development as an investment in human beings, aimed at improving the condition and quality of human life. Thus social development planning focuses on total human development including productive capacity, participatory skills, and cultural experiences, and on the development of all sections of the population. It is. Also directed toward enhancing the capacities and opportunities of the present generation without diminishing the potential of future generations.

The human resource approach to social development is also linked with the concept of human rights. A United Nations report, referred to earlier, which examined the human resource approach in the light of human rights, found the two notions complementary. Each calls for the universal provision of social services and the development of specialised services to realise individual potentialities. The report concluded that the human resource approach concentrates on the general supply of qualified persons to fill the occupational, social, and political roles that are essential to the functioning of modern urban-industrial societies. 'It does not place equalisation of social opportunities in the foreground. It is quite possible that in a condition of extremely uneven and concentrated modernisation and income distribution, the human resource approach could coincide with the continuing marginalisation of large population strata. Thus the question of human resource development cannot be separated from the general question of rights, opportunities, and general human well-being.'

The conflicting orientations in the conception of human development get reflected in the setting of priorities, choice of instruments, and allocation of resources. For example, a social development plan may encounter a policy dilemma between universal primary education and the training of middle-level technicians. Similarly, primary health care and nutritional measures are often juxtaposed with specialised medical and health services. An alternative strategy might combine universal provisions of primary health care and primary education against the development of higher education and specialised medicine. These are illustrations of conflicting orientations in any human development strategy. The fundamental problem of public social policy is to identify the right balance between different strategic measures. Again, the balance will change with changing priorities at different stages of national development.

A human development strategy may address itself to the question of achieving the broad goals of social development. It may be geared toward enhancing the capacities of all sections of the population and promoting the multiple roles of producer, consumer, citizen and family member. The strategy requires universal provision of social services such as education, health, housing, nutrition, vocational training, and recreation. Universality may be combined with special social provisions to meet the needs of weak and vulnerable groups in society. Positively discriminating policies define selective services as a social right based on the needs of specific, disadvantaged categories, groups, and territorial areas. The amount, range and quality of social services along with questions of accountability and access are other issues that pertain to the human development strategy. In a specific context, these issues are largely defined according to the stage of national development reached, social priorities, cultural preferences, and political commitment to a particular concept of social development. It is usually assumed that the level of social services corresponds to the level of national income or the income of certain sectors or regions. Furthermore, increases in the social services are proportionate to increases in the national income. An analysis of many national development plans would seem to confirm these assumptions.

Social Integration Strategy

Social development is also characterised by an integrative approach aimed at bringing isolated and peripheral groups, communities and regions into the main stream of national development. In any country there are numerous social groups—ethnic, tribal, caste, and occupational—and various regional communities which do not feel identified with the development priorities of the larger society. They cannot participate in and share the benefits of social and economic development unless special measures and institutional arrangements are adopted to break their isolation and build up their capability for effective participation in decision and action. The problems of such groups tend to be circular, and special planning for them requires a package of mutually supportive measures.

An integrative strategy might be directed toward reducing or eliminating any disparities between different regions, social groups or communities. This requires a careful analysis and assessment of the social situation and of the potential impact of a particular social measure on various social groups. In a particular political context, the social development strategy may be geared toward mobilising resources for one set of social priorities to the neglect of others. For example, many national development plans have given high priority to local community or regional development but have often failed to reflect serious concern for the disadvantaged groups of the population.

Social integration strategies are frequently marked by general conflict. One such strategic conflict is identified in the arena of autonomy vs. integration. Many regions or social groups, however peripheral their place in national space, do not like to lose their self-identity or merge into the larger social system. Special measures adopted to change their status strengthen separate identity and continuation of privileged status. Another strategic conflict could be identified at the level of resource transfer. An integrative strategy often involves transfer of social and economic resources from one region to another region, from affluent to weak and disadvantaged groups. This will have political and social repercussions. Under these conditions, not every social and institutional innovation designed to promote integration will be a viable and acceptable measure. Conflict situations demand a careful social and political diagnosis. Attention to political costs and benefits is inevitable in all national integration strategies, for the achievement of social development goals depends upon the proper selection of means.

2

Evaluation and Ethics of Social Work

Social Problems: Perspectives and Definitions

How are social problems identified and defined? Sociologists have introduced four ways to identify social problems: (1) through public opinion; (2) as conditions that decision makers view as undesirable but able to be corrected; (3) as conditions that have a negative impact on individual and social well-being; and, (4) as products of collective behaviour and the organisation of social movements.

Polling for Problems

The first way to identify social problems, through public opinion, assumes that social problems can be pinpointed by studying the opinions, attitudes, and beliefs of the members of society. Individuals share many ideas, opinions, and values that result in general agreement that certain social conditions represent social problems (for example, criminal violence and mental illness). Some have suggested, in fact, that one method of identifying social problems would be a kind of majority vote in which social problems would be identified through the use of public opinion polls. This approach would tie the identification of social problems directly to public awareness and to public opinion about society's ills.

Taken alone, however, this approach has several drawbacks. Rarely is there consensus about the undesirability of any social condition. Instead, conflicting notions regarding what is or is not a social problem is the more common state of affairs. Another drawback of this method is that the public may be misinformed about particular social issues. Sometimes there have been deliberate attempts to mislead the public, but, more commonly, because social problems are complex issues that cannot be understood without knowledge of a vast amount of information, public opinion is often based on faulty logic, folk beliefs, or misunderstandings. Restrictive attitudes toward marijuana use, for example, typically rest on the premise that it is addictive or that it leads to the use of addictive drugs, although neither popular belief is rooted in fact.

Moreover, public opinion is shaped and influenced by powerful interest groups in society and may, therefore, only reflect the biases held by society's opinion makers. Thus, while measuring social problems through public opinion polls may appear to be a democratic and egalitarian method of identifying their severity, not everyone's values and attitudes are given equal weight in defining social problems this way.

Those persons who are in positions of power are those who control the legal, economic, and political institutions and make many of the decisions that affect our choices, values, and attitudes. These decision makers also tend to be white, male, middle-aged, and in the upper middle class. They are capable of influencing public opinion and structuring institutions to reflect their particular values and interests.

Although powerful individuals exert profound influence over both the government and the communications media, because of (heir positions they are frequently unaware of the problems confronting the majority of the American people. As a result, groups within society often must actively publicize their problems in order to bring them to the attention of these decision makers. The incidence of lung disease among coal miners, for example, was long regarded as a fact of life by mine owners — and even by many workers — until intensive union action influenced the decision makers to enact legislation providing safeguards against hazardous working conditions and compensation to those affected by them. Similarly, racial and sexual discrimination were of little concern to the majority of the white male power structure until the black power movement and the feminist movement made it impossible for the decision makers to avoid confronting these issues. These examples point to the fact that mass action is often a prerequisite for social change.

Correctable Conditions

A second approach used to identify social problems is to see them as conditions that decision makers view as undesirable and decide can be ameliorated by social action. A major shortcoming of this approach, however, is that conditions believed by decision makers as resisting corrective measures would not he identified as social problems. Thus, the problems associated with a society dominated by giant corporations or the military-industrial complex (considered by many to be the inevitable outgrowth of the socioeconomic system in this country) would be considered beyond the scope of social problems analysis.

There is reason to doubt that the American public would put complete faith in its decision makers' opinions. Recent public opinion polls also show, surprisingly, that most Americans say they do not have great confidence in those who run our major institutions. A national survey taken in 1985 found that only 32 per cent of the American public said they had a great deal of confidence in those running the military; 30 per cent said they had a great deal of confidence in the White House; only 28 per cent expressed a great deal of confidence in the Supreme Court; 23 per cent had a great deal of confidence in TV news; a mere 17 per cent said they had a great deal of confidence in those running major companies; and only 16 per cent said they had a great deal of confidence in the Congress and the press.

Furthermore, relying on decision makers to identify conditions that can be corrected places even greater control over society's resources in the hands of powerful interest groups in society. Typically, potential solutions to social problems necessitate changes, sometimes minor and sometimes major, in the social, political, and economic status quo. Those members of society who have the power to effect such change tend to be those interested in maintaining the status quo. Consequently, they may be conservative in their attitudes and slow-moving in their actions. Weapons manufacturers, for example, are not likely to be enthusiastic about cutting the defence budget to provide more adequate health care for the American population.

Table : Public Confidence in Major Institutions[a]

	1985	*1975*	*1966*
Medicine	39%	43%	73%
Colleges and universities	35	36	61
Military	32	24	61
White House	30	—	—
Supreme Court	28	28	50
Television news	23	35	—
Organised religion	21	32	41
Executive branch of federal government	19	13	41
Local governments	18	—	—
Major companies	17	19	55
State governments	16	—	—
Congress	16	13	42
Press	16	20	29
Organised labour	13	14	—
Law firms	12	16	—

Source: The Harris Survey (Orlando, Florida: Tribune Media Services, December 1985).

Unless they believe their own social status to be in jeopardy, people in power are generally reluctant to enact changes in social policy. During the Great Depression, for example, the prospect of a socialist revolution that would have changed the class structure and redistributed property was very threatening to those in positions of wealth and power.

By recognising poverty as a social problem and adopting social policies in the form of New Deal legislation, political leaders succeeded in stabilising their own positions in the social structure. Similarly, enactment of the Superfund legislation in 1980, which provides revenue for the cleanup of toxic waste dumps, made those responsible for the pollution liable for cleanup. However, enactment of this legislation came only after numerous parties had filed suits against companies that produced toxic wastes.

Any change in social policy is likely to have adverse effects on some portions of the population. Given these considerations, it would appear that linking the identification of social problems directly to individual opinions, whether of the powerful or the ordinary, may not be the most fruitful way to identify social problems. Nonetheless, it is a way of gauging public response to various social problems and getting some indication of the degree of support and resistance to changes needed to solve the problem at hand.

Determining Negative Impact

A thud way to identify social problems is to see them as conditions that have a negative impact on individual and social well-being and are identified by sociological analysis of the structure and organisation of society. Rather than relying on public opinion or political interests to determine when a social condition is a social problem, or identifying only those problems powerful people believe to be capable of solution, this third method places the identification of social problems in the hands of professional experts—trained people who will use the knowledge and values of science in their assessments. On the basis of such evaluations, social problems are "conditions deemed detrimental to human well-being on the basis of reasonable evidence."

Of the many social conditions one may deem detrimental to personal and social well-being, not all are serious enough to be labeled and treated as social problems. Hence, one important task of those who categorize social conditions is an assessment of their seriousness. According to Jerome Manis, indicators of the harmfulness or seriousness of social conditions are the *magnitude,* the *severity,* and the *primacy* of detrimental conditions.

The magnitude of a social problem refers to the actual size or extent of the condition. How many people are affected? What is the extent of the problem? For number of people—both as users and as indirect victims? Or, how often does rape occur? What is the impact of the prevalence of rape on the behaviour of women? Since public notions about the extent of various social problem are likely to be misleading, measuring the actual extent of a problem is an important requirement for determining its seriousness. The severity of a social condition is determined by its actual harmfulness for the individual and for society. How great a negative impact does the condition have on personal well-being, physical and emotional security, and on the ability of social institutions to function? For example, if most working women report that they have, at one time, been victims of sexual harassment, how does this affect their job performance? How does it affect their attitudes toward men? How does it influence the productivity of the work force?

The primacy of a social problem refers to the importance of a condition as a cause of other harmful conditions. Social conditions "that have many severe effects are more serious than those with lesser ones." Poverty, for example, which is related to malnutrition, poor health, inadequate housing, and low educational attainment, among other things, is a major social problem because of its multiple ramifications. Likewise, mental illness, coupled with cutbacks in social services (along with other factors) has resulted in dramatic increases in the number of homeless.

This method of identifying social problems rests on inquiry and investigation to determine the impact of possible social problems on individuals and societies. Rather than accepting popular beliefs or political pronouncements, it asks questions and relies on empirical data for the answers, and it assumes that the judgment of experts in measuring the magnitude, severity, and primacy of a social problem will be better informed than that of the general public. Conceived in this way, social problems are subject to sociological analysis.

Social Problems as Social Movements

All three of the above means of identifying social problems assume that social problems are objective conditions that exist in the society and that call attention to themselves either because of public opinion about them, their identification by persons in powerful positions, or by their severity and consequent analysis by social scientists. A fourth way by which sociologists have understood social problems is to see them as a form of collective behaviour.

Collective behaviour is an area of sociology that studies such phenomena as crowd behaviour and social movements.

Sociologists who view social problems through the perspective of collective behaviour argue that "social problems are fundamentally products of a process of collective definition instead of existing independently as a set of objective social arrangements with an intrinsic makeup." In other words, they define social problems as identified by social movements organised specifically to call attention to a problem.

Those who take this approach ask, "What is the process by which society comes to recognise its social problems?" They point out that current sociological theory does not enable us to identify social problems. Instead social problems are recognised by sociologists only after entrepreneurs or organised social movements successfully call attention to them. Those who work from this perspective do not see social problems just in terms of objective measures of their incidence, detrimental effects, or severity, but see them also as the result of collective social definition. For example, child abuse is a problem that has long existed in our society, but it took the collective activity of the feminist movement and other organisations to define child abuse as a social problem.

Identifying social problems as the result of collective behaviour perhaps sounds similar to the approach of polling for problems, but in the collective behaviour approach collective definition is different from simply the sum of individual attitudes and opinions. Instead the collective definition hinges on the formation of groups that become mobilised around particular problems. Smoking, for example, though long recognised as posing serious health hazards, has only recently become identified as a social problem as the result of social action by antismoking groups. The collective behaviour approach also sees social problems as points around which there can be competing interests, objectives, and solutions. The more powerful and effective groups or movements will be most influential in defining whether something is problematic. The use of legitimate drugs provides a case in point. Although the National Commission on Marijuana and Drug Abuse defines a drug as any substance, other than food, that by its chemical nature affects the structure or function of a living organism, we do not define extensive and repeated use of prescription drugs as a social problem. Were a social movement to develop that defined such drug use as problematic, it is quite likely that major drug companies would resist such a definition.

Herbert Blumer, a major spokesperson for this perspective, identifies five phases in what he calls "the career of a social problem": (1) emergence of a social problem; (2) legitimation of the problem; (3) mobilisation of action with regard to the problem; (4) the formation of an official plan of action; and, (5) the transformation of the official plan to its empirical implementation." We can think of the emergence of domestic violence as a social problem defined in this way. Although wife-beating has occurred for many years (in fact, throughout history), its recognition as a social problem is a relatively recent phenomenon.

As battered wives themselves, in affiliation with the feminist movement, begun to speak out about domestic violence, they organised battered women's shelters and a public campaign designed to call attention to the extent of wife abuse in this culture. Once domestic violence emerged as a social issue, social scientists documented the problem and disseminated this information through scholarly journals and the mass media. These activities led to further mobilisation around the problem of wife-beating, and various communities formulated policies designed to alleviate the problem.

Similarly, just as social movements can call attention to social problems, so can social problems "disappear" when their advocates lose their effectiveness. For instance, while there is little evidence that occupational safety and health is less serious now than it was in the 1970s, it currently does not receive as much attention, since advocates for reform on this issue have lost much of their influence.

By conceptualising social problems as the products of collective behaviour, sociologists also recognise that there are conflicting opinions and beliefs about social problems and that one's vantage point on the problem will influence how the problem is defined, juvenile delinquency, for example, has a different meaning to the delinquents themselves than it does to those with the authority to oversee delinquency. A sociological perspective on social problems takes into account the multiple dimensions and meanings that social problems have. Peter Berger, a noted sociologist, puts it this way:

The sociological problem is not so much why things "go wrong" from the viewpoint of the authorities and the management of the social scene, but how the whole system works in the first place.... Take a settlement house in a lower-class slum district trying to wean away teenagers from the publicly disapproved activities of a juvenile gang. The frame of reference within which social workers and police officers define the "problems" of this situation is constituted by the world of middle-class, respectable, publicly approved values. It is a "problem" if teenagers drive around in stolen automobiles, and it is a "solution" if instead they will play group games in a settlement house. But if one changes the frame of reference and looks at the situation from the viewpoint of the leaders of the juvenile gang, the "problems" are defined in the reverse order. ¼ What is a "problem" to one social system is the normal routine of things in the other and vice versa. Loyalty and disloyalty, solidarity and deviance, are defined in contradictory terms by the representatives of the two systems. ¼ The "problems" that the sociologist will want to solve concern an understanding of the entire' social situation, the values and modes of action in both *systems, and the way in which the two systems coexist in space and time. Indeed, this very ability to look at a situation from the vantage points of competing systems of interpretation is ¼ one of the hallmarks of sociological consciousness."*

Seeing social problems from a collective behaviour perspective underscores that there is no single interpretation of the nature, causes, or consequences of social problems. Likewise, there are likely to be multiple suggestions about the proper solutions to social problems.

Defining Social Problems

Based on the above discussion, it is fair to say that social problems have both objective and subjective dimensions. Their objective dimensions, while not always noticed or understood by the average person, can be studied through sociological analysis and include their extent, impact on groups of people, and relationship to social institutions. In addition, social problems, like other social phenomena, are subject to collective definition and, therefore, have a subjective basis as well. *Therefore, we can define social problems as conditions in the society affecting individual and social well-being, as identified through a process of collective definition and subject to sociological analysis of the relationship of these conditions to social structure and social change.*

In sum, all four of the above approaches are useful to our understanding of social problems. Our definition of social problems emphasizes their complexity and indicates that no single solution to, explanation of, or perspective on a given problem is adequate for a full understanding of problematic conditions in society. Understanding social problems in this way should help us develop a long-term view of social problems and imagine complex potential solutions, as opposed to the short-run, crisis management, "Band-Aid" approach all too common in popular thinking and official responses to social problems.

CHARITIES ADMINISTRATION IN INDIA

The Nonprofit Sector

Charity is defined as giving voluntarily to those in need. It covers the giving of both money, and of the self through service to the needy. The term is also used to denote an institution or organization, which helps those in need. Though the roots of charity are to be found in religious belief and practice, charitable trusts and voluntary organizations are its secular and institutional manifestation.

Those who wished to work together for social reform or to provide service to the poor and needy-formed associations or societies for the purpose. Religious organizations, especially Christian missions, also took up work to help the poor to improve their condition. This was the genesis of what came to be referred to as voluntary organizations. With the freedom struggle and Gandhiji's advocacy of voluntary constructive work to improve the lot of the masses, many more voluntary organizations were formed. Those who were unable to serve society directly, but were able to provide money and other material resources, either established charitable institutions like *dharamshalas,* schools, orphanages, women's homes and the like, and donated funds to run them, or established endowments to provide monetary he lp in perpetuity to some charitable cause.

The beginning of the industrial revolution in India led to establishment of large fortunes, and gave a fillip to the establishment of endowed foundations to support welfare and development work. Later, inspired by Gandhiji's message that rich businessmen should look upon themselves as trustees of society and hold their wealth in trust for the less fortunate, many wealthy families and businesses added to the numbers of foundations and trusts, just as his message of constructive work to bring about national development led to the formation of many voluntary agencies.

During the 19th and early 20th century such organizations received legal recognition through the enactment of laws such as the Registration of Societies Act 1860, and the Indian Trusts Act 1882. Such enactments gave public recognition to the intention of the founders and extended the protection of the law to their income and property, and to their office bearers. The British Government in India also recognized that it could not, by itself, provide for all the welfare and development needs of society, and therefore sought to encourage private charitable contributions for public purposes by giving incentives. This included award of official titles and exempting donated income from the income tax. The Income Tax had been introduced in 1860, and in 1922, the government granted 50% tax exemption to individuals on donations for charitable purposes.

After Independence the numbers of voluntary organizations expanded to meet national development goals, especially when it became apparent that the governmental programs were inadequate to respond to the development needs of the deprived sections of the society. The Government of independent India continued and extended the tax concessions given earlier, fully aware of its own limitations in meeting social needs. The Finance Act of 1948 extended the exemption, earlier given only to individuals, to companies making charitable contributions. The Companies Act of 1956 introduced Sec 25 to enable individuals and corporations to set up nonprofit companies for charitable purposes. The Income Tax Act of 1961 broadened the definition of charitable purpose, which is in force today. Charity is now defined as " relief of the poor, education, medical relief, and the advancement of any other object of general public utility not involving the carrying on of any activity for profit." The broadening of the definition of charity thus brought within its ambit a very wide range of organizations working for both welfare and development, and not only those working for relief of distress.

These measures, coupled with high tax rates, led to the formation of several charitable trusts and organizations.

Collectively all such organizations are today referred to as the nonprofit sector, (NPO sector) which has grown almost exponentially over the last few decades. Today the non-profit sector comprises organizations that

- Donate money for charitable causes, (trusts and foundations)
- Charitie s for the welfare of the poor and the needy, (charitable organizations)
- Organizations that are development oriented, (NGOs)
- Organizations engaged in advocacy, protection of human rights, research and resource centres, environmental conservation et al., (intermediary support organizations, umbrella groups, networks,) and,
- Associations of all kinds, including chambers, associations of lawyers and chartered accountants, who are not public benefit but mutual benefit organizations, though nonprofit making.

Traditionally many of them would not have come within the ambit of "charity".

Nature and Scope of Nonprofit Sector

Non-profit organizations (NPOs) have certain common characteristics. These are:

- Formal: institutionalised to some extent or, if not registered, demonstrating a definite program or aims and objects, as well as rules and regulations of governance;
- Private: institutionally separate from the government;
- Self-governing: not controlled by the government or any other outside entity;

- Not-for-profit: non-profit-distributing;
- Voluntary: involving some meaningful degree of voluntary participation, either in the actual conduct of the organization's activities or in the management of its affairs;
- Non-religious: not primarily involved in the promotion of religious worship or religious education. This automatically excludes from voluntary organizations any temples, churches, synagogues, mosques, and other places where religious worship takes place, but includes not-for-profit service organizations affiliated to religious institutions, e.g., schools run by the *Arya Samaj* or Christian missionaries;
- Non-political: not primarily involved in promoting candidates for elected office, etc. India today has a vigorous nonprofit sector playing a pivotal role in accelerating the process of social and economic development. There has been a rapid expansion in the numbers of non-profit organizations in India. The sector has also matured in terms of outreach, sophistication of approach, diversity in types of organizational forms, the amounts invested in the sector and the employment it offers to people at all skill levels. According to a recent study of the non-profit sector in India by Participatory Research in Asia (PRIA) there are as many as 1.2 million non-profit organisations operating in the country, approximately half of whom are not registered. In the year 2000 this sector was providing paid employment to as many as 2.7 million people and mobilising resources to the tune of Rs. 17,922 crores. Non-profit organizations in India today encompass a wide-range of activities, including designing and implementing innovative programs in various sectors of development, research, documentation, and training and advocacy. They range from very small people's organizations to highly sophisticated and technologically advanced research and health care or educational institutions.

Legal Status

Legally, these various organizations become a legal entity by registering either as a;

- Public Charitable Trust under the Registration of Documents Act, or under the Bombay Public Trusts Act 1950, in Maharashtra and Gujarat, or their equivalents in some of the states.
- Registered Society under the Registration of Societies Act 1860 or its equivalent in force in various states.
- Section 25 Nonprofit Company under the Companies Act 1956.

Definition of Terms

Hereafter, this broad composite entity including foundations, NGOs, and large charitable institutions like colleges and hospitals, and service clubs, membership associations, chambers of commerce and similar organizations is referred to as the Non-profit Sector; non donating, voluntary organizations providing development services of all kinds are referred to as NGOs, and collectively as the Voluntary Sector.

What are referred to here as Charities or the Charities Sector are only those nonprofit organizations (donating and non donating) which work for public benefit. This is the sector, which is the prime focus of this research. Thus it does not concern itself with mutual benefit non-profit associations such as professional bodies, chambers and the like.

NEED FOR THE STUDY

Importance of the Sector

With the liberalization of the Indian economy, the enhanced focus on development, and the increasing awareness of the importance of human resource development, especially of women and children, there is a growing awareness amongst the government and the general public that the government machinery alone cannot adequately meet the demands of the situation, and that non-profit organizations can play a very vital role in bringing change and development because of their social and non commercial orientation, and closer interaction with local people.

Moreover, NPOs help to build a strong civil society, act as a vehicle for social cohesion, and are a bridge between the government and citizens. Because of this it is necessary to create conditions, which are conducive to its growth. A conducive environment includes an enabling legal and fiscal framework, which allows voluntary non-profit organizations to

- Come into existence in a manner that is easy and inexpensive and without restraint;
- Exist and operate free of undue interference; and
- Have direct and indirect (through tax benefits) access to funds, whether these come from private sources, the state or through economic activities of the organizations themselves.

The Legal and Fiscal Framework

By and large the basic legal framework governing the sector satisfies these conditions. Charity is on the concurrent list of subjects where both the Centre and the states are competent to legislate. There are 4 main laws governing the nonprofit sector, each of which is administered by an agency specifically created for the purpose. These are:

- The Registration of Societies Act of 1860 and its versions enacted by different states, and a corresponding Registrar of Societies to deal with organizations registered under the Societies Act.
- A variation of the Indian Trusts Act of 1882 is in operation in different states. Maharashtra and Gujarat have offices of the Charities Commissioner to oversee charities in these states; Tamil Nadu has a department of Religious and Charitable Endowments, and other states have something similar for charitable trusts.
- The Companies Act, Section 25 deals with nonprofit companies from the office of the Registrar of Companies, and
- The Income Tax Act is concerned with providing fiscal benefits to NPOs, administered through the Directorates of Income Tax Exemption.

In addition, there is the Foreign Contributions Regulatory Act, (FCRA) applicable all over India, enacted to meet the special condition of inflow of foreign funds to charitable organizations. The FCRA was essentially meant to control external funds, which could be used to threaten national security. However, in practice it has come to regulate the receipt and spending of foreign funds irrespective of security concerns.

Need for Administrative Reform

The non-profit sector has grown within this basic legislative framework, which sets out the parameters within which it can operate. However, during a hundred plus years of growth, rapid economic and social changes have changed the parameters within which the sector operates. On the one hand, both state and society expect it to take on much more than was initially expected, and for which it is not well prepared either in terms of financial, human or organizational resources. On the other, the state has not fully recognized this need for more resources and for a more liberal and facilitative approach to enable charities to operate more effectively. In short, the laws have not kept pace with changed circumstances or with need. From time to time, as will be noticed in detail later, the state has attempted to review these laws through consultations with the charities sector. The latest such effort was the Task Force established by the Planning Commission, Government of India in October 2000 to review, analyse and suggest ways in which the present acts, rules and procedures can be modified or simplified to facilitate the growth and development of the voluntary sector. However, its recommendations are yet to be implemented.

Moreover, it did not go into the administrative functioning of the agencies, merely noting in its report submitted in July 2001, that though there is scope and need to change parts of certain laws, the problem is not only with the formulations of the laws but also in their administration, with either cumbersome procedures or lack of understanding on the part of those who administer the charity laws, of the unique nature of the charities sector.

It also noted other lacunae which do not lie in the realm of laws as such, but in the administrative sphere, which if remedied could enhance the functioning of the sector. These are:

- A need to review and redefine accepted definitions of popularly used concepts – "charity", "non-profit", "voluntary", "civil society", "development organizations" and so on, especially for interpretations of the laws and regulations.

- Lack of authentic official statistics pertaining to the sector and lack of access for bonafide purposes, to information collected by the government;
- The lack of a mechanism for redressing grievances without recourse to the courts;
- Lack of a permanent forum for ongoing interaction between civil society and government so as to find a voice in policy making;

To achieve socio economic and sustainable development an effective state is necessary and there are growing pressures on governments and or ganizations round the world to be more responsive to the demands of internal and external stakeholders for good governance, accountability, effectiveness and achievement of tangible results. It is this pressure and need for administrative reform, which have prompted the present exercise.

Availability of Resources

A subset of this need for reform is connected to the availability of resources for charities to ensure sustainability and future growth.

To enable it to discharge its obligations properly, charities, like all other organizations, need resources. PRIA's study of the non-profit sector quoted earlier, found that of the Rs. 17.922 crores mobilised by non donating, non-profit organizations in the year 2000, 32.4 percent of the funds were from government sources, 31 percent were self generated and only 16.6 percent were private funds from Indian as well as foreign donors.

Government funds ensure stability and continuity, and lend credibility to the organization and its programmes. Government support to voluntary organizations has existed since 1950s, when the government started providing funds to NGOs through the Central and State Welfare Boards, and other government departments, and has increased steadily over the years, from Rs. 150 crores in the Seventh Plan to Rs. 462 crores in the year 2001-02. However, government support is far from adequate to meet their needs, government funds are difficult to access, lack flexibility, and are beset by delays.

Foreign assistance to the voluntary sector from multilateral and bilateral funders, routed through the government, though it has declined from a high of $ 500 million in 1980-81, is still substantial at an average of $ 250 million per year. In addition are the amounts contributed by private foreign donors. In the year 2000-01, 14,598 organisations including large religious trusts received Rs. 4,535 crores ($ 1 billion) as funds from private foreign donors.

Though there has been an increase of 15 percent per annum in funds from foreign sources, only 7.4 percent of the total receipts of voluntary organisations are foreign funds. The inflow of foreign funds is restricted due to the provisions of the Foreign Contribution Regulatory Act, which makes it mandatory for organisations to be registered with them or have prior permission before receiving foreign funds. Foreign funders have their own criteria for funding and for managing programmes that are usually complicated and difficult to understand for the smaller NGOs. The funds from this source are also unstable as they are driven by geopolitical considerations and can be withdrawn anytime. In fact foreign funds are on the decline or becoming more difficult to access, and foreign donors are increasingly encouraging local resource mobilization.

Therefore it is imperative that an additional alternative source of funds, viz, donations and grants from Indian trusts and foundations, and individuals is developed.

Though a recent research study by Sampradaan Indian centre for Philanthropy (SICP), indicates that 96% of urban individual households donate in charity, a major portion goes for ad hoc charity to individuals in need (50% of the total donated,) or to religious organizations, (29% of total) and only 21 percent of the total amounts donated goes to voluntary organizations.

There is, therefore, a need to increase charitable contributions from private sources, including from donating trusts. It is in this context of the need to stimulate private charity for development that tax incentives to donors provided by the Income tax law become important. Moreover, because of the dependence of nonprofit organizations on donations and grants from government and well wishers and the uncertain as well as the particular characteristics of their income stream, with few chances to generate income of their own, their income and expenditure patterns are also substantially different from those of government and the commercial sector, and these need to be understood, if the tax regime is not to cause undue hardship.

Therefore how facilitative or restrictive the IT administration is matters greatly to the charities sector. But whatever committees and commissions of enquiry have been constituted for review of the tax administration so far, such as the Direct Taxes Enquiry Committee (1958-59) the Wanchoo Committee on Direct Taxes (1971), the Raja Cheliah Committee, or the Public Accounts Committees, have had the limited mandate of checking tax evasion and misuse of tax benefits. They did not approach the problem from the point of view of the need of the charities Sector for resources for healthy development. Nor were they concerned with promoting internal good governance.

Public Accountability

Though inadequate in terms of need, the resources mobilized by the charities sector are still sizable. Not only do charitable organizations receive funds directly from the public, but they are also indirect beneficiaries of public benevolence. They receive grants from government out of the tax revenues contributed by society. Besides, government foregoes tax by offering exemptions on income tax and other taxes such as excise, as well as land at concessional rates. Therefore the public, apart from the government and the sector, has an important stake in seeing that charities are transparent and credible in terms of their governance and use of funds.

Instances of misuse of tax provisions, fraud, and poor governance by some sections of the sector appear to be increasing, and have brought issues of ethics and values underlying voluntary work, and the accountability of voluntary organisations to the government and the public. In particular, there are two categories of misuse, which need to be checked. One is that by large hospitals and educational institutions, which by claiming to be charitable, or promising to reserve a certain percentage of their services for the poor, have availed of benefits like land nominal or concessional rates, exemption from excise duties and the like, apart from exemption of income from tax, but have gone back on their promises. They are running these organizations as business ventures. A second category is organizations, which exist only on paper, and have been established only to launder black money or to avail of grant funding.

If the misuse is not checked, public trust in the nonprofit sector will be eroded, and because of a few black sheep the whole sector stands to have its image tarnished. This will also affect the chances of NPOs receiving funds from the public as well as donors. The possibility of increasing private charitable resources is not only a function of tax incentives and education of potential donors on the need to give, but also of accountability of nonprofit organizations. If the public perceives that charitable resources are not being properly used, it will reduce, not increase the flow of private resources to the nonprofit sector. Therefore proper regulation of NPOs for tax and other legal compliance is very necessary.

People will support charities if they can see that charities are meeting their legal obligations. Regulatory effectiveness, in turn depends on charities perceiving distinct advantages of complying with legal regulations; or its converse, see distinct disadvantages of not complying with legal requirements. Nonprofit organizations will comply with the law if they see that the regulator

- acts with integrity
- is open about its decisions and performance;
- is committed to high standards of service and
- is willing to work with the sector in seeking knowledge and innovation, and if
- compliance is not burdensome with complex and time consuming procedures.

They will not comply if they feel that they can get away with wrongdoing and there will be no adverse consequences for them. Though self-regulation of the charities sector to ensure good governance and accountability is very necessary and better than heavy state regulation, there will still be a need for an effective state mechanism to enforce the law in case of transgression of a code of good conduct. A self-regulatory body cannot administer legal sanctions, or adjudicate in disputes regarding property of trusts, or give protection of the law to office bearers discharging their official duties.

Effective Regulation and Compliance Education

In sum the above discussion raises the following points:

- How effective have our charity laws and the charity administration been in
  - o ensuring public confidence in charitable organizations by ensuring good governance, and
  - o encouraging charity through the concessions provided?
- What are the problems faced by NPOs in getting registration, tax exemptions and in complying with the laws?
- Is there in place a system for appealing the decisions made by the regulator. How effective is the present system of grievance redressal?
- Does the public have access to information about charities, and is there a public forum for debating issues related to the regulation of the charities sector?
- Does our charities administration play an educative role as distinct from the regulatory role, educating charities about legal requirements, providing the general public with information about the regulatory process, and educating the public about nonprofit organizations and how they operate? Should they play this role or should it be left to another organization?

These are the questions to which this study seeks answers.

Recent Developments

The study of the charities administration has become timely for three other reasons: One, there is a disturbing trend towards using the charity regulatory framework and administrative agencies for political purposes. Various states have enacted their own Registration of Societies Act in place of the central

Act of 1860. These amendments to the simpler and more liberal 1860 Act allow for much greater degree of state control over voluntary organizations, with powers to the state agencies to supersede the existing managements or to appoint state officers to the managing boards. It is reported that some states like Tamil Nadu and UP have used such provisions for political reasons.

Instances have also been reported in Maharashtra of political appointment of trustees to rich temple and other trusts like the Siddhi Vinayak Trust and others to control the vast funds at their command. And most recently, newspapers have reported the use of the charity laws to selectively send notices to activist groups involved in critiquing or protesting against the government after the Gujarat and Mumbai riots.

Two, the present Prime Minister, has, time and again, stressed the importance of the nonprofit sector in accelerating development and distributive justice, as also the need for administrative reform to meet public aspirations, and to see that the benefits of development reach all. Several state governments too, the Maharashtra and Gujarat governments among others, have set up State Law Commissions to review several of the laws which are old and in need of amendments.

The Maharshtra Law Commission has reviewed both the Bombay Public Trusts Act and the Registration of Societies Act and has made recommendations for new enactments to replace these, especially keeping in view the inadequacy of the present administrative structure to meet emergent needs, though it is important to note that their draft recommendations have called forth protest about certain recommendations from the charities sector in Maharashtra.

Three, globally too there is much interest in charities infrastructure reform and experiments with new models. For instance U.K., Canada, Australia, New Zealand, etc. are reviewing the effectiveness of their charity laws in the context of changed demands. It is possible to learn from their experience.

OBJECTIVES OF REVIEW

It is against this background and context that the present review of the charities administration has been undertaken to highlight areas for reform and to suggest institutional alternatives.

Its objective is twofold:

- To strengthen the voluntary sector's capacity to meet the challenges of the future, and especially to meet the public demand for more accountability, and
- To improve the state- nonprofit sector interface.

SOCIAL WORK- PROFESSIONAL VALUES AND ETHICS

In this section, we consider the value base of social work and the implications it has for practice and the professional status of social work.

VALUES, ETHICS AND REGULATION

In discussions about the value or ethical base of social work, a distinction has to be drawn between two competing notions. One is of 'ethics' as relating to the value base of social work and in providing a set of principles or values on which those involved in social work base their actions - a kind of moral code. In this sense ethics and values can be treated synonymously. However, 'ethics' will also often refer to certain rules and regulations which govern the behaviours of professionals such as social workers. As such, they are more to do with the regulation and monitoring of professional activity. Banks (Banks, 2003) cautions:

Don't take codes of ethics too seriously - they are as much rhetorical, educational and regulatory devices as they are grounds to practice for professionals facing ethical dilemmas.

Our concern is more with the value basis of social work. The concern of some social work commentators is that there has been increasing emphasis on the notion of ethics or ethical codes in terms of the regulation of behaviours and less emphasis on the core values or principles on which social work as an activity should be based. Regulation has become more important than promotion of core values. Though the establishment of the Scottish Social Services Council for example may be seen to be a good thing, it may do more in terms of regulation than in the protection of professional identity (Community Care, 17 June 2004).

Social work has undergone many changes in the second half of the 20th century in terms of organisational context and the nature of the social and political environment in which it operates. What is remarkable is how constant have been the key principles on which social work is seen to be based. Though the key principles have remained constant, they have of course been read and re read in different ways at particular points in time.

Code of Ethics: International Federation of Social Work

In the recent new shortened ethical document proposed by the International Federation of Social Work, key values are presented which would have been accepted by social workers from much earlier periods in the history of social work. Few social workers would disagree with them because of their rather general nature. As seen above, the definition of social work proposed by the IFSW contains reference to human rights and social justice and it is not surprising that the Code of Ethics privileges such notions. In the IFSW Code (IFSW (International Federation of Social Workers), 2004):

Social work is based on respect for the inherent worth and dignity of all people, and the rights that follow from this. Social workers should uphold and defend each person's physical, psychological, emotional and spiritual integrity and well-being. This means:

1. Respecting the right to self-determination - Social workers should respect and promote people's rights to make their own choices and decisions, irrespective of their values and life choices, provided this does not threaten the rights and legitimate interests of others.
2. Promoting the right to participation - Social workers should promote the full involvement and participation of people using their services in ways that enable them to be empowered in all aspects of decisions and actions affecting their lives.
3. Treating each person as a whole - Social workers should be concerned with the whole person, within the family, community and societal and natural environments, and should seek to recognise all aspects of a person's life.

4. Identifying and developing strengths - Social workers should focus on the strengths of all individuals, groups and communities and thus promote their empowerment.

Further, through their commitment to the promotion of social justice, social workers should challenge negative discrimination on whatever grounds; recognise diversity whether it be individual, family or community based; challenge unjust policies; and work in solidarity by challenging the conditions that contribute to social exclusion, stigmatisation or subjugation and work towards an inclusive society (IFSW (International Federation of Social Workers), 2004).

The inability to operate according to such core principles may also in part account for the fact that many social workers leave the profession. For that reason what have been referred to as 'golden hellos' (Unison, 2004) - payments to encourage social workers to work in areas short of social workers; or 'golden handcuffs' (Unison, 2004) - payments to entice social workers not to leave, will not in themselves address the crisis facing social work. The issue is not one of logistics and redistribution of resources but rather about the very basis and key principles on which contemporary social work operates. What the literature does reveal is that for those who leave the profession, or indeed many who remain within it, the situation in which they practice does not allow them to fulfil their commitment to key principles.

'Social work' is also a concept that is not readily understood by the public whose views on social work are equally influenced by its association with scandals, especially those involving children (Scottish Executive, 2005). Research using general public survey methods suggests that social work has a negative public image and is poorly understood, although there are some signs that this image is beginning to be less held (ibid.). The impact on public understanding and acceptance of social work has clearly been influenced by cases involving children. In any review of the future of social work it will be important to gauge public opinion as one element of the social context in which social work operates.

What is also particularly interesting is that, though there are key differences in what the definition of social work may be, such values as contained in the IFSW statement are also embodied in the national association code of ethics for countries such as France, Germany and the Russian Federation (IFSW (International Federation of Social Workers), 2004). There is a universality of such key values over time and place whether it be for the 'social worker', 'educateur' or 'social pedagogue' (Kornbeck, 2002). Though there may be disagreement about the most appropriate structural or organisational context there is little disagreement about the core values of social work.

The importance of maintaining a set of core values for social work also contributes to the notion of the professionalisation of social work - that it has its own distinctive values which demarcate it from other professions. The concern of some is that it is precisely because social work may have lost contact with these values that it has also lost its professional identity. Similarly, by not promoting these core values, the boundary between what social workers and other professionals do may be somewhat eroded.

What this discussion of professional values and ethics serves to highlight is that despite the many organisational and structural changes which have impacted on social work, the core values have remained relatively constant. This is significant for any review of social work because-

The maintenance of core values and principles is central to professional identity. The difficulty of implementing core values and principles in the context of current organisational and structural arrangements is problematic for social workers Future developments in the profession of social work should be based on a commitment in practice to key values and principles.

PROFESSIONAL SOCIAL WORK IN INDIA - ISSUES AND CHALLENGES

Social Work is a discipline involving the application of social theory and research methods to study and improve the lives of people, groups, and societies. It incorporates and uses other social sciences as a means to improve the human condition and positively change society's response to chronic problems. It is a profession committed to the pursuit of social justice, to the enhancement of the quality of life, and to the development of the full potential of each individual, group and community in the society. It seeks to simultaneously address and resolve social issues at every level of society and economic status, but especially among the poor and sick. Social workers are concerned with social problems, their causes, their solutions and their human impacts. They work with individuals, families, groups.

In the developed countries, only professionally qualified persons with social work education can intervene with the psycho-social problems of individuals and practitioners must obtain a license or be professionally registered. Unfortunately in India, in spite of the fact that the number of social work schools, institutes and departments of colleges and universities have been growing slowly but steadily during the initial six decades and growing rapidly over the last one decade or so, the quality of professional social work education and training and professional standards of practice have been declining and as a result, there is a serious damage to the 'professional status and image' of social work. With innumerable departments of social work mushrooming each day, professional social work education is being commercialized and issues of quality, credibility and ethical standards are compromised by the different stakeholders.

Professional Social Work Education began in India in 1936 with the establishment of TATA Institute of Social Sciences. For the past more than 7 decades, there has been an unprecedented growth in the number of Schools/Departments/ Institutes offering Social Work education all over the country. In India, currently there is a wider number of Institutions offering Social Work Education with different specializations. One of the serious issues in Social Work Education is the lack of uniformity in curriculum and standards of practice among the professionals in different settings. In spite of earlier efforts taken by prominent Social Work Educators, still in India, we do not have a Council for Social Work Education. In the absence of a National Council, there is no system of accrediting Social Work Institutions, standardization of Social Work Education, Practices and Licensing of Social Work Practitioners. There are considerable variations in the content and quality of BSW and MSW Curricula among the different institutions spread all over the country. Even though there are national level bodies representing social work schools and professional social workers, there has been a lack of consistent, coordinated and sustained efforts on the part of these bodies to accomplish the goal of establishing a national council and other institutional mechanisms for standardization, accreditation and licensing for social work. Even the active associations of social workers at national and state levels are satisfied with regular programmes of academic interest such as seminars, conferences and workshops which are organized efficiently but seldom move beyond those sporadic and geographically scattered events and dread the path of working for the enhancement of the quality and professional status of social work. The advent of Social work Education in Tata Institute of Social Sciences in 1936 as a post world war development and later the appointment of medical social workers in JJ hospital indicated the acceptance of social work as profession in India. With its knowledge base spanning fields like psychology, Sociology, Medicine, Psychiatry, Development theories, Management and Welfare administration, it was meant to produce professionals who can be fittingly called social doctors or social engineers. But after more than seven decades since its beginning, social work profession in India is unfortunately groping in the dark for its professional space. The “change agents “as social workers are called seem at a loss to change this increasing ambiguity of identity.

A CIITZENS' AUDIT OF EDUCATION

Hundreds of NGOs, institutions, people's organisations, and individuals recently joined hands to conduct a survey, district by district, of the state of education in the country. Their findings have been summarised in the First Annual Survey of Education Report (ASER). Ashwin Mahesh reports.

31 January 2006 - How well can Indian children read and write? It is well known that although raising literacy levels has been a goal endorsed by virtually every government, hundreds of millions of citizens remain outside the reach of this promise even today. It is also no secret that the quality of public education across the country is inadequate; enrolment in school alone is not enough to ensure that today's children too will not fall prey to the same forces that kept their parents illiterate. These generalities, however, are too sweeping, and do not provide

meaningful indicators to the state of public education in India. An important first step to creating measurable change in the future, therefore, is to properly understand the current state.

This assessment has now been attempted. Hundreds of prominent NGOs, institutions, people's organisations, and individuals joined hands to conduct a district-by-district survey of the country recently, in a national effort led by the NGO, Pratham.

Between Nov 11 and Dec 18, volunteers visited randomly picked villages in each district of India and surveyed 20 randomly chosen households in each village. In each household, children in the age group of 6-14 years were interviewed and tested for basic reading, writing, and arithmetic on a one-on-one basis. In all, Pratham and its partners surveyed nearly 6 lakh children in 2.4 lakh households from 12,000 villages in 525 rural districts; the result is the First Annual Status of Education Report (ASER), released recently.

ASER asked simple questions, designed to provide a good first look at the state of education. Do children have a school? Can children read? Can they write? Can they do basic arithmetic? Are there teachers in schools? Are enrolled children attending school? Based on the answers, ASER has ranked the states and districts, and plans to do this every year until 2010 - the deadline for achieving quality universal elementary education. Following the 2005 report, the district and state level groups will interact with state and district governments. ASER 2005 is expected to become a tool in the hands of people so that they can monitor, and help in improving in the status of education around them.

Some findings ;

- Nearly 1.4 crore children are out of school; this situation is especially worse in Bihar, Rajashtan and Jharkand, where 10% or more of school-age children are not enrolled.
- The gender gap in the percentage of children out of school, however, has dropped. In 2001, it was estimated that 2 out of 3 dropouts were girls, but this study finds that only a little more than half (52-55%) of the children out of school are gilrs.

- In three out of four schools visited by volunteers collecting data, the teachers were present, as they are expected to be. In several states, all the teachers assigned to surveyed schools were present. Unexpectedly, however, teacher absenteeism was high in Kerala, where 3 out of 10 schools visited did not have any teacher present.
- The really worrisome findings from ASER relate not to attendance and demographics, but to learning. The tests of reading ability were quite simple (a short paragraph at the grade 2 level), but even then 35% of children aged 7-14 could not pass this test, and 60% of the children could not read a simple story, also at grade 2 level. This situation was in fact worse in states like Tamilnadu and Gujarat, where the usual indicators (school availability, enrolment, teachers, etc.) are all good. Students in Bihar and Chhatisgarh fared better, despite really poor education infrastructure indicators for their states.

ROLE OF THE PROFESSIONAL

The main tasks of professional social workers can include a variety of services such as case management (linking clients with agencies and programs that will meet their psychosocial needs), medical social work, counselling (psychotherapy), human services management, social welfare policy analysis, policy and practice development, community organizing, advocacy, teaching (in schools of social work), and social science research.

Professional social workers work in a variety of mainly public settings, including: grassroots advocacy organizations, hospitals, hospices, community health agencies, schools, international organizations, employee assistance, philanthropy, and even the military. Some social workers work as psychotherapists, counsellors, psychiatric social workers, community organizers or mental health practitioners.

Types of Professional Intervention

There are three general categories or levels of intervention. The first is "Macro" social work which involves society or communities as a whole. This type of social work practice would include policy forming and advocacy on a national or international scale. The second level of intervention is described as "Mezzo" social work practice. This level would involve work with agencies, small organizations, and other small groups. This practice would include policy making within a social work agency or developing programs for a particular neighbourhood.

The final level is the "Micro" level that involves service to individuals and families. There are a wide variety of activities that can be considered social work and professional social workers are employed in many different types of environments. The following list details some of the main fields of social work.

Social Work Perspectives

Perspectives are ways of viewing and thinking about practice. They are used as a framework to assist clients in therapy or other social work settings

There are four main perspectives social workers employ: Ecosystemic/Ecological System, Feminist, Generalist, and Strengths Perspectives.

Ecosystemic/Ecological System-This perspective honours the mutual relationship between individuals and their environment. It looks at the goodness of fit between the individual's capacities and the environment's resources and capacities.

Feminist-This perspective examines the impact of societal beliefs, stereotypes and practices as the related to gender and sex roles. It values the feminine attributes of clients and attempts to address societal patriarchy, androcentrism and sexist practices which seek to oppress and exploit women.

Generalist-An approach to practice that involves a holistic understanding of the client on multiple levels-individual, family, community, organizational. This approach integrates various models and theories to help understand the client's situation and uses an eclectic mix of interventions and techniques. Inherent in this perspective is a collaborative process in which the client and the worker have mutual responsibility.

Professional Associations

There are a number of professional associations for social workers. The purpose of these associations is to provide ethical guidance, and other forms of support for their members and social workers in general. The International Federation of Social Workers (IFSW) the International Association of Schools of Social Work (IASSW), and the National Association of Social Workers (NASW) are among the professional associations that exist to enhance the profession of social work. *Network of Professional Social Workers* is a fast growing professional network of Social Workers across the globe. Network of Professional Social Workers aims to connect social workers beyond their local and national associations across the globe. Network of Professional Social Workers effectively uses Social networking media such as Linkedin, Face Book etc. to network with Social Workers across many countries and initiate discussions on various issues affecting Social Work Profession. Network of Professional Social Workers Group list serve, NPSW.

3

Philosophy and Ideology of Social Work

PHILOSOPHY AND IDEOLOGY

The New Principles

The idea that philosophical systems are solely an ideological expression of definite class interests provided the basis for the establishment of two fundamental 'laws' of the history of philosophy. Both of them were formulated by Zhdanov and accepted by all Marxist-Leninist historians in Poland.

If the disputes of various philosophical schools reflect the class struggle taking place in an antagonistic society, and if the main line of class division in such a society always differentiates two classes, those of the exploiters and of the exploited masses, there are also two main philosophical schools of thought struggling with each other throughout the ages, those of idealism and materialism.

Furthermore, since social progress is the process of change that leads from a class-ridden to a classless society and the struggle for the abolition of classes is bound up with the development of the materialist outlook, the 'scientific history of philosophy', that truly and adequately reflects the historical process, is the 'history of the birth, rise and development of the materialist world outlook and its laws'. So far as materialism grew and developed by constant disputes with various idealist trends, the 'history of philosophy is at the same time the history of the struggle of materialism with idealism'.

This assumption is neither a matter of convention nor a mere classification of philosophical currents, comparable to any other classificatory division, but the 'fundamental historical law of philosophical development'. This can be seen from the fact that the solution of many particular philosophical problems is supposedly determined in advance by the thinker's choice between materialism and idealism.

The second 'law' of the scientific history of philosophy regards the teaching of Marx as a philosophical revolution. It has resulted in the creation of a new philosophy 'differing qualitatively from all previous philosophical systems, however progressive they were'. Consequently, there are two epochs in the development of philosophy: the period prior and posterior to Marx and Engels whose life work forms the great divide.

From these two fundamental laws of philosophical development three subsidiary methodological rules were derived. The first and most important extended the class determination of philosophy from schools of thought to particular thinkers and to their particular views.

A 'concrete interpretation' requires the assignment to any philosopher of a definite position with respect to the class struggle of his time, the description of his share in the consolidation or destruction of the existing economic basis and its ideological superstructure. Any ascertainable philosophical deviation in the thinker's views from the prevailing ideological patterns should be reduced to socio-economic causes, to strains and stresses within the social class, to which he belonged, and to the shift in class relations.

The second methodological rule recommended that advantage should be taken of the results obtained by the application of the first directive to assess the relative importance of a given thinker for the development of the scientific materialist world outlook. In this manner Marxist-Leninist methodology gains an objective and universal criterion by means of which it can make the right selection of facts and order them according to their relative significance. This establishes the third rule which enjoins the historian to trace the direction of progress in philosophy and to assign to particular thinkers a place in it in accordance to whether they managed, in the specific conditions of their times, to discover and to resolve problems that promoted the objectively ascertainable course of social progress.

The three methodological rules had some direct and far-reaching implications. First, they made havoc of the relative independence of philosophical thought with respect to the material conditions of life, recognised by Engels in his old age and nominally endorsed by Marxist-Leninists, including Zhdanov. Second, they ascribed a high rank of philosophical importance to various writers, who so far have only been marginally considered in the history of philosophy (though they have a place in the history of social or political thought). The history of philosophy, wrote Kroński, has to give an extensive account of the 'great plebeian thinkers', such as Thomas More, Winstanley, Mably and Morelly; of the ideologists of the bourgeois revolution, e.g. Milton, and the precursors of socialism – Robert Owen and the French utopian socialists. According to the same criteria, Herzen, Belinsky and, generally, the so-called Russian revolutionary democrats, assume the most important place in the period between Hegel and Marx. This ran counter to the opinion of Marx and Engels who, understandably, assigned this rank to Feuerbach. As far as the history of philosophy in Poland was concerned, the methodological rules of Marxist-Leninist historiography implied an upheaval and a complete revaluation of the prevailing tradition. In particular, Edward Dembowski, a Polish revolutionary democrat (according to the Marxist-Leninist classificatory categories) and the leader of an abortive peasant rising in 1846, to which Marx and Engels referred in laudatory terms, was to be given, jointly with Herzen and Belinsky, the most elevated rank, for they all, in Kroński's opinion, rose to the greatest philosophical heights in the period prior to Marx.

The scissor-and-paste history of philosophy, combined with Zhdanov's peremptory instructions, was firmly established in Poland by 1952. Its methodological rules were applied, above all, in a large-scale effort to adjust as much as possible the pattern of social, ideological and philosophical developments in nineteenth century Poland to that in Russia, as established by Soviet historians. The most cursory and commonplace references to Poland, made by Marx and Engels, every sentence, however trivial, of Lenin and Stalin concerned with the approach to historical inquiry or with the ideological development in the past, were scrutinised with reverence and the utmost care to serve as an unconditionally accepted guidance for historical research. Two of Lenin short contributions, In Memory of Herzen and Two Utopias, were of particular importance.

The main historical categories – those of revolutionary nobles, bourgeois democrats, and revolutionary democrats – which served to differentiate various political and ideological movements in nineteenth century Poland, were taken from In Memory of Herzen. They were applied and adjusted to Polish conditions in a great number of contributions that appeared in the years 1952-1956. The ideological transformations in Russia and Poland in the preMarxian period were described as essentially similar. They ran parallel to and interacted with each other. To show in detail that this had actually been the case and that the reception of Marxism-Leninism in Poland had proceeded in a 'correct manner' became the objective which was moved by the taskmasters of historical inquiry to the centre of interest.

The task assigned by Zhdanov to the historian of philosophy turned out to be extremely burdensome and difficult, if not impossible to accomplish. For the extension of what had to be considered in a historical-philosophical inquiry was expanded to an unmanageable size. It included not only ontology, the theory of knowledge, methodology, logic and ethics, but also, and above all, aesthetics, the theory of art, historiosophy, social philosophy, philosophy of religion, politics, science, economics, and ideology. At any rate, these were the problems which a historian of the nineteenth century philosophy in Poland, as it was conceived by Marxist-Leninists, should have investigated. The same applied to other periods. Generally, the conception of philosophy as a world outlook and of its history as a synoptic vision comprising political, social, economic, and philosophical thought, cultural trends and artistic currents, disregarded the accepted distinctions and self-imposed limitations. It also abolished the difference between philosophers at one extreme, philosophical journalists and polemical writers of political tracts for the times at the other. It resulted in insuperable difficulties of which, at first, Marxist-Leninist historians were unaware and which they regarded as a sign of their superiority over the traditional historian of philosophy.

There is a passage in Lord Acton Inaugural Lecture on the Study of History in which he pointed out the confusion ensuing from a study of history, if it does not display in its course specific and distinctive characteristics of its own. Mastery, he argued, is acquired by resolved limitations a historian is a master of detail, without which his synthesis loses itself in the realm of fantasy. At the time when Marxist-Leninists were embarking upon their new course Tatarkiewicz gave the same advice to the historian of philosophy: he should not try to do everything at once; self-imposed limitations and principles of selection are unavoidable in his inquiry. Marxist-Leninists discovered the justice of this view when from making plans they passed on to their implementation. For they were unable to retain control over their all-inclusive subject-matter; they got lost in the tangle of the sum total of views on man, society, history, religion, politics, literature, morals, and the like. They became trapped in trivialities and generalities unsupported by the study of detailed and concrete facts. On the other hand, the assumption that the history of philosophy can be represented as a mere response to socio-economic needs and the corollary of this assumption that an alleged social and political significance should be imputed to every philosophical view, overreached the evidence. The historian's attention, focussed at the wrong place, impeded the progress of his study. Since the examination of particular facts was neglected, a typical Marxist-Leninist historical contribution contained very little of interest to the history of philosophy in the specific meaning of this term.

There was yet another difficulty no less formidable than the first. For their methodology put Marxist-Leninists under the obligation of relating the phenomena of the superstructure to those of the basis. This presupposed the existence of an economic and social history with a wealth of detailed material, generalisations and syntheses. But economic and social history as advanced as the philosophic programme required was non-existent.

This does not mean that no economic history of Poland was available. On the contrary, Franciszek Bujak (1875-1953) and Jan Rutkowski, mentioned before, have created thriving schools of research, and the latter produced the first comprehensive Economic History of Poland. This work did not, however, satisfy the requirements of Marxist-Leninists, for, in their opinion, it was based on entirely false theories and could be used only as a source of materials. Strange as it may appear, economic history as a specialised branch of historical inquiry was suppressed during the Stalinist period, since such a specialisation was considered to be harmful. A short essay that discussed various views on and succinctly described some aspects of the development of capitalism in Poland in the first half of the nineteenth century was practically all that was made available to the historian of philosophical thought. Although a MarxistLeninist historian should have had a wide and detailed command over the history of economic and social development, he was left entirely to his own resources with practically no help from economic historians.

To acomplish his assigned task, a historian of philosophy had first to change into an economic and social historian, and, as he was not equipped and prepared to perform this role, what he did was to make a short-cut of an impermissible sort. Over and over again he turned in a vicious circle. First, he deduced his economic and social data from various historical material at hand and later related the inferred state of affairs largely to the same material from which he started. This procedure was either actually displayed before the reader's eyes or made apparent by stereotype descriptions as much alike as if they came from the same mould. Moreover, it has been said that the influence of ideology shows nowhere more strongly than in economic history. Marxist-Leninist economic history affords a striking instance of the justice of this observation. When the historians finally recognised the amateurishness and irresponsibility of their procedure, they also confessed that it always filled those who had to resort to it with an unconcealed dismay.

IDEOLOGY

An ideology is a set of ideas that constitutes one's goals, expectations, and actions. An ideology can be thought of as a comprehensive vision, as a way of looking at things (compare worldview), as in common sense and several philosophical tendencies, or a set of ideas proposed by the dominant class of a society to all members of this society (a "received consciousness" or product of socialization). The main purpose behind an ideology is to offer either change in society, or adherence to a set of ideals where conformity already exists, through a normative thought process. Ideologies are systems of abstract thought applied to public matters and thus make this concept central to politics. Implicitly every political tendency entails an ideology whether or not it is propounded as an explicit system of thought. It is how society sees things.

History

The term "ideology" was born in the highly controversial, philosophical and political debates and fights of the French Revolution and acquired several other meanings from the early days of the First French Empire to the present. The word *ideology* was coined by Destutt de Tracy in 1796 assembling the parts *idea* (near to the Lockean sense) and *-logy*. He used it to refer to one aspect of his "science of ideas". (To the study itself, not the subject of the study.) He separated three aspects, namely: ideology, general grammar and logic, considering respectively the subject, the means and the reason of this science. He argues that among these aspects ideology is the most generic term, because the science of ideas also contains the study of their expression and deduction.

According to Karl Mannheim's historical reconstruction of the meaning-shifts of ideology, the modern meaning of the word ideology was born when Napoleon Bonaparte (as a politician) used it in an abusive way against "the ideologues" (a group which included Cabanis, Condorcet, Constant, Daunou, Say, Madame de Staël and Tracy), to express the pettiness of his (liberal republican) political opponents.

Perhaps the most accessible source for the near-original meaning of *ideology* is Hippolyte Taine's work on the Ancien Regime (first volume of "Origins of Contemporary France"). He describes ideology as rather like teaching philosophy by the Socratic method, but without extending the vocabulary beyond what the general reader already possessed, and without the examples from observation that practical science would require. Taine identifies it not just with Destutt De Tracy, but also with his milieu, and includes Condillac as one of its precursors. (Tracy read the works of Locke and Condillac while he was imprisoned during the Reign of Terror.)

The word "ideology" was coined long before the Russians coined "intelligentsia", or before the adjective "intellectual" referred to a sort of person, i.e. an intellectual. Thus these words were not around when the hard-headed, driven Napoleon Bonaparte took the word "ideologues" to ridicule his intellectual opponents. Gradually, however, the term "ideology" has dropped some of its pejorative sting, and has become a neutral term in the analysis of differing political opinions and views of social groups. While Karl Marx situated the term within class struggle and domination, others believed it was a necessary part of institutional functioning and social integration.

Analysis

Meta-ideology is the study of the structure, form, and manifestation of ideologies. Meta-ideology posits that ideology is a *coherent system of ideas*, relying upon a few basic assumptions about reality that may or may not have any factual basis, but are subjective choices that serve as the seed around which further thought grows.

According to this perspective, ideologies are neither right nor wrong, but only a relativistic intellectual strategy for categorizing the world. The pluses and minuses of ideology range from the vigour and fervour of true believers to ideological infallibility. Excessive need for certitude lurks at fundamentalist levels in politics and religions.

The works of George Walford and Harold Walsby, done under the heading of systematic ideology, are attempts to explore the relationships between ideology and social systems.

David W. Minar describes six different ways in which the word "ideology" has been used:

1. As a collection of certain ideas with certain kinds of *content*, usually normative; a
2. As the *form or internal logical structure* that ideas have within a set;
3. By the role in which ideas play in *human-social interaction*;

4. By the role that ideas play in the *structure of an organization*;
5. As meaning, whose purpose is *persuasion*; and
6. As the *locus* of social interaction, possibly.

For Willard A. Mullins, an ideology is composed of four basic characteristics:

1. it must have power over cognition
2. it must be capable of guiding one's evaluations;
3. it must provide guidance towards action;
4. and, as stated above, must be logically coherent.

Mullins emphasizes that an ideology should be contrasted with the related (but different) issues of *utopia* and *historical myth*.

The German philosopher Christian Duncker called for a "critical reflection of the ideology concept" (2006). In his work, he strove to bring the concept of ideology into the foreground, as well as the closely connected concerns of epistemology and history. In this work, the term ideology is defined in terms of a system of presentations that explicitly or implicitly claim to absolute truth.

Though the word "ideology" is most often found in political discourse, there are many different kinds of ideology: political, social, epistemological, ethical, etc.

IDEOLOGY AS AN INSTRUMENT OF SOCIAL REPRODUCTION

In the Marxist economic base and superstructure model of society, *base* denotes the relations of production, and *superstructure* denotes the dominant ideology (religious, legal, political systems). The economic base of production determines the political superstructure of a society. Ruling class-interests determine the superstructure and the nature of the justifying ideology—actions feasible because the ruling class control the means of production. For example, in a feudal mode of production, religious ideology is the most prominent aspect of the superstructure, while in capitalist formations, ideologies such as liberalism and social democracy dominate. Hence the great importance of the ideology justifying a society; it politically confuses the alienated groups of society via false consciousness, such as in the case of commodity fetishism—the belief that value is inherent to a commodity, rather than external, added to it via labour.

The ruling class affect their social reproduction by the dominant ideology's representing—to every social-economic class—that the economic interests of the ruling class are the economic interests of the entire society. Some explanations, György Lukács proposes ideology as a projection of the class consciousness of the ruling class. Antonio Gramsci uses cultural hegemony to explain why the working-class have a false ideological conception of what are their best interests.

Chronologically, the dominant ideologies in Capitalism are:

1. classical liberalism
2. modern liberalism
3. social democracy
4. neo-liberalism.

Corresponding to these three capitalist stages of development:

1. extensive stage
2. intensive stage
3. contemporary capitalism (late capitalism).

The Marxist formulation of "ideology as an instrument of social reproduction" is conceptually important to the sociology of knowledge, viz. Karl Mannheim, Daniel Bell, and Jürgen Habermas et al. Moreover, Mannheim has developed, and progressed, from the "total" but "special" Marxist conception of ideology to a "general" and "total" ideological conception acknowledging that all ideology (including Marxism) resulted from social life, an idea developed by the sociologist Pierre Bourdieu.

Louis Althusser's *Ideological State Apparatuses*

Louis Althusser proposed a materialistic conception of ideology, which made use of a special type of discourse: the lacunar discourse. A number of propositions, which are never untrue, suggest a number of other propositions, which are. In this way, the essence of the lacunar discourse is what is *not* told (but is suggested).

For example, the statement "All are equal before the law", which is a theoretical groundwork of current legal systems, suggests that all people may be of equal worth or have equal "opportunities". This is not true, for the concept of private property over the means of production results in some people being able to own more (*much* more) than others, and their property brings power and influence (the rich can afford better lawyers, among other things, and this puts in question the principle of equality before the law).

Althusser also proffered the concept of the Ideological State Apparatus to explain his theory of ideology. His first thesis was "*ideology has no history*": while individual ideolog*ies* have histories, interleaved with the general class struggle of society, the general form of ideology is external to history. His second thesis, "*Ideas are material*", explains his materialistic attitude, which he illustrates with the "scandalous advice" of Pascal toward unbelievers: "kneel and pray, and then you will believe". For Althusser, beliefs and ideas are the products of social practices, not the reverse. What is ultimately important for Althusser are not the subjective beliefs held in the "minds" of human individuals, but rather the material institutions, rituals and discourses that produce these beliefs.

Feminism as Critique of Ideology

Naturalizing socially constructed patterns of Behaviour has always been an important mechanism in the production and reproduction of ideologies. Feminist theorists have paid close attention to these mechanisms. Adrienne Rich e.g. has shown how to understand motherhood as a social institution. However, feminism is not a homogeneous whole, and some corners of feminist thought criticize the critique of social constructionism, by advocating that it disregards too much of human nature and natural tendencies. The debate, they say, is about the normative/naturalistic fallacy—the idea that just something "being" natural does not necessarily mean it "ought" to be the case.

POLITICAL IDEOLOGIES

Many political parties base their political action and program on an ideology. In social studies, a Political *Ideology* is a certain ethical set of ideals, principles, doctrines, myths or symbols of a social movement, institution, class, or large group that explains how society should work, and offers some political and cultural blueprint for a certain social order. A political ideology largely concerns itself with how to allocate power and to what ends it should be used. Some parties follow a certain ideology very closely, while others may take broad inspiration from a group of related ideologies without specifically embracing any one of them.

Political ideologies have two dimensions:

1. *Goals*: how society should work (or be arranged).
2. *Methods*: the most appropriate ways to achieve the ideal arrangement.

An ideology is a collection of ideas. Typically, each ideology contains certain ideas on what it considers to be the best form of government (e.g. democracy, theocracy, etc.), and the best economic system (e.g. capitalism, socialism, etc.). Sometimes the same word is used to identify both an ideology and one of its main ideas. For instance, "socialism" may refer to an economic system, or it may refer to an ideology which supports that economic system.

Ideologies also identify themselves by their position on the political spectrum (such as the left, the centre or the right), though this is very often controversial. Finally, ideologies can be distinguished from political strategies (e.g. populism) and from single issues that a party may be built around (e.g. legalization of marijuana). Philosopher Michael Oakeshott provides a good definition of ideology as "the formalized abridgment of the supposed sub-stratum of the rational truth contained in the tradition." Studies of the concept of ideology itself (rather than specific ideologies) have been carried out under the name of systematic ideology.

Political ideologies are concerned with many different aspects of a society, some of which are: the economy, education, health care, labour law, criminal law, the justice system, the provision of social security and social welfare, trade, the environment, minors, immigration, race, use of the military, patriotism and established religion.

Today, many commentators claim that we are living in a post-ideological age, in which redemptive, all-encompassing ideologies have failed, and this is often associated with Francis Fukuyama's writings on "the end of history.".

Epistemological Ideologies

Even when the challenging of existing beliefs is encouraged, as in science, the dominant paradigm or mindset can prevent certain challenges, theories or experiments from being advanced. There are critics who view science as an ideology in itself, or being an effective ideology, called scientism. Some scientists respond that, while the scientific method is itself an ideology, as it is a collection of ideas, there is nothing particularly wrong or bad about it.

Other critics point out that while science itself is not a misleading ideology, there are some fields of study within science that are misleading. Two examples discussed here are in the fields of ecology and economics.

A special case of science adopted as ideology is that of ecology, which studies the relationships among living things on Earth.

Perceptual psychologist James J. Gibson believed that human perception of ecological relationships was the basis of self-awareness and cognition itself. Linguist George Lakoff has proposed a cognitive science of mathematics wherein even the most fundamental ideas of arithmetic would be seen as consequences or products of human perception—which is itself necessarily evolved within an ecology.

Deep ecology and the modern ecology movement (and, to a lesser degree, Green parties) appear to have adopted ecological sciences as a positive ideology. Some accuse ecological economics of likewise turning scientific theory into political economy, although theses in that science can often be tested. The modern practice of green economics fuses both approaches and seems to be part science, part ideology.

This is far from the only theory of economics to be raised to ideology status—some notable economically-based ideologies include mercantilism, mixed economy, social Darwinism, communism, laissez-faire economics, and free trade. There are also current theories of safe trade and fair trade which can be seen as ideologies.

Psychological Research

Psychological research increasingly suggests that ideologies reflect motivational processes, as opposed to the view that political convictions always reflect independent and unbiased thinking. Research in 2008 proposed that ideologies may function as prepackaged units of interpretation that spread because of basic human motives to understand the world, avoid existential threat, and maintain valued interpersonal relationships. The authors conclude that such motives may lead disproportionately to the adoption of system-justifying worldviews. Psychologists have generally found that personality traits, individual difference variables, needs, and ideological beliefs seem to have a common thread.

Ideology and Semiotic Theory

According to the semiotician Bob Hodge, ideology "identifies a unitary object that incorporates complex sets of meanings with the social agents and processes that produced them. No other term captures this object as well as 'ideology'. Foucault's 'episteme' is too narrow and abstract, not social enough. His 'discourse', popular because it covers some of 'ideology's' terrain with less baggage, is too confined to verbal systems. 'Worldview' is too metaphysical, 'propaganda' too loaded. Despite or because of its contradictions, 'ideology' still plays a key role in semiotics oriented to social, political life". Authors such as Michael Freeden have also recently incorporated a semantic analysis to the study of ideologies.

In Everyday Society

In public discussions, certain ideas arise more commonly than others. Often people with diverse backgrounds and interests may find themselves thinking alike in ways startling to those from other backgrounds. Social scientists might explain this phenomenon as evidence of ideologies.

Dominant ideologies appear as "neutral", holding to assumptions that are largely unchallenged. Meanwhile, all other ideologies that differ from the dominant ideology are seen as radical, no matter what the content of their actual vision may be. The philosopher Michel Foucault wrote about the concept of apparent ideological neutrality. Ideology is not the same thing as philosophy. Philosophy is an analytic method for assessing ideologies and belief systems. Some attribute to ideology positive characteristics like vigour and fervour, or negative features like excessive certitude and fundamentalist rigor. Organizations that strive for power will try to influence the ideology of a society to become closer to what they want it to be. Political organizations (governments included) and other groups (e.g. lobbyists) try to influence people by broadcasting their opinions.

When most people in a society think alike about certain matters, or even forget that there are alternatives to the status quo, we arrive at the concept of hegemony, about which the philosopher Antonio Gramsci wrote. Such a state of affairs has been dramatized many times in literature: *Nineteen Eighty-Four* by George Orwell; *Brave New World* by Aldous Huxley; and *A Wrinkle in Time* by Madeleine L'Engle. Noam Chomsky and Edward S. Herman have argued that social ideological homogeneity can be achieved by restricting and filtering the political, social, and economic information transmitted by mass communication.

PHILOSOPHY AS IDEOLOGY

Philosophy can also be thought of as ideology. An ideology is, by comparison with wisdoms, a more highly organized body of opinion. It usually serves programs of action and organizational needs. Philosophy as ideology is what we normally find in schools. For licensing purposes, state departments of education require schools, public and private, to have available a document that states the school's "philosophy" of education. Significantly, such school philosophies can be acquired pre-packaged. Educational accrediting agencies publish books of them that school planners and directors can use to choose among different philosophies of education like so many items on a menu. Here is an example of such an educational ideology:

The social development of elementary school students proceeds as the child becomes aware of the various authority structures that operate throughout the school, the community, the region, and the nation. We believe the school must help the child establish a perspective on the responsibilities and opportunities inherent in the multitude of authority systems in a democratic social order.

The point of ideology is to provide extensive suggestion as to how to structure and control an organization. This may be subject to debate. Although the example above mentions a"democratic social order," given its emphasis on authority, one could imagine that with this ideology, a school run like a miniature police-state could be rationalized.

In developing an ideology, the wisdoms of individuals, prophetic or otherwise, is called on to justify policies and day-to-day procedures. But did Moses, Jesus or Mohammed ever talk or write about hall passes, or detentions? No. What philosophy as ideology requires is an imagination that stretches the original intents and statements into broader or novel applications. Sometimes this imagination goes far beyond any reasonable interpretation. Indeed, deeply pious people may complain that the ideology of a church organization violates the essential spirit of the prophetic teachings, as when they complain that teachers in their schools fail exercise forgiveness as often as they should. A key point here is that organizational demands often substantially change the spirit of the original philosophy. Deep moral concerns may be lost in service of expediency.

Philosophy as Critical Inquiry

The American Philosophical Association, which represents professional academic philosophers in the critical tradition, characterizes the activities of philosophy this way:

Properly pursued, philosophy enhances analytical, critical and interpretive capacities that are applicable to any subject-matter, and in any human context. It cultivates the capacities and appetite for self-expression and reflection, for exchange and debate of ideas, for life-long learning, and for dealing with problems for which there are no easy answers.

The distinguishing characteristic of philosophy as critical inquiry is its focus on careful questioning and systematic appraisal, with no special respect given to the sources of the opinions examined. It doesn't matter who said or wrote what. Nor does it matter what effect critical inquiry might have on an organization. The point of the activity is not to honour individuals or to bolster organizations, but to try to get to the truth. Most importantly, in philosophy as critical inquiry, any statement purporting to be truth is challengable. But what are the rules for making such a challenge more than just an expression of dislike? What rules there are have been developed through millennia in a literature tracing back to Plato and earlier. We will look more closely at these rules for challenge and investigation later.

Assumptions of the Tradition of Critical Inquiry. Early on in critical philosophy, Greek philosophers distinguished between what they saw as "received opinion" and "truth." This distinction mirrors the difference between what we are calling wisdoms— and their derived ideologies — on the one hand, and critical inquiry on the other. Received opinion might be true, but it was the task — those ancient philosophers believed — not of traditional or religious authorities but of critical analysis to determine if it was so. There is a potential here for significant conflict. It is important that a central story in the history of philosophy is that of Socrates. He was condemned to death by the Athenian Court for "impiety" and "corrupting youth" by teaching them critical inquiry.

To emphasize an important point, however, critical inquiry is not confined to the irreligious. The tools of critical inquiry have long been recognized as useful by religiously committed philosophers in their struggle with the wisdoms of competing religious groups. There are recognized critical philosophers in many major religions. Islamic, Jewish and Christian philosophers have practiced in the tradition of critical inquiry.

Philosophy as critical inquiry treats knowledge as tentative. For practical purposes we might accept something as true, yet later change our mind if the evidence warrants. Notice how different this is from the conceptions of philosophy as wisdoms or ideologies. Wisdoms and ideologies present what they offer as absolutes. Those who offer us such absolutes insist at some point that inquiry must stop, questioning is no longer allowed. Critical inquiry, by contrast, will always — in theory, at least— allow questioning to proceed.

To reiterate, just because something is commonly believed to be true, is not considered in critical philosophy to be an adequate reason for accepting it. Since it is method, not personal authority that establishes truth, critical philosophy does not encourage us to become followers, or true believers. Rather, each person is required to think for himself or herself, following certain procedures which do not prejudice the outcome. Educators are well-served by learning these procedures, especially in a pluralistic society like ours where so many wisdoms and ideologies compete.

FIELD OF SOCIAL WORK

The growing complexities of the society have made man more vulnerable and helpless and given rise to various types of social problems. Social Work implies bringing of various resources in helping people with such problems and alleviate their suffering. Social workers try to lessen and prevent social problems caused by factors such as poverty, unemployment, alcoholism, lack of health services, family maladjustments, physical, mental and emotional handicaps, anti-social behaviour, and poor housing.

Social work was once the domain of philanthropists, and done voluntarily. However today, with changing social values and norms, the problems are more complex and effect larger number of people especially in the urban areas and tackling such problems requires people not with just good heart but also with special skills. As a matter of fact it has become quite a sought after career offering reasonable financial returns.

The field of social work encompasses a variety of subjects like sociology, psychology, education, criminology, industrial relations and personnel management and medical sciences and career opportunities would depend on an individual's area of specialisation. There are job openings both in the government as well as non-governmental sectors. Openings in the governmental sector are mainly in the community development projects pertaining to health, rural development and tribal welfare etc. Work in the non-governmental sector i.e. in NGOs' is more varied and can be specific to either urban or rural area. Postgraduates in Social Work (MSW) also have job opportunities in the industrial and corporate sector.

NATURE OF THE WORK

Social work is a profession for those with a strong desire to help improve people's lives. *Social workers* assist people by helping them cope with and solve issues in their everyday lives, such as family and personal problems and dealing with relationships. Some social workers help clients who face a disability, life-threatening disease, social problem, such as inadequate housing, unemployment, or substance abuse. Social workers also assist families that have serious domestic conflicts, sometimes involving child or spousal abuse. Additionally, they may conduct research, advocate for improved services, or become involved in planning or policy development. Many social workers specialize in serving a particular population or working in a specific setting. In all settings, these workers may also be called *licensed clinical social workers*, if they hold the appropriate State mandated license.

Child, family, and school social workers provide social services and assistance to improve the social and psychological functioning of children and their families. Workers in this field assess their client's needs and offer assistance to improve their situation. This often includes coordinating available services to assist a child or family. They may assist single parents in finding day care, arrange adoptions, or help find foster homes for neglected, abandoned, or abused children. These workers may specialize in working with a particular problem, population or setting, such as child protective services, adoption, homelessness, domestic violence, or foster care.

In schools, social workers often serve as the link between students' families and the school, working with parents, guardians, teachers, and other school officials to ensure that students reach their academic and personal potential. They also assist students in dealing with stress or emotional problems. Many school social workers work directly with children with disabilities and their families. In addition, they address problems such as misbehavior, truancy, teenage pregnancy, and drug and alcohol problems and advise teachers on how to cope with difficult students. School social workers may teach workshops to entire classes on topics like conflict resolution.

Child, family, and school social workers may be known as child welfare social workers, family services social workers, or child protective services social workers. These workers often work for individual and family services agencies, schools, or State or local governments.

Medical and public health social workers provide psychosocial support to individuals, families, or vulnerable populations so they can cope with chronic, acute, or terminal illnesses, such as Alzheimer's disease, cancer, or AIDS. They also advise family caregivers, counsel patients, and help plan for patients' needs after discharge from hospitals. They may arrange for at-home services, such as meals-on-wheels or home care. Some work on interdisciplinary teams that evaluate certain kinds of patients, such as geriatric or organ transplant patients.

Some specialize in services for senior citizens and their families. These social workers may run support groups for the adult children of aging parents. Also, they may assess, coordinate, and monitor services such as housing, transportation, and long-term care. These workers may be known as gerontological social workers.

Medical and public health social workers may work for hospitals, nursing and personal care facilities, individual and family services agencies, or local governments.

Mental health and substance abuse social workers assess and treat individuals with mental illness or substance abuse problems. Such services include individual and group therapy, outreach, crisis intervention, social rehabilitation, and teaching skills needed for everyday living. They also may help plan for supportive services to ease clients' return to the community when leaving in-patient facilities. They may provide services to assist family members of those who suffer from addiction or other mental health issues. These workers may work in outpatient facilities, where clients come in for treatment and then leave, or in inpatient programs, where patients reside at the facility. Some mental health and substance social workers may work in employee-assistance programs. In this setting, they may help people cope with job-related pressures or with personal problems that affect the quality of their work. Other social workers work in private practice, where they are employed directly by the client. These social workers may be known as *clinical social workers*, *occupational social workers*, or *substance abuse social workers*. (Counselors and psychologists, who may provide similar services, are discussed elsewhere in the *Handbook*.)

Other types of social workers include *social work administrators, researchers, planners* and *policymakers*, who develop and implement programs to address issues such as child abuse, homelessness, substance abuse, poverty, and violence. These workers research and analyze policies, programs, and regulations. They identify social problems and suggest legislative and other solutions. They may help raise funds or write grants to support these programs.

NATURE AND FUNCTION OF SOCIAL WORK

In this section, we consider the nature and function of social work in anticipation of the discussion on the role of the social worker.

DEFINING SOCIAL WORK

Any attempt to explore the role and function of the social worker must of necessity seek to answer or at the very least address one basic question - what is social work? Our concern here is not to indulge in semantics though there is a serious issue about the language within which social work is framed and to which we will return later. Rather, our purpose is to identify the main definitions of social work as a social movement.

The logic for this is very simple. Without some agreed notion of what it is that constitutes social work, it is well nigh impossible to determine what the role of the social worker might be; what skills and expertise social workers should have; what training and education is appropriate for social workers; and what it is that distinguishes social work from other professions.

Differences in what is taken to be social work can also account in part for the gap between what social workers say they want to achieve and accomplish and what they are able to achieve within the constraints of the institutional settings within which they operate. It may also partly account for the gap in expectations of those who seek to enter the profession of social work and what they experience when they are in a work situations. It may also account for the fact that materials and documentation relating to the training courses offered by training institutions rarely (though with some exceptions) offer intending students any definition of what social work is.

Cree (Cree, 2003) states that 'It is almost impossible to find a simple definition of social work with which everyone is likely to agree'. Thompson (Thompson, 2000) suggests 'Social work is what social workers do'. For Cree (Cree, 2003), though the Thomson position is not seen by her to be very helpful, goes on to state that:

We should not expect to find unanimity in books about social work, or even in accounts of social workers. Social work is always subject to competing claims of definition and practice, and cannot be separated from the society in which it is located. Rather social work has to be seen as a collection of competing and contradictory discourses that come together at a particular moment in time to frame the task of social work.

SOCIAL WORK AS A CONTESTED CONCEPT

From this perspective, social work is what social work is seen to legitimately be. This of course presents no statement as to the actual nature and function of social work. It does though emphasise the importance that what social work is, is subject to a process of what Askeland and Payne (Askeland and Payne, 2001) call 'validation'. That is, a process of legitimation validates what is seen to be the nature of social work from a variety of conflicting definitions and assumptions. Social work is a truly contested concept and at any point in time there are competing definitions. What is clear is that what social work is taken to be has as much been about whose definition is seen as legitimate rather than which definition.

Social work has always been subject to competing claims of definition and practice, as social workers, politicians, service users and policy makers have struggled to lay claims on what social work is, and what it might be.

And

To understand social work, therefore, we must understand how knowledge is validated within the profession (Askeland and Payne, 2001).

What this inevitably implies is that there is no universal body of knowledge for social workers. What is seen to be valid knowledge or indeed the function of social work is defined by many others outwith the profession including academics, educators, professionals, administrators, politicians, users, carers and the media. There can be no doubt that within these different constituencies, there are very different views and assumptions about social work and its function, fuelled by vested interests and media representation, especially of problematic cases and scenarios.

This of course makes it very difficult to identify what are the appropriate skills and expertise needed for social work. It also accounts for the fact that social work as a movement has since its earliest days been associated with continual change and critical reflection on what it is; how best and where best it can be exercised. It also makes it very difficult to establish a clear professional identity for social work when the concept itself is subject to the views and assumptions of competing constituencies. Similarly, accepted or validated notions of social work which are embedded in the organisational structures of public social services may be entirely unacceptable to those with a more radical bent (Searing, 2004). For some, the resolution of this near chaos in competing statements about the nature and function of social work resides in the importance of social workers themselves determining what their specific professional identity is in order to ward off conflicting, indeed detrimental, notions about social work and its role.

DEFINING SOCIAL WORK: THE INTERNATIONAL FEDERATION OF SOCIAL WORK

However, one particular statement of the nature of social work has been agreed in the international community and has been accepted by the many constituencies within the UK and the international community (though Cree and others do not see it as in itself an acceptable statement). In 2001, the International Association of Schools of Social Work and the International Federation of Social Work agreed the following definition:

The social work profession promotes social change, problem-solving in human relationships, and the empowerment and liberation of people to enhance well-being. Utilising theories of human behaviour and social systems, social work intervenes at points where people interact with their environments. Principles of human rights and social justice are fundamental to social work (IASSW (International Association of Schools of Social Work), 2001).

Though of a very general nature, what the IFSW statement does at least present is a set of agreed commitments for social work. In particular, it promotes change, and also locates the social work task at the interface between the individual and the social; the individual and his/her environment. Similarly, it also identifies the importance of social justice and rights and working with disempowered members of our communities. It underlines the affinity between social work, the human rights conventions and the more recent legislation that strengthens the enforcement of human rights. And again, though of a general nature it does accord with statements made by others as to what constitutes the primary function of social work:

* Social work is committed to rights and justice (Clark, 2002).
* [social workers'] concern is for the individual and helping them achieve change, a certain quality of life and/or protection from harm or harming others (ADSW (Association of Directors of Social Work), 2004).

Davies put the notion of helping the vulnerable more forcibly when he asserted that: the essence of social work is maintenance: maintaining a stable, though not a static society, and maintaining the rights of and opportunities for those who in an unplanned uncontrolled community would go to the wall.

Social work from this perspective then is about assisting, supporting and enabling certain sections of the community. For that reason, one constancy in the history of social work has been its concern with those who suffer from the negative effects of social inequalities. For many this concern with inequality and poverty has become increasingly important because of what is seen to be the growing gap in modern societies between the rich and the poor or disadvantaged. For many (Community Care, 17 June 2004) there has never been a more important time for social work to establish itself as a credible profession working to ensure that the interests of less advantaged sections of the community are promoted and protected.

In a society where the gaps between the haves and have nots have widened and continue to widen, the social policy role of social work is going to be of major significance (Bamford, 1990).

and social work might be

... really concerned with freeing the poor and the marginal underclass from subordination and exclusion (Ferraro, 2003).

SOCIAL WORK AND SOCIAL CONTROL

What is also clear is that whatever the legitimate or validated notion of social work is seen to be, from other perspectives, social work can be seen to be an agent of social control. Far from addressing the inequalities with which we live, it may well play an important role in sustaining or perpetuating the very social and economic system which promotes such inequalities. Rather than liberating, it can be viewed as oppressive and for that reason not true to the core values on which it claims to be based (Jordan and Parkinson, 2001; Jordan, 2004).

Social Work as an Integrating Force

Munday (2003) and others also suggest European systems of social work also have a social integration function. On this view social work has as a key function the integration or reintegration of sections of the community with mainstream society. What would be lost from this perspective if social work did not exist would be the necessary support and assistance offered to the most vulnerable sections of society and the abdication of any responsibility to ensure their social inclusion. If social work did not fulfil that task it is difficult to envisage what agency or body would. In the connection it may be added that other agencies are only likely ever to take on parts of the role of social work in a piecemeal and selective way; the integrated view that characterises social work would be lost.

A Radical Social Work?

The demand for a radical social work which truly addresses the situation of those in need has been another constancy in the development of social work since the 1960s (Jones et al., 2004). Many of the current critiques of social work as a profession have embedded within them comments which do echo the concerns of those more inclined to a radical perspective on the role of social work. The argument has been made that the current structures through which social work is realised may not best serve those who are in need, and social work may do little more than perpetuate the very system which creates their vulnerability. A number of commentators (for example Bailey and Brake, 1975; Jordan and Jordan, 2000) have expressed their concern that by working with those who are most disadvantaged by the inequalities imposed by the economic system, social work may well contribute to the perpetuation of that very system. It is such a situation that Jordan (Jordan and Jordan, 2000) and others seek to address by proposing 'constructive social work'.

SOCIAL WORK AND POLICY FAILURE

A related position is that the function of social work may well be to deal with the failure of other policy areas such as crime, health or education. Social work is then seen to be charged with not simply dealing with those in need but rather with addressing the shortcomings of key policy areas in the public services.

From these kinds of arguments then, whatever it is that social workers are expected to do or want to do at a face to face or micro level, at the macro level, social work may well have other functions. What the literature then suggests is that

* There are competing definitions of social work
* Social work has a number of wider social functions
* The function of social work is highly contested
* Social work plays an important function in social integration
* Social work may fulfil a social control function
* Social work is expected to address the failure of social policies.

The tension for social work has of course always been bridging the tension between the personal and the political (Halmos, 1965); between supporting clients and controlling them or subjecting them to forms of surveillance; between meeting the needs of clients or addressing the social and political situation in which they find themselves. Though the IFSW statement on the nature of social work does note the importance of social justice, it could be criticised for saying little about the importance of seeing the service user/client/citizen in the context of his/her local community. In fact, it may well understate the value of community social work. One of the threads that has been woven through the history of social work and the organisational structures through which social work is to be realised, is the importance of seeing the client/service user as a member of a local community.

The Kilbrandon report (Kilbrandon, 1964), the Seebohm report (Seebohm, 1968), the Barclay report (Barclay, 1982) and the Griffiths report (Griffiths, 1988) all evidence this. They all reflect the recurring emphasis on the importance of working not just with individuals but with individuals as members of communities.

These reports highlight that community social work could play a significant role in supporting community members to address the circumstances in which they find themselves. The paradox is that although this is seen to be the clear value of a community social work approach, organisational and structural changes in the way social work services are provided are seen to have inhibited its growth and development.

The argument made against the value of community social work, especially from the radical perspective is of course also that such an approach does not address the causal factors which propel many social work clients/service users into disadvantage and poverty. The model for a future social work offered by Jordan, drawing on the Australasian experience in offering what he calls a 'constructive social work', provides solutions to this dilemma and emphasises the importance of the local and the community. As we discuss later the 'constructive' approach takes a user centred approach to social work and recognises the importance of addressing family, local and national issues.

SUMMARY

In summary, several implications can be drawn from the contested nature of social work and the fact that it is seen to have a number of wider functions. In particular, the absence of a clear definition of social work - or at least a definition agreed by all - means that it will continue to be difficult to identify just what the skills, knowledge and expertise are required by social workers.

Establishing just what legitimate role social workers can play will also be somewhat problematic in the absence of an agreed basis for the development of the 'profession' of social work. The fact that there are competing notions of social work maintained by different constituencies, including practitioners, users, politicians, policy makers, and the public does suggest that there is a need to establish clearly an agreed and accepted statement on the nature and function of social work.

4

Origin and Development of Social Work in India

PHILANTHROPY IN INDIA

Philanthropic funding in India is not only insufficient in overall monetary value but also inefficient in flowing to the people with the greatest need. According to the Bain report*, India's giving in 2006 was $5 billion compared to $300 billion in the US. Like other nations, wealth in India is concentrated with a few with nearly 40% of household wealth controlled by the top 5%. Yet, the higher the education and wealth, the lower the generosity ratio. Evidently, there is a need to generate more resources but there is also a need to apply these resources effectively to ensure social returns are maximised. There are over 3 million non profits in the India but less than 500 are scale organizations in terms of giving and impact (greater than $100,000 in annual income).

In addition, only 10% of giving in India comes from corporates and individuals versus 75% from individuals alone in the US. Private philanthropy has huge promise as it can reward innovation and undertake greater risks than government funding. We believe India's growing wealthy must intensify their giving, and examine the outcomes of their donations. However many donors are simply not conscious of the greater impact that they could be having if they took a more strategic approach.

There are two major reasons why philanthropic funding is not as effective as it could be.

Firstly, funding tends to be short-term. This means non profits are caught in a constant cycle of raising funds, unable to plan for the long-term and unable to focus on their impact. Real social change takes time and one-off donations, or one-year funding means programs get started, but may not reach the momentum to bring about real social change.

Secondly it is highly restrictive – donors will often specify what they want the funds to be spent on, and usually this is program costs – textbooks, buildings, medicines. This is important,but if an organisation is going to scale and create greater impact then funding has to be put into the more "unpopular", but equally vital areas such as monitoring and evaluation, salaries for staff, training and planning. It is not possible for an organization to be effective if it does not have talented staff, effective plans, a vision for growth and a method for demonstrating its impact.

The exciting news is that philanthropy in India is expected to increase on the back of greater wealth accumulation and better channels for donations owing to the economic boom in the country. HNIs in India are numerous with over 115,000 in 2009, and are a fast-growing segment. At this stage, if critical hurdles faced by donors, support networks and charities are addressed and resources are applied effectively, then maximum impact can be achieved for the most number of people. Dasra is committed to helping philanthropists understand this complex area and make informed choices.

VEDIC PERIOD

The Vedic Period (or Vedic Age) is the period during which the Vedas, texts related to early Indo-Aryan religion, were being composed, during the period of roughly the mid second to mid first millennium BCE. The associated culture, sometimes referred to as Vedic civilization, was centered in the northern and northwestern parts of the Indian subcontinent.

Chronologically, its early phase overlaps with the Late Harappan period and its late phase with the rise of the Mahajanapadas (early Indo-Aryan kingdoms in India). After the end of the Vedic period, the Mahajanapadas in turn gave way to the Maurya Empire (from ca. 320 BCE), the golden age of classical Sanskrit literature.

Overview

The reconstruction of the history of Vedic India is based on text-internal details. Linguistically, the Vedic texts could be classified in five chronological strata:

Rigvedic: The Rigveda is by far the most archaic of the Vedic texts preserved, and it retains many common Indo-Iranian elements, both in language and in content, that are not present in any other Vedic texts. Its creation must have taken place over several centuries, and apart from that of the youngest books (first part of 1 and all of 10), would have been complete by 1000(?) BCE. Archaeologically, this period may correspond with the Swat culture, the *Cemetery H* culture of the Punjab and the *Ochre Coloured Pottery culture* (OCP) further east. There is no widely accepted archaeological or linguistic evidence of direct cultural continuity from the Indus Valley civilization.

Mantra language: This period includes both the mantra and prose language of the Atharvaveda (Paippalada and Shaunakiya), the Rigveda Khilani, the Samaveda Samhita (containing some 75 mantras not in the Rigveda), and the mantras of the Yajurveda. Many of these texts are largely derived from the Rigveda, but have undergone certain changes, both by linguistic change and by reinterpretation. Conspicuous changes include change of *vishva* "all" by *sarva*, and the spread of the *kuru-* verbal stem (for Rigvedic *krno-*). This is the time of the early Iron Age in north-western India, corresponding to the *Black and Red Ware* (BRW) culture, and the kingdom of the Kurus, dating from ca. the 10th century BCE.

Samhita prose: This period marks the beginning of the collection and codification of a Vedic canon. An important linguistic change is the complete loss of the injunctive. The Brahmana part ('commentary' on mantras and ritual) of the Black Yajurveda (MS, KS, TS) belongs to this period. Archaeologically, the *Painted Grey Ware* (PGW) culture from ca. 900 BCE corresponds, and the shift of the political centre from the Kurus to the Pancalas on the Ganges.

Brahmana prose: The Brahmanas proper of the four Vedas belong to this period, as well as the Aranyakas, the oldest of the Upanishads (BAU, ChU, JUB) and the oldest Shrautasutras (BSS, VadhSS).

Sutra language: This is the last stratum of Vedic Sanskrit leading up to c. 500 BCE, comprising the bulk of the Œrauta and Grhya Sutras, and some Upanishads (e.g. KathU, MaitrU). All but the five prose Upanishads are post-Buddhist). Videha (N. Bihar) as a third political centre is established.

Epic and Paninian Sanskrit: The language of the Mahabharata and Ramayana epics, and the Classical Sanskrit described by PaGini is considered post-Vedic, and belongs to the time after 500 BCE. Archaeologically, the rapid spread of *Northern Black Polished Ware* (NBP) over all of northern India corresponds to this period. The earliest Vedanta, Gautama Buddha, and the Pali Prakrit dialect of Buddhist scripture belong to this period.

Historical records set in only after the end of the Vedic period, and remain scarce throughout the Indian Middle Ages. The end of Vedic India is marked by linguistic, cultural and political changes. The grammar of Panini marks a final apex in the codification of Sutra texts, and at the same time the beginning of Classical Sanskrit. The invasion of Darius I of the Indus valley in the early 6th century BCE marks the beginning of outside influence, continued in the kingdoms of the Indo Greeks, new waves of immigration from 150 BCE (Abhira, Shaka), Kushan and ultimately the Islamic Sultans. The most important historical source of the geography of post-Vedic India is the 2nd century Greek historian Arrian whose report is based on the Mauryan time ambassador to Patna, Megasthenes.

RIGVEDIC PERIOD

The origin of the Vedic civilization and its relation to the Indus Valley civilization, Indo-Aryan migration and Gandhara Grave culture related cultures remains controversial and politically charged in Indian society, often leading to disputes on the history of Vedic culture. The Rigveda is primarily a collection of religious hymns, and allusions to, but not explanation of, various myths and stories, mainly in the younger books 1 and 10. The oldest hymns, probably in books 2–7, although some hold book 9, the Soma Mandala, to be even more ancient, contain many elements inherited from pre-Vedic, common Indo-Iranian society. Therefore, it is difficult to define the precise beginning of the "Rigvedic period", as it emerges seamlessly from the era preceding it. Also, due to the semi-nomadic nature of the society described, it cannot be easily localized, and in its earliest phase describes tribes that were essentially on the move.

Rigvedic Aryans have a lot in common with the Andronovo culture and the Mittanni kingdoms as well as with early Iranians. The Andronovo culture is believed to be the site of the first horse-drawn chariots.

Political Organization

The *grama* (wagon train), *vis* and *jana* were political units of the early Vedic Aryans. A *vish* was a subdivision of a *jana* or "krishti", and a *grama* was a smaller unit than the other two. The leader of a *grama* was called *gramani* and that of a *vish* was called *vishpati*.

The *rashtra* (polity) was governed by a *rajan* (chieftain, 'king'). The king is often referred to as *gopa* (protector) and occasionally as *samrat* (supreme ruler). He governed the people with their consent and approval. He was elected from a restricted class of 'royals' (rajanya). There were various types of meetings such as the *vidhata* or "Sabha". Gana was the non-monarchial assembly that is a parallel one to the monarchial assemblies of that period headed by Jyestha the same was referred in Buddhist text named Jettaka. The Sabha, situated outside of settlement, was restricted to the Vratyas, bands of roving Brahmins and Kshatriyas in search of cattle, with a common woman (pumscali) while the vidatha was the potlatch-like ritual distribution of bounty.

The main duty of the king was to protect the tribe. He was aided by several functionaries, including the *purohita* (chaplain) and the *senani* (army chief; *sena*: army). The former not only gave advice to the ruler but also was his chariot driver and practiced spells and charms for success in war. Soldiers on foot (*pattis*) and on chariots (*rathins*), armed with bow and arrow, were common. The king employed *spaœ* (spies) and *dutas* (messengers). He collected taxes (originally ceremonial gifts, *bali*), from the people which he had to redistribute.

Society and Economy

The concept of *varna* (class) and the rules of marriage were rigid as is evident from Vedic verses (RV 10.90, W. Rau 1957). The status of the Brahmins and Kshatriyas was higher than that of the Vaishyas and Shudras. The Brahmins were specialized in creating poetry, preserving the sacred texts, and carrying out various types of rituals. Functioning as intellectual leadership, they also restricted social mobility between the varnas, as in the fields of science, war, literature, religion and the environment. The proper enunciation of verses in ritual was considered essential for prosperity and success in war and harvests. Kshatriyas amassed wealth (cattle), and many commissioned the performance of sacrifices. Kshatriyas helped in administering the polity, maintained the structure of society and the economy of a tribe, and helped in maintaining law and order.

In the Early Vedic Period all the three upper classes Brahmins, Kshatriyas, and Vaishyas were considered as — relatively— equal Arya, but in the Later Vedic Age the Brahmins and Kshatriyas became upper class. The Vaishyas were pastoralists and farmers; the Shudras were the lower class; they included artisans and were meant to serve the upper three classes. As the caste system became deep-rooted there were many restrictions and rules which were to be followed.

Cattle were held in high esteem and frequently appear in Rigvedic hymns; goddesses were often compared to cows, and gods to bulls. Agriculture grew more prominent with time as the community gradually began to settle down in post-Rigvedic times. The economy was based on bartering with cattle and other valuables such as salt or metals. Families were patrilineal, and people prayed for the abundance of sons. The Society was strictly organized in a system of four varna (classes, to be distinguished from caste, jati)

VEDIC RELIGIOUS PRACTICES

The Vedic forms of belief are the precursor to modern Hinduism. Texts considered to date to the Vedic period are mainly the four Vedas, but the Brahmanas, Aranyakas and the older Upanishads as well as the oldest Shrautasutras are also considered to be Vedic. The Vedas record the liturgy connected with the rituals and sacrifices performed by the 16 or 17 Shrauta priests and the purohitas. The rishis, the composers of the hymns of the Rigveda, were considered inspired poets and seers (in post-Vedic times understood as "hearers" of an eternally existing Veda, *Shrauta* means "what is heard").

The mode of worship was performance of sacrifices which included the chanting of Rigvedic verses, singing of Samans and 'mumbling' of offering mantras (Yajus). The priests executed rituals for the three upper classes (varna) of Vedic society, strictly excluding the Sudras. People offered for abundance of rain, cattle, sons, long life and gaining 'heaven'.

The main deities of the Vedic pantheon were Indra, Agni (the sacrificial fire), and Soma and some deities of social order such as Mitra–Varuna, Aryaman, Bhaga and Amsa, further nature deities such as Surya (the Sun), Vayu (the wind), Prithivi (the earth). Goddesses included Ushas (the dawn), Prithvi and Aditi (the mother of the Aditya gods or sometimes the cow). Rivers, especially Saraswati, were also considered goddesses. Deities were not viewed as all-powerful. The relationship between humans and the deity was one of transaction, with Agni (the sacrificial fire) taking the role of messenger between the two. Strong traces of a common Indo-Iranian religion remain visible, especially in the Soma cult and the fire worship, both of which are preserved in Zoroastrianism. The Ashvamedha (horse sacrifice) has parallels in the 2nd millennium BC Andronovo culture, in Rome and old Ireland, was continued in India until at least the 4th century AD and revived under Jai Singh II of Amber in 1716 AD.

Vedic religion evolved into the Hindu paths of Yoga and Vedanta, a religious path considering itself the 'essence' of the Vedas, interpreting the Vedic pantheon as a unitary view of the universe with 'God' (Brahman) seen as immanent and transcendent in the forms of Ishvara and Brahman. These post-Vedic systems of thought, along with later texts like Upanishads, epics (namely Gita of Mahabharat), have been fully preserved and form the basis of modern Hinduism. The ritualistic traditions of Vedic religion are preserved in the conservative Shrauta tradition, in part with the exception of animal sacrifice, which was mostly abandoned by the higher castes by the end of the Vedic period, partly under the influence of the Buddhist and Jain religions, and their criticism of such practices.

THE LATER VEDIC PERIOD

The transition from the early to the later Vedic period was marked by the emergence of agriculture as the dominant economic activity and a corresponding decline in the significance of cattle rearing. Several changes went hand in hand with this. For instance, several large kingdoms arose because of the increasing importance of land and long distance trade. The late Vedic period, from ca. 500 BCE onward, more or less seamlessly blends into the period of the Middle kingdoms of India known from historical sources.

Kingdoms

The late Vedic period was marked by the rise of the sixteen *Mahajanapadas* referred to in some of the literature. The power of the king and the Kshatriyas greatly increased. Rulers gave themselves titles like *ekarat* (the one ruler), *sarvabhauma* (ruler of all the earth) and *chakravartin* ('who moves the wheel'). The kings performed sacrifices like *rajasuya* (royal consecration), *vajapeya* (including a chariot race) and, for supreme dominance over other kings, the ashvamedha (horse sacrifice).

The coronation ceremony was a major social occasion. Several functionaries, in addition to the purohita and the senani, took part. The role of the people in political decision making and the status of the Vaishyas as such was greatly decreased.

ISLAM IN INDIA

Islam is the second-most practiced religion in the Republic of India after Hinduism, with more than 13.4% of the country's population (over 138 million as per 2001 census).

Islam arrived in India in the 12th century and has since become a part of India's rich religious and cultural heritage. Over the years, there has been significant integration of Hindu and Muslim cultures across India and the Muslims have played a prominent role in India's economic rise and cultural influence.

Matters of jurisdiction involving Muslims in India related to marriage, inheritance and wakf properties are governed by the Muslim Personal Law, and the courts have ruled that Sharia or Muslim law, holds precedence for Muslims over Indian civil law. India is the only country in the world where the government subsidizes the airfare for the Hajj pilgrimage, spending ₹47,454 per passenger as of 2007.

POPULATION

India's Muslim population is the world's third largest and the world's largest Muslim-minority population. Most of the Muslims in India belong to Indian ethnic groups, with minor to obvious levels of gene flow from outside, primarily from Persia and Central Asia.

The largest concentrations-about 47% of all Muslims in India, according to the 2001 census—live in the 3 states of Uttar Pradesh (30.7 million) (18.5%), West Bengal (20.2 million) (25%), and Bihar (13.7 million) (16.5%). Muslims represent a majority of the local population in Lakshadweep (93% in 2001) and Jammu and Kashmir (67% in 2001). High concentrations of Muslims are found in the eastern states of Assam (31%) and West Bengal (25%), and in the southern state of Kerala (24.7%). Officially, India has the third largest Muslim population (after Indonesia and Pakistan).

Growth Rate

Muslims in India have a much higher total fertility rate (TFR) compared to that of other religious communities in the country. Because of higher birthrates and an influx of migrants from neighbouring Bangladesh, the percentage of Muslims in India has risen from about 10% in 1991 to 13% in 2001. The Muslim population growth rate is higher by more than 10% of the total growth compared to that of Hindus. However, since 1991, the largest decline in fertility rates among all religious groups in India has occurred among Muslims.

Demographers have put forward several factors behind high birthrates among Muslims in India. According to sociologists Roger and Patricia Jeffery, socio-economic conditions rather than religious determinism is the main reason for higher Muslim birthrates. Indian Muslims are poorer and less educated compared to their Hindu counterparts. Noted Indian sociologist, B.K. Prasad, argues that since India's Muslim population is more urban compared to their Hindu counterparts, infant mortality rates among Muslims is about 12% lower than those among Hindus.

However, other sociologists point out that religious factors can explain high Muslim birthrates. Surveys indicate that Muslims in India have been relatively less willing to adopt family planning measures and that Muslim women have a larger fertility period since they get married at a much younger age compared to Hindu women. A study conducted by K.C. Zacharia in Kerala in 1983 revealed that on average, the number of children born to a Muslim woman was 4.1 while a Hindu woman gave birth to only 2.9 children. Religious customs and marriage practices were cited as some of the reasons behind the high Muslim birth rate. According to Paul Kurtz, Muslims in India are much more resistant to modern contraceptive than are Hindus and, as a consequence, the decline in fertility rate among Hindu women is much higher compared to that of Muslim women. The National Family and Health survey conducted in 1998-99 highlighted that Indian Muslim couples consider a substantially higher number of children to be ideal for a family as compared to Hindu couples in India. The same survey also pointed out that percentage of couples actively using family planning measures was more than 49 percent among Hindus against 37 percent among Muslims. A 1996 survey conducted in the Lucknow district revealed that 34 percent of the Muslim women believed that family planning went against dictates of their religion while none of the Hindu women surveyed believed that religion was a barrier against family planning.

According to a 2006 committee appointed by the Indian Prime Minister, by the end of the 21st century India's Muslim population will reach 320 to 340 million people (or 18% of India's total projected population). Swapan Dasgupta, a prominent Indian journalist, has raised concerns that the higher Muslim population growth rate in India could adversely effect the country's social harmony. Phillip Longman, a renowned demographer, remarked that the substantial difference between Muslim and Hindu birthrates could contribute to ethnic tension in India.

HISTORY OF ISLAM IN INDIA

Contrary to popular belief, Islam came to South Asia prior to Muslim invasions of India. Islamic influence first came to be felt in the early 7th century with the advent of Arab traders. Trade relations have existed between Arabia and the Indian subcontinent from ancient times. Even in the pre-Islamic era, Arab traders used to visit the Malabar region, which linked them with the ports of South East Asia. According to Historians Elliot and Dowson in their book *The History of India as told by its own Historians*, the first ship bearing Muslim travelers was seen on the Indian coast as early as 630 AD. H.G. Rawlinson, in his book: *Ancient and Medieval History of India* claims the first Arab Muslims settled on the Indian coast in the last part of the 7th century AD. Shaykh Zainuddin Makhdum's "Tuhfat al-Mujahidin" also is a reliable work. This fact is corroborated, by J. Sturrock in his *South Kanara and Madras Districts Manuals*, and also by Haridas Bhattacharya in *Cultural Heritage of India Vol. IV*. It was with the advent of Islam that the Arabs became a prominent cultural force in the world. The Arab merchants and traders became the carriers of the new religion and they propagated it wherever they went.

The first Indian mosque is thought to have been built in 629 A.D, purportedly at the behest of Rama Varma Kulashekhara, who is considered the first Indian Muslim, during the life time of Muhammad (c. 571–632) in Kodungallur, Kerala by Malik Bin Deenar.

In Malabar, the Mappilas may have been the first community to convert to Islam as they were more closely connected with the Arabs than others. Intensive missionary activities were carried out along the coast and a number of natives also embraced Islam. These new converts were now added to the Mappila community. Thus among the Mappilas, we find, both the descendants of the Arabs through local women and the converts from among the local people.

In the 8th century, the province of Sindh (in present day Pakistan) was conquered by an Arab army led by Muhammad bin Qasim. Sindh became the easternmost province of the Umayyad Caliphate. In the first half of the 10th century, Mahmud of Ghazni added the Punjab to the Ghaznavid Empire and conducted several raids deeper into modern day India. A more successful invasion came at the end of the 12th century by Muhammad of Ghor. This eventually led to the formation of the Delhi Sultanate.

Arab-Indian Interactions

There is much evidence in history to show that Arabs and Muslims interacted with India and Indians from the very early days of Islam, if not before the arrival of Islam in Arabia. Arab traders transmitted the numeral system developed by Indians to the Middle East and Europe.

Many Sanskrit books were translated into Arabic as early as the Eighth century. George Saliba writes in his book 'Islamic Science and the Making of the European Renaissance' that "some major Sanskrit texts began to be translated during the reign of the second Abbasid caliph al-Mansur [754-775], if not before; some texts on logic even before that, and it has been generally accepted that the Persian and Sanskrit texts, few as they were, were indeed the first to be translated."

Spread of Sufi Islam

Sufis (Islamic mystics) played an important role in the spread of Islam in India. They were very successful in spreading Islam, as many aspects of Sufi belief systems and practices had their parallels in Indian philosophical literature, in particular nonviolence and monism. The Sufis' orthodox approach towards Islam made it easier for Hindus to practice. Hazrat Khawaja Muin-ud-din Chishti, Qutbuddin Bakhtiar Kaki, Nizam-ud-din Auliya, Shah Jalal, Amir Khusro, Sarkar Sabir Pak, Shekh Alla-ul-Haq Pandwi, Ashraf Jahangir Semnani, Sarkar Waris Pak, Ata Hussain Fani Chishti trained Sufis for the propagation of Islam in different parts of India. Once the Islamic Empire was established in India, Sufis invariably provided a touch of colour and beauty to what might have otherwise been rather cold and stark reigns. The Sufi movement also attracted followers from the artisan and untouchable communities; they played a crucial role in bridging the distance between Islam and the indigenous traditions. Ahmad Sirhindi, a prominent member of the Naqshbandi Sufi advocated the peaceful conversion of Hindus to Islam. Imam Ahmed Rida Khan contributed a lot by defending traditional and orthodox Islam in India by his famous work Fatawa Razvia.

Ahmadiyya Islam

India has a significant Ahmadiyya population. Most of

them live in Rajastan, Orissa, Haryana, Bihar, Delhi, Uttar Pradesh, and a few in Punjab in the area of Qadian. In India, Ahmadis are considered to be Muslims by the Government of India. This recognition is supported by a court verdict (Shihabuddin Koya vs. Ahammed Koya, A.I.R. 1971 Ker 206). There is no legislation that declares Ahmadis non-Muslims or limits their activities, but they are not allowed to sit on the All India Muslim Personal Law Board, a body of religious leaders India's government recognises as representative of Indian Muslims.

ISLAM IN INDIA

The Muslims are about 12% of India's population. But their influence on the Indian society was much stronger. The main reason was that there were many Muslims rulers in different parts of India. Most of the Muslim rulers of India were invaders from the west.

Islam was established in Saudi Arabia. But most of Islam's spreaders in India arrived from non-Arab countries (It must be noted that Arab traders and travellers had arrived into India even before Islam was established in Arabia. These Arabs probably had their own places of worship, later on transformed into mosques.). The first spreaders of Islam in India were individuals who saw in spreading Islam a holy precept. They began coming to India from the 11th century. They arrived in India from Bukhara, Turkey, Iran, Yemen and Afghanistan. The most famous preacher of Islam in India was Khwaja Chishti, who arrived from Iran and his sect is called Sufism. But the accepted assumption in India is that most of India's Muslims were converted to Islam through the sword. Meaning the Indians were given an option between death or adopting Islam. The third option was getting examined in Islam religion along with heavy taxes- Jeziya (poll tax) and Kharaj (property tax).

The process of converting Indians to Islam began in the 8th century, when the Arabs began invading north India and present day Pakistan. After the Arabs other Muslims invaded India. These invasions by Muslims in India were not continuous and not all Muslim invaders were Islamic fanatics. One of the Mughal emperors, Akbar, was very liberal and he even established a new religion, Din E Elahi, which included in it, beliefs from different religions. In some of the monuments built by Akbar symbols of different religions are visible. In contrast with Akbar his great grand son, Aurangazeb, was a fanatic Muslim and during his term the non-Muslims suffered a lot. Many worshipping sites of different religions were destroyed and transformed into mosques.

Most of the Indian Muslims converted to Islam were belonged to the lower classes of the Indian society. Besides these Muslims there are also Muslims who belonged to the ruling families of the different Indian kingdoms. Some of these rulers were Hindus who actually belonged to the warrior castes of the Hindu society and adopted Islam. Others are descendants of Muslim rulers who invaded India. The different Muslim rulers of India also brought to their kingdoms Muslim mercenaries, businessmen and slaves from different parts of the world like Russia; Afghanistan; Turkey; Arab countries and Africa. These people remained in India, married local Indians and converted them to Islam. Because of the different origins as stated and because of other reasons the Muslims of India refer to themselves not only as Muslims but also with other titles.

In general the Muslims of India like the Muslim world is divided into two main sects, Sunni and Shia. And just like in the whole Muslim world there is tension between these two sects. Each sect has many different schools. There are also Muslims who claim to be the descendants from the daughter of Prophet Muhammad and the men in this community add the title Syed before their names. Other claim to be the descendants from the first Muslims and add the title Sheik. Along with these Muslim world divisions, the Indian Muslims also have other divisions.

Different communities who adopted Islam in different ways have different community names. In west India the Bohra and Khoja are Muslim communities who adopted Islam influenced by different Muslim preachers. The Khojas also split into different communities. The leader of the Khoja (Nizari) community is Aga Khan. The Nawait are descendants of Arab and Persian immigrants. In south India in the state of Kerala, the Mophilla community is descendants from Arab merchants. A well known Indian Muslim community is Pathan. The Pathan are Muslims who arrived from Afghanistan. They normally have their surname as Khan. The Pathan have an image of being brave, honest and righteous. Many Indians who adopted Islam adopted the surname Khan and they claim that they are Pathans, which is not always true. The original Pathans claim that they originate from the Tribes of Israel.

In the beginning of the 20th century, some reformist Muslims organizations evolved in India who wanted to adjust Islamic philosophy to the modern world. These organizations wanted to cancel polygamy and were in favor of women education.

CHRISTIANITY IN INDIA

Christianity is India's third-largest religion, with approximately 24 million followers, constituting 2.3% of India's population. The works of scholars and Eastern Christian writings state that Christianity was introduced to India by Thomas the Apostle, who visited Muziris in Kerala in 52 CE to proselytize amongst Kerala's Jewish settlements Although, the exact origins of Christianity in India remain unclear, it is generally agreed that Christianity in India is almost as old as Christianity itself and spread in India even before it spread in many, predominantly Christian, nations of Europe.

Today Christians are found all across India and in all walks of life, with major populations in parts of South India, the Konkan Coast and the North-East. Indian Christians have contributed significantly to and are well represented in various spheres of national life. They include former and current chief ministers, governors and chief election commissioners. Indian Christians also have one of the highest literacy, work participation and sex ratio figures among the various religious communities in India. Most Christians in India are Catholic (Latin rite). The Eastern rites include the Syro-Malabar Catholic Church and the Malankara Orthodox Syrian Church, which are prominent in Kerala. Other churches include the Mar Thoma Syrian Church, Church of South India (CSI), the Church of North India (CNI), Presbyterian Church of India, Indian Pentecostal Church, The Pentecostal Mission and other evangelical groups. The Christian Church runs thousands of educational institutions and hospitals contributing significantly to the development of the nation.

EARLY CHRISTIANITY IN INDIA

According to Indian Christian traditions, the apostle Thomas arrived in Kodungallur (also Muziris), Kerala established the Seven Churches and evangelized in present day Kerala and Tamil Nadu.

As with early Christianity in the Roman Empire, it is assumed that the initial converts were largely Jewish proselytes among the Cochin Jews who are believed to have arrived in India around 562BC, after the destruction of the First Temple. Many of these Jews presumably spoke Aramaic like St. Thomas, also a Jew by birth, who is credited by tradition with evangelizing India.

More likely to be historical than the tradition that the apostle Thomas himself went to India is the claim of Eusebius of Caesarea that Pantaenus, the head of the Christian exegetical school in Alexandria, Egypt went to India during the reign of the Emperor Commodus and found that Christians already existed in India, and that these Christians were using a version of the Gospel of Matthew with "Hebrew letters." This is plausibly a reference to the earliest Indian churches using the Syriac New Testament, which we know to have been the case. Pantaenus' evidence thus indicates that Syriac-speaking Christians had already evangelized parts of India by the late 2nd century.

An early 3rd-century Syriac work known as the *Acts of Thomas* connects the tradition of the apostle Thomas' Indian ministry with two kings, one in the north and the other in the south. The year of his arrival is widely disputed due to lack of credible records. According to one of the legends in the *Acts*, Thomas was at first reluctant to accept this mission but the Lord overruled the stubborn disciple by ordering circumstances so compelling that he was forced to accompany an Indian merchant, Abbanes, to his native place in northwest India, where he found himself in the service of the Indo-Parthian king, Gondophares. The apostle's ministry reputedly resulted in many conversions throughout this northern kingdom, including the king and his brother. The *Acts of Thomas* identifies his second mission in India with a kingdom ruled by King Mahadwa, one of the rulers of a 1st-century dynasty in southern

India. According to the tradition of the *Mar Thoma* or "Church of Thomas," Thomas evangelized along the Malabar Coast of Kerala State in southwest India, though the various churches he founded were located mainly on the Periyar River and its tributaries and along the coast, where there were Jewish colonies. He reputedly preached to all classes of people and had about seventeen thousand converts, including members of the four principal castes. According to legend, St. Thomas attained martyrdom at St. Thomas Mount in Chennai and is buried on the site of San Thome Cathedral.

Critical historians treated the *Acts of Thomas* as an idle tale and denied the historicity of King Gundaphorus until modern archeology established him as an important figure in North India in the latter half of the 1st century. Many coins of his reign have turned up in Afghanistan, the Punjab, and the Indus Valley. Remains of some of his buildings, influenced by Greek architecture, indicate that he was a great builder.

Although little is known of the immediate growth of the church, Bar-Daisan (AD 154-223) reports that in his time there were Christian tribes in North India which claimed to have been converted by Thomas and to have books and relics to prove it. But at least by the time of the establishment of the Second Persian Empire (AD 226), there were bishops of the Church of the East in northwest India, Afghanistan and Baluchistan, with laymen and clergy alike engaging in missionary activity.

Although there was a lively trade between the Near East and India via Mesopotamia and the Persian Gulf, the most direct route to India in the 1st century was via Alexandria and the Red Sea, taking advantage of the Monsoon winds, which could carry ships directly to and from the Malabar coast. The discovery of large hoards of Roman coins of 1st-century Caesars and the remains of Roman trading posts testify to the frequency of that trade. Historian Vincent A. Smith wrote, *"It must be admitted that a personal visit of the Apostle Thomas to South India was easily feasible in the traditional belief that he came by way of Socotra, where an ancient Christian settlement undoubtedly existed. I am now satisfied that the Christian church of South India is extremely ancient...* ".

India had a flourishing trade with Central Asia, Mediterranean, and Middle East, both along mountain passes in the north and sea routes along the western and southern coast, well before the start of Christian era, and it is likely that Christian merchants settled in Indian cities along trading routes.

The Chronicle of Seert describes an evangelical mission to India by bishop David of Basra around the year 300; this metropolitan reportedly made many conversions, and it has been speculated that his mission took in areas of southern India. According to *Travancore Manual*, Thomas of Cana, a Mesopotamian merchant and missionary, brought a mission to India in 345 AD. He brought 400 Christians from Baghdad, Nineveh, and Jerusalem to Kodungallur. He and his companion Bishop Joseph of Edessa sought refuge under King Cheraman Perumal from persecution of Christians by the Persian king Shapur II. The colony of Syrian Christians established at Kodungallur may be the first Christian community in South India for which there is a continuous written record. A number of historians claim that Thomas of Cana was confused with the 1st century apostle Thomas by India's Syrian Christians sometime after his death and became their Apostle Thomas in India.

Jesus in India Theories

There are also two sets of distinct accounts of Jesus travelling through India. According to the first set of accounts, Jesus traveled and studied in India between the ages of twelve and thirty. According the second set of accounts, Jesus did not die on the cross, but after his apparent death and resurrection he journeyed to Kashmir to teach the gospel, and then remained there for the rest of his life. The origin of the first set of accounts is attributed to Russian author Nicolas Notovitch who published the book *La vie Inconnue du Jesus Christ* (The Unknown life of Jesus Christ) in 1894. Other writers have suggested, however, that Notovitch's claims were a hoax.

The origin of the second set of accounts is attributed to Kashmiri author Mirza Gulam Ahmed who published the book *Masih Hindustan Mein* (Jesus in India) in 1899. These two accounts are generally not presented in combination. While travel between Middle-East and India was common during those times, these accounts are not given serious thought and treated as speculation since there is no historical account, either in early Christian writings or Indian historical accounts, to either confirm or refute Jesus traveling to India.

Medieval Period

The Syrian Malabar Nasrani community was further strengthened by various Persian immigrant settlers, the Christian-Jewish Knanaya colonies of 3rd century, Manichaeanism followers, Babylonian Christians settlers of 4th century AD, the Syrian settlements of Mar Sabor Easo and Proth in 7th century AD and the immigrant Persian Christians from successive centuries. Archaeological excavations at Pattanam show that the ancient port town of Muziris was in modern Kerala. The Periplus of the Erythraean Sea describes it as a port of "leading importance". The Kerala Syrian Church was in communion with the Assyrian Church of the East till the Portuguese arrival in the late 15th century. Bishops came from Syria.

The South Indian epic of Manimekalai (written between 2nd and 3rd century CE) mentions the Nasrani people by referring to them by the name Essanis. The embassy of Alfred in 833 CE described the Syrian Christians as being prosperous and enjoying high status in the Malabar coast. Marco Polo also mentioned the Nasranis and their ancient Church in the Malabar coast in his writings Il Milione.

The Saint Thomas Christians still use the Syriac language, (a dialect of Aramaic, also the language which Jesus spoke) in services. This group, which existed in Kerala relatively peacefully for more than a millennium, faced considerable persecution from Portuguese evangelists in the 16th century. This later wave of evangelism spread Catholicism more widely along the Konkan coast.

The French Dominican missionary Jordanus Catalani was the first European to proselytise in India. He arrived in Surat in 1320. After his ministry in Gujarat he reached Quilon in 1323. He not only revived Christianity but also brought thousands to the Christian fold. He brought a message of good will from the Pope to the local rulers. As the first bishop in India, he was also entrusted with the spiritual nourishment of the Christian community in Calicut, Mangalore, Thane and Broach (north of Thane).

Modern Period

Portuguese missionaries reached the Malabar Coast in the late 15th century. They made contact with the St. Thomas Christians in Kerala (who were following Eastern Christian practices at that time) and sought to introduce the Catholicism among them. Throughout this period, foreign missionaries also made many new converts to Christianity. Early Roman Catholic missionaries, particularly the Portuguese, led by the Jesuit St. Francis Xavier (1506-52), expanded from their bases on the west coast making many converts. With the Papal bull *Romanus Pontifex* the patronage for the propagation of the Christian faith in Asia was given to the Portuguese. The Portuguese colonial government in Goa supported the mission in India with incentives for baptized Christians.

They offered rice donations for the poor, good positions in the Portuguese colonies for the middle class and military support for local rulers. As a result of these incentives many converted Indians were opportunistic *Rice Christians*, who practiced their old religion alongside Christianity. This was seen as a threat to the immaculateness of the Christian belief. St. Francis Xavier, in a 1545 letter to John III of Portugal, requested an Inquisition be installed in Goa.

However the Inquisition, considered one of the most violent institutions in the History of Goa targeted Hindus, Jews, and many newly converted Christians, was only installed eight years after St.Francis Xavier's death. Modern-day Goa has a substantial Roman Catholic population with around 30% of the population professing the faith. The undecayed body of St. Francis Xavier is still on public view in a glass coffin at the *Basilica of Bom Jesus* in Goa. Mangalore is another significant region on the west coast which has a huge Christian population. In 1321, the French Dominican friar Jordanus Catalani of Severac (in south-western France), who also worked in Quilon arrived in Bhatkal, a place near Mangalore and established a missionary station there. Many locals were converted to Christianity by Jordanus.. The Portuguese were however unable to establish their presence in Mangalore as a result of the conquests of the Vijayanagara ruler Krishnadevaraya and Abbakka Rani of Ullal, the Bednore Queen of Mangalore. Most of Mangalorean Catholics were not originally from Mangalore but are descendants of Goan Catholics who fled Goa during the Portuguese-Maratha Wars and the Goan Inquisition. The origin of Christianity in North Konkan, was due to the proselytizing activities of the Portuguese in the 16th century. The French Dominican friar Jordanus Catalani of Severac (in south-western France) started evangelizing activities in Thana. On the occasion of *The Golden Jubilee of Queen Victoria*, the Christians of North Konkan, who were known as *Portuguese Christians* discarded that name and adopted the designation *East Indians*.

The first Protestant missionaries to set foot in India were two Lutherans from Germany, Bartholomaus Ziegenbalg and Heinrich Pluetschau, who began work in 1705 in the Danish settlement of Tranquebar. They translated the Bible into the local Tamil language, and afterwards into Hindustani. They made little progress at first, but gradually the mission spread to Madras, Cuddalore and Tanjore. Today *bishop of Tranquebar* is the official title of a bishop in the Tamil Evangelical Lutheran Church (TELC) in South India which was founded in 1919 as a result of the German Lutheran Leipzig Mission and Church of Sweden Mission. The seat of the Bishop, the Cathedral and its Church House ("Tranquebar House") is in Tiruchirappalli. Beginning in the 18th century, Protestant missionaries began working throughout India, leading to the growth of different Christian communities.

In 1793, William Carey, an English Baptist Minister came to India as a Missionary. He worked in Serampore, Calcutta, and other places as a missionary. He started the Serampore College. He translated the Bible into Bengali. He worked until his death in 1834. The London Missionary Society was the first Protestant mission in Andhra Pradesh which established its station at Visakhapatnam in 1805. Anthony Norris Groves, a Plymouth Brethren missionary came to India in 1833. He worked in the Godavari delta area until his death in 1852. John Christian Frederick Heyer was the first Lutheran missionary in the region of Andhra Pradesh. He founded the Guntur Mission in 1842. He studied Sanskrit and medicine in Baltimore, and set sail for India from Boston in 1841 with three other missionary couples on the ship *Brenda*. He travelled to India a second time in 1847, spending a decade, mainly in the Guntur district of Andhra Pradesh state, in southern India, where he ministered and performed yeoman service to the people there. Supported initially by the Pennsylvania Ministerium, and later by the Foreign Mission Board of the General Synod, Heyer was also encouraged and assisted by British government officials. He established a number of hospitals and a network of schools throughout the Guntur region. Mormon missionaries, including Hugh Findlay, arrived in Bombay and Pune in the early 1850s, but did not meet with success.

During the 19th century, several American Baptist missionaries evangelized in the northeastern parts of India. In 1876, Dr. E. W. Clark first went to live in a Naga village, four years after his Assamese helper, Godhula, baptized the first Naga converts. Rev. and Mrs. A.F. Merrill arrived in India in 1928 and worked in the southeast section of the Garo Hills. Rev. and Mrs. M.J. Chance spent most of the years between 1950-1956 at Golaghat working with the Naga and Garo tribes. Even today the heaviest concentrations of Christians in India continue to be in the Northeast.

VEDIC RELIGION

The Vedic period religions laid the foundation of the religious practices that are continued till date in modern India. These religions arose from the sacred scriptures that were composed during the Vedic period. These scriptures founded the very base of Hinduism in India. The scriptures that talk of the various religious practices are basically the four Vedas namely Rig Veda, Yajur Veda, Sama Veda and Atharva Veda. The Upanishads are also considered to be a part of the Vedas and contain valuable information regarding the rituals and religions of Vedic Age.

The principles of religions in Vedic Era were basically laid down by the priests, who were the highest class of people in the society. They were the ones who performed the rituals, chanted hymns and read out holy texts in temples and functions. The texts recorded in the Vedas were supposed to have divine power and were to be chanted perfectly with the right tone, pronunciation and emphasis. This was believed to make the hymns effective to the hilt and gain the maximum power out of it.

Religion in Early Vedic Period

Religion in early Vedic period revolved around crude forms of worshipping which basically includes nature worship. This means that people in the early Vedic period worshipped different forms of nature as god like sun, earth, moon, wind, rain, and other natural phenomena. Since there were no scientific explanations for natural phenomena like rain, thunder, wind, etc. people feared them and thus worshipped them. Chanting of prayers and hymns were a common practice to invoke the Gods and it was normal to sacrifice animals in the name of religion.

Religion in Later Vedic Period

The later Vedic age saw the increase in powers of the priests and they formed the highest class in the society. Religious practices were refined and worship of Gods in the form of idols gained importance. Animal sacrifice also increased during this period. With rituals and hymns taking centre stage, the evolution of Hindu religion took place. Nature worship gave rise to new beliefs and new Gods. The duty of imparting the religious know how to people was the duty of the priests.

SOCIO-RELIGIOUS REFORM MOVEMENTS IN INDIA

Reckoning the millennia of Indian history, one can hardly think of a greater contrast than the one that existed between eighteenth-century and twentieth-century India. On the one hand India had a stagnating traditional culture and society at very low ebb, while on the other hand India possessed a still traditional society in the throes and the creative excitement of modernising itself, of emerging as a new nation, remaining thoroughly its own and rooted in its culture, yet taking its place in the contemporary world. The nineteenth century was the pivotal century that saw the initiation of this process that brought about an enormous transformation in the religious, social, economic, political, and cultural spheres.

The transformation came for the involvement of some interrelated factors among which the first is the total impact of the British Raj. It influenced Indian life through many channels: administration, legislation, trade, the creation of a network of communications, inchoative industrialisation and urbanisation, all had great influence not only on the many Indians who became directly involved in them, but also on society as a whole, because every measure in some way interfered with some traditional patterns of life. In the cultural field too the British exerted pressure through the work of scholars, educators, and missionaries, Orientalists, utilitarian, or evangelical. The entire effect of this influence acted on the life and ideas of the people in multiple ways, forcing them to adjust their patterns of life to the new circumstances and thus effecting a continuum of social change.

Under these circumstances, the reformers excelled as landmarks in this gradual adaptation to new conditions. These are the Indians who consciously reacted to the new situation and advocated deliberate changes in social and religious attitudes and customs, involving a break with tradition itself. They saw change not as a slow adaptive process, but as a positive value in itself, and contrasted it with the negativity of existing patterns. As a group they had a great impact on nineteenth-century India, though they were not by far the only factor in effecting change.

Social and religious reformers were, naturally, not a new phenomenon in Hinduism. In fact in some ways the very nature of Hinduism is to be continuously adaptive and reformist. Yet the nineteenth-century reform movement was in general distinguished from previous Hindu reform by a cluster of new characteristics. It became closely conjoined to a political movement, and consequently sought to influence political authority, administration, and legislation. This political movement became very soon an all-India nationalist movement, and reform acquired a nationalist flavour and an all-India extension. Whereas previously social reform was inextricably interwoven with religious motivation and religious reform, in the nineteenth century the relationship of the two oscillated, and sometimes secular and rationalistic motives were the decisive ones, though in fact the century did produce a few reformers who remained totally within the traditional pattern, and whose influence on the period remained insignificant. Among them the most noteworthy are Swami Narayana of

Gujarat, initiator of a sect bearing his name, and Mahatma Ramalingam of Tamil Nadu.

The reformers themselves had no doubts as to the main stimulants of this new spirit. The British administration, English education, and European literature brought to India a constellation of fresh ideas which constituted a challenge to the new intellectuals. Rationalism as the basis for ethical thinking, the idea of human progress and evolution, the possibility of 'scientifically' engineering social change, the concept of natural rights connected with individualism, were all alien to traditional society. An equally strong influence was exerted by the ideas and the work of the Christian missionaries. Although some later nationalist writers tend to discount this influence, the nineteenth-century reformers themselves, starting with Ram Mohan Roy, did not hesitate to give credit where it was due, and acknowledged their indebtedness in no uncertain terms, even while vigorously opposing certain aspects of missionary activity.

In the first decades of the nineteenth century, India had already produced a small new social group, the English-educated intelligentsia, mostly closely associated with British administration or British trade. It was amongst these people that several ideas of reform first arose and constant contact with Britishers and European ideas made them look upon some social and religious characteristics of their own society with horror and disgust. Social reform in this first stage was mostly prompted by the desire of these people to cope with the difficulties which they experienced themselves and which were experienced too by others belonging to their European-influenced group. There was not as yet any concern for the mass of the people, or any desire to transform the structure of society at large. What they wanted was to reshape their lives according to the new standards and values they were discovering. They sought to clarify their own ideas, and propagate them among their kindred intelligentsia. Thus, this first stage was a time when the reformer was almost exclusively concerned with his own group, a time also when political concern was inceptive and when it was generally held that personal social reform needed to be based upon the solid foundation of religious reform.

Bengal was first to undergo significant British influence and to produce the new English-educated group. By the early 1800s a crystallization of different reactions to Western influence was noticed, and there emerge three distinct groups, the radicals, the reformers, and the conservatives. Ram Mohan Roy (1772-1833) was the first great modern reformer, and has for good reason been called 'The Father of Modern India'. In the religious sphere Ram Mohan's main target of attack was the Hindu system of idolization, its mythology and cult. He proposed as an alternative a deistic type of theism, strongly influenced by European deism and the ideology of the Unitarians. As a social reformer, Ram Mohan's interest was mainly in the appalling condition of women in Hindu society, an interest that was to dominate the social reform movement for many decades. He is rightly famous for his long and successful campaign for the abolition of sati, the self-immolation of widows on the funeral pyres of their husbands, and he fought incessantly against child marriage and for female education. The crowning achievement of Ram Mohan's organizational efforts was the foundation of the Brahmo Sabha (later known as Brahmo Samaj) in 1828. The Socio-Religious Reform movements of the 19th century in West Bengal, Maharashtra, Uttar Pradesh and Punjab aimed at checking the influence of Christian Missionaries. The missionaries wished to convert Indians to Christianity. They also wished to purge Hindu society of social evils such as Sati and infanticide. The aim of Brahmo Samaj was to save middle class families of Bengal from adverse effects of Christianity.

After the death of Ram Mohan Roy, Debendranath Tagore (1817-1905) took over its leadership and gave it a new direction. He drew up a declaration of faith, established a theological school, sent out the first Brahmo missionaries, and created a new liturgy, the 'Brahmo Rites'. He himself was inclined towards the contemplative and the bhakti aspect of Hinduism, and averse to Ram Mohan's rationalism. With a stress on devotion, ethical duties, and the near-Vedic but non-idolatrous Brahma rites, the Samaj moved closer to the mainstream of Hinduism, as it grew quickly in numbers.

Later with Keshab Chandra Sen (1838-84) a new wind started to blow in the Samaj. He was an iconoclastic reformer, repudiating all Hindu cults, rejecting caste and the seclusion of women. In religion he had a new 'universalistic' tendency, with strong leanings towards Christianity. During this time Bengal also produced the scholar Iswara Chandra Vidyasagar (1820-91) who took up the widow remarriage movement, the first social reform cause that was taken up all over the country, and who saw it to a successful conclusion. The reform he advocated and saw become law, namely that a high-caste widow could legally remarry, affected few individuals and in fact was taken advantage of by very few for many years to come. Nevertheless, the widow remarriage movement was very important because it became the inspiration of other reform movements all over the country.

The growing religious and social reform awareness started in Maharashtra from 1840. In this early stage, Gopal Hari Deshmukh (1823-92), known as Lokahita-wadi, denounced loudly that typical feature of Maharashtra, the absolute intellectual and moral dominance of Brahmans over Hindu life. His friend and collaborator Jotiba Govind Phule (1827-90), of low caste, took up this fight against brahmanic oppression in his voluminous prose and poetic works, and gave it concrete form in his organization for the uplift of the low castes, the Satyasodhak Samaj. In 1867 Maharashtra brought forth its own organization of religious and social reform, the Prarthana Samaj. The theism of the Prarthana Samaj was similar to that of its Bengali counterpart, but it was consciously linked with the bhakti tradition of the Maharashtrian saints. They invoked their own medieval bhakti tradition as another reform movement that was evolutionary, not revolutionary. They also had a different attitude towards the connection between religious and social reform.

Another important figure of Indian Socio Religious reform movement was Dayananda Saraswati (1824-83) who in 1875 published his major work the Satyarth Prakash and founded his reform society, the Arya Samaj. Dayananda's theological vision was one that emerged neither from a personal mysticism nor from Western ideas, but from the intimate observation of the corrupt Hinduism of his day. He attacked polytheism, idolatry, and the many superstitious beliefs and rites connected with them, and the stranglehold of the brahmans on sacred lore and religious practice. He had the vision of a primeval monotheism, above the paraphernalia and hostilities of all human creeds. According to him, this religion was in fact the original Vedic religion, which was contained in the four Vedas. It was his aim to propagate the truth of that religion, to reinstate it in its purity, and thereby to reinstate the Indian people in their forgotten glory. Thus Dayananda's religion, whilst denouncing much of contemporary Hinduism, kept close to orthodoxy in several basic ways: belief in the Vedas, and in karma and transmigration, and allegiance to the six darshanas and to the various Hindu names for the one God.

From 1880 two important tendencies which had been stirring in the previous decades occupied the Indian scene: nationalism and political action. From now on individuals and groups openly identified themselves with an Indian nation, a new concept in Indian history. This predominance of nationalism and politics now began to exert influence on the ideas of religious and social reform which had previously prevailed. Nationalism itself developed two patterns, a religious one and a secular one, and each school assigned a different place to social reform.

Two early outstanding examples of the new religious nationalism are Bankim and Tilak. It is very striking how the religious nationalism of both in fact had deep provincial roots, and may be seen as Bengali and Maharashtrian nationalism respectively. Bankim Chandra Chatterjee (1838-94) found Bengal divided between the traditionalist orthodox and the progressive reformers.

His religion combines the humanism of Positivism with the activist interpretation of the Krishna myth and of the Bengali cult of the Mother Goddess. His novels in particular awoke in the Bengalis, first the middle class, and later the masses, a self-confidence and pride in their language and their religion. Another personality from Maharashtra, Bal Gangadhar Tilak (1857-1920) took initiative to promote Hinduism as the only basis of this new spirit. He also inaugurated new Hindu festivals, the Ganapati festival and the Sivaji festival, thus reaching the populace with his ideas of Hindu nationalistic activism, instilling in them a pride in their glorious Maharashtrian past. He advocated the severance of social reform and political agitation.

It was in the 1880s that the social reform movement in India at last became organised on a national basis. It was a Bombay Parsi, Behramji Malabari (1853-1912), who launched the issue that set social reform on its way to becoming consciously national: the campaign for the legal checking of infant marriage by an Age of Consent Bill. Further in 1892 the Madras Hindu Social Reform Association came into being, led mostly by radical reformers. In Bengal, where social change had advanced rapidly, social reform went into a depression. Reformations like uplifting of women and widows, society, religion, castes etc. It was in the north that the first new caste organizations arose. Castes were traditionally well organized and held effective power over their members. What was new was that associations of related castes came into being. These were voluntary bodies to which caste leaders attached their own groups. Their prime concern was the welfare of the members, but their programme included many of the ideals and principles advocated by social reformers, so that the National Social Conference officially acknowledged them as reform societies.

In 1887 the Kayastha Conference was formed in Lucknow, comprising the group of subcastes. The early split of the organization into a reformist and an orthodox section testifies to the eager reformist ideas of a good number of its leaders. Another important organization was that of the Vaishyas, established in 1891. In this period the caste organizations kept away from politics, but in the twentieth century they assumed in several areas of India very great political importance, in fact frequently dominating the political game.

The first two decades of the twentieth century saw Indian politics engaged in the great debate between the moderates and the extremists, and in their struggle for control of the Congress. The development of the social reform movement, however, was intimately connected with that debate and that struggle. The main objections of the extremists against the moderate leadership were two: that in aims and methods the moderates were completely British-oriented and therefore slow and unpatriotic; and that they did not reach down to the mass of the people. The extremists' advocated militancy based on national and religious identification and wanted involvement of the masses. In the last two decades of the nineteenth century social reform was dominated by the nationalistic secularists. The revivalist extremists naturally opposed this approach vehemently, as being denationalizing and degrading because it was based on European ideas and aspired to European models. So an intense debate between the reformers and the revivalists ensued. The revivalists succeeded in demonstrating that a purely nationalistic motive and a Hindu model could be the inspiration for whatever reform the reformer envisaged. But they proved more than that: they showed that Hindu nationalism and an ideal Hindu society had a mass appeal that was absent in Western-type reform. These arguments were irresistible, and the reform movement as a whole changed its image and its model in the direction of revivalist Hindu nationalism, and swerved towards a concern for the mass of the people.

Moreover, under the impact of British rule India was transformed into one administrative unit with the same legal system all over the country. The country has also become united economically as one unit with the development of all India's internal trade and foreign trade. This action was greatly helped by the development of new means of transport such as railways. It also included communication system such as new postal system and telegraph. This administrative and economic unification greatly contributed to the generation of national consciousness. The very existence of foreign rule acted as a unifying factor. All over the country people saw that they were suffering at the hands of the same enemy, and that is British rule.

By the 1920s the Indian religious and social reform movement had lost its peculiar identity as an important and distinct phenomenon of Indian life. Among the many reasons of this, one was the appearance on the national stage of Mahatma Gandhi.

5

Social Reform Movements

REFORM MOVEMENT

A reform movement is a kind of social movement that aims to make gradual change, or change in certain aspects of society, rather than rapid or fundamental changes. A reform movement is distinguished from more radical social movements such as revolutionary movements.

Reformists' ideas are often grounded in liberalism, although they may be rooted in utopian, socialist or religious concepts. Some rely on personal transformation; others rely on small collectives, such as Mahatma Gandhi's spinning wheel and the self sustaining village economy, as a mode of social change. Reactionary movements, which can arise against any of these, attempt to put things back the way they were before whatever successes of the new movement(s), or prevent any such successes in the first place.

GREAT BRITAIN/UNITED KINGDOM: LATE 18TH CENTURY TO EARLY 20TH

The Radical Movement

The Radical movement campaigned for electoral reform, a reform of the Poor Laws, free trade, educational reform, postal reform, prison reform, and public sanitation. Originally this movement sought to replace the exclusive political power of the aristocracy with a more democratic system empowering urban areas and the middle and lower classes. Following the Enlightenment's ideas, the reformers looked to the Scientific

Revolution and industrial progress to solve the social problems which arose with the Industrial Revolution. Newton's natural philosophy combined a mathematics of axiomatic proof with the mechanics of physical observation, yielding a coherent system of verifiable predictions and replacing a previous reliance on revelation and inspired truth. Applied to public life, this approach yielded several successful campaigns for changes in social policy. Eventually, this reform movement led to formation of the Liberal Party in 1859. Later, wealthy business owners and high ranking officials created the Conservative Party to counter the rising strength of the liberals in Parliament.

One of the actions taken was the Reform Bill of 1832, which provided the rising middle classes more political power in urban areas while lessening the representation of districts undisturbed by the Industrial Revolution. Despite determined resistance from the House of Lords, this Bill gave more parliamentary power to the liberals, while reducing the political force of the working class, leaving them detached from the main body of middle class support on which they had relied. Having achieved the Reform Act of 1832, the Radical alliance was broken until the Liberal-Labour alliance of the mid-Victorian period.

The Chartist Movement

The Chartist movement sought universal suffrage. An historian of the Chartist movement observed that "The Chartist movement was essentially an economic movement with a purely political programme." A period of bad trade and high food prices set in, and the drastic restrictions on Poor Law relief were a source of acute distress. The London Working Men's Association, under the guidance of Francis Place, found itself in the midst of a great unrest. In the northern textile districts the Chartists, led by Feargus O'Connor, a follower of Daniel O'Connell, denounced the inadequate Poor Laws. This was basically a hunger revolt, springing from unemployment and despair. In Birmingham, the older Birmingham Political Union sprang to life under the leadership of Thomas Attwood. The Chartist movement demanded basic economic reforms, higher wages and better conditions of work, and a repeal of the obnoxious Poor Law Act.

The idea of universal male suffrage, an initial goal of the Chartist movement, was to include all males as voters regardless of their social standing. This later evolved into a campaign for universal suffrage. This movement sought to redraw the parliamentary districts within Great Britain and create a salary system for elected officials so workers could afford to represent their constituents without a burden on their families.

The Women's Suffrage Movement

Many consider Mary Wollstonecraft's *Vindication of the Rights of Woman* (1792) to be the source of the reformers' long-running campaign for feminist inclusion and the origin of the Women's Suffrage movement. Harriet Taylor was a significant influence on John Stuart Mill's work and ideas, reinforcing Mill's advocacy of women's rights. Her essay, "Enfranchisement of Women," appeared in the *Westminster Review* in 1851 in response to a speech by Lucy Stone given at the first National Women's Rights Convention in Worcester, Massachusetts in 1850, and it was reprinted in the United States. Mill cites Taylor's influence in his final revision of *On Liberty,* (1859) which was published shortly after her death, and she appears to be obliquely referenced in Mill's *The Subjection of Women.*

A militant campaign to include women in the electorate originated in Victorian times. Emmeline Pankhurst's husband, Richard Pankhurst, was a supporter of the women's suffrage movement, and had been the author of the Married Women's Property Acts of 1870 and 1882. In 1889, Pankhurst founded the unsuccessful Women's Franchise League, but in October 1903 she founded the better-known Women's Social and Political Union (Suffragettes), an organization famous for its militancy. Led by Pankhurst and her daughters, Christabel and Sylvia, the campaign culminated in 1918, when the Parliament of the United Kingdom passed an act (the Representation of the People Act 1918) granting the vote to women over the age of 30 who were householders, the wives of householders, occupiers of property with an annual rent of £5, and graduates of British universities.

Reform in Parliament

Earl Grey, Lord Melbourne and Robert Peel were leaders of Parliament during the earlier years of the British reform movement. Grey and Melbourne were of the Whig party, and their governments saw parliamentary reform, the abolition of slave trading throughout the British Empire, and Poor Law reform. Peel was a Conservative, whose Ministry took an important step in the direction of tariff reform with the abolition of the Corn Laws.

Benjamin Disraeli and William Ewart Gladstone, as leaders of Great Britain's Conservative and Liberal parties, respectively, served as Prime Ministers during the later years of Great Britain's era of reform. Disraeli saw British control of the Suez Canal and named Queen Victoria the Empress of India.

Gladstone approached politics differently. Among the reforms he helped Parliament pass was a system of public education in the Elementary Education Act 1870. In 1872, he saw the institution of a secret ballot to prevent voter coercion, trickery and bribery. By 1885 Gladstone had readjusted the parliamentary district lines by making each district equal in population, preventing one MP from having greater influence than another.

HINDU REFORM MOVEMENTS

Several contemporary groups, collectively termed Hindu reform movements, strive to introduce regeneration and reform to Hinduism. Although these movements are very individual in their exact philosophies they generally stress the spiritual, secular and logical and scientific aspects of the Vedic traditions, creating a form that is egalitarian that does not discriminate based on Jati (caste or subcaste), gender, or race. Thus, most modern Hindu reform movements advocate a return to supposed ancient, egalitarian forms of Hinduism, and view aspects of modern Hinduism, such as discrimination and the caste system, as being corrupt results from colonialism and foreign influence.

Active Hindu communities are to be found in all parts of the world. In particular, countries of the former Soviet Union and Poland have thriving Hindu communities due to the missionary work of the Hare Krishnas. Most of the Hindu movements, with the exception of the Hare Krishna movement, reflect a more Smarta-like ideology.

There are groups in India that are actively engaged in getting women and those from socially disadvantaged jatis to become priests of Vedic ritual. One of the foremost movements in breaking the caste system and educating the downtrodden was the Lingayat movement spearheaded by Basavanna in the 12th century in Anubhava Mantapa in Kalyani of Karnataka. The less accessible Vedas were rejected and parallel Vachanas were compiled.

The new movements look up to Swami Vivekananda; Rabindranath Tagore; Ramana Maharshi; Shri Aurobindo (for his *Integral Yoga*); A.C. Bhaktivedanta Swami Prabhupada (founder of the modern Hare Krishna movement); Swami Sivananda, Swami Rama Tirtha; Narayana Guru,Jagadguru Swami Sathyananda Saraswathi, Paramhansa Yogananda; Shrii Shrii Anandamurti.

More recently, the work of Maharishi Mahesh Yogi, Sathya Sai Baba, Shirdi Sai Baba, Swami Muktananda, Swami Chinmayananda, Maharishi Dayananda Saraswati, Shriram Sharma Acharya, Sri Sri Ravi Shankar, and Mata Amritanandamayi has inspired millions to create new centres of spiritual development. In the intellectual field, the writings of Ananda Coomaraswamy, Ram Swarup, Sita Ram Goel, Subhash Kak and David Frawley have been influential.

In social work, Mahatma Gandhi, Vinoba Bhave, Baba Amte and Shrii Shrii Anandamurti have been most important. Sunderlal Bahuguna created the *chipko* movement for the preservation of forestlands according to the Hindu ecological ideas.

The Rashtriya Swayamsevak Sangh or RSS was founded by Keshav Baliram Hegdewar in 1925. The goal was to unite Hindus, make them rise over their caste differences and work to achieve a Hindu Rashtra; the ideology of the Sangh, closely associated with political Hinduism, came to be known as Hindutva.

In Indonesia several movements favour a return to Hinduism in Java, Sumatra, Kalimantan, and Sulawesi. Balinese Hinduism, known as Agama Hindu Dharma, has witnessed great resurgence in recent years. Shrii Prabhat Rainjan Sarkar (founder of Ananda Marga) initiated a new renaissance in the Indian world of samgeet.

SOCIAL REFORMERS

India has produced numerous social reformers who have played a significant role in making India a more progressive and forward looking country. These social reformers have fought against several social evils such as Sati, widow remarriage, child marriage, casteism et al. Here is a brief profile of famous Indian social reformers.

Dayanand Saraswati

Dayanand Saraswati was one of the most radical socio-religious reformers in the history of India. Swami Dayanand Saraswati was the founder of Arya Samaj and propagated egalitarian approach of the Vedas at a time when widespread casteism was prevalent in the society.

Raja Ram Mohan Roy

Raja Ram Mohan Roy is known as the 'Maker of Modern India'. He was the founder of the Brahmo Samaj, one of the first Indian socio-religious reform movements. He played a major role in abolishing the role of Sati. Raja Rammohan Roy was a great scholar and an independent thinker.

Ramakrishna Paramhansa

Ramakrishna Paramhansa was one of the foremost Hindu spiritual leaders of the country. His teachings are still deeply revered by the people. He also played a key role in the social reform movement in Bengal in 19th century.

Swami Vivekananda

Swami Vivekananda was one of the most influential spiritual leaders of Vedanta philosophy. He was the chief disciple of Ramakrishna Paramahansa and was the founder of Ramakrishna Math and Ramakrishna Mission. Swami Vivekananda was the living embodiment of sacrifice and dedicated his life to the country and yearned for the progress of the poor, the helpless and the downtrodden.

Vinoba Bhave

Vinobha Bhave's original name was Vinayak Narahari Bhave. He was born in a Brahmin family on September 11, 1895 at the village of Gagoda in Kolaba district of Maharashtra.

He was greatly influenced by his mother Rukmini Devi. Vinoba Bhave was well-read in the writings of Maharashtra's saints and philosophers.

Kiran Bedi

Kiran Bedi is truly an icon of heroism. She was the first Indian woman to join the Indian Police Services. She was born on June 9, 1949 at Amritsar in Punjab. She is one of the most renowned police officers, who have put in their whole hearted effort in serving the society.

Medha Patkar

Medha Patkar is a well known social activist of India. She was born on 1st December in the year 1954. Prior to becoming a social reformer, she completed her M.A. in Social Work from Tata Institute of Social Sciences (TISS).She left Ph. D. in the midst and got actively involved in the agitations conducted by tribals and peasants of Maharashtra, Madhya Pradesh and Gujarat.

Shanta Sinha

Shanta Sinha, the Ramon Magsaysay award winner, has recently been appointed for the post of chairperson of the National Commission for Protection of Child Rights. She is the founder secretary trustee of the Mamidipudi Venkatarangaiya (MV) Foundation, Secunderabad.

Baba Amte

Baba Amte is one of the greatest social reformers India's ever had. He gave his lucrative career as barrister for social service. He was so great a person that he dedicated his entire life to the care and rehabilitation of leprosy patients.

Jyotiba Phule

Jyotirao Govindrao Phule, who was a prominent activist, thinker and social reformer from the Indian state of Maharashtra during the 19th century, was also famous by the name of Mahatma Jyotiba Phule. During his time, he tried bringing in positive renovations in the spheres of education, agriculture, caste system, social position of women et al.

Shahu Chhatrapati

Shahu Chhatrapati was the Maharaja or the king of the Indian princely state of Kolhapur. Also known by the name of Rajarshi Shahu, he was known to be a great social reformer of his time. Shahu Chhatrapati was born on 26 June in the year 1874 as Yeshwantrao Ghatge.

THE HINDU REFORMATION

"...Thus it may be said that as early as 1820 India had come into the direct current of European thought and had begun to participate in the fruits of Europe's intellectual quest. The Brahmo Samaj lived up to this ideal. Its social message was Westernization, to purge Hinduism of the customs and superstitions with which it was overlaid, to raise the status of women, to bridge the yawning gulf between popular and higher Hinduism, to fight relentlessly against caste, social taboo, polygamy and other well entrenched abuses. To the educated Hindu, who felt unsettled in mind by the attack of the missionaries, the Brahmo Samaj provided the way out.

The Brahmo tradition has become so much a part of the Indian way of life now, that one is inclined to overlook its distinctive contribution. It does not lie primarily in the fact that it enabled Hinduism to withstand the onslaught of the missionaries, but in that it introduced the modern approach to Indian problems..."

The Hindu Reformation of the nineteenth century is one of the great movements of the age which by its massiveness and far-reaching significance takes its place with the most vital developments of modern history.

As it was a slow process and took place under the cover of British authority and was not always obvious to the outsider, it has so far escaped attention. A further reason why, in spite of its tremendous import, it passed unnoticed is that, by its very nature, it was an internal movement which did not touch or influence outside events. But India's independence and emergence into the modern world would hardly have been possible without the slow but radical adjustments that had taken place within the fold of Hinduism for a period of over 100 years.

In order to appreciate this movement fully it is necessary to understand what the position of Hinduism was in the beginning of the nineteenth century. 700 years of Islamic authority over the Indo-Gangetic Plains from Delhi to Calcutta had left Hinduism in a state of depression. It was the religion of a subject race, looked down on with contempt by the Muslims as idolatry. It enjoyed no prestige and for many centuries its practice had been tolerated only under considerable disadvantage in various areas. It had no central direction, no organization and hardly any leadership. When the British took over the rulership of Northern India, Hinduism for the first time in 700 years stood on a plane of equality with Islam. But a new and even more dangerous portent appeared on the stage.

The missionaries, feeling that there was almost a virgin field here in a society which appeared to be on the point of dissolution, took up the work of conversion. Islam, though it proselytized by fits and starts, had no separate machinery for carrying its message to the people. The Christian missionaries were different. They used no physical force, which Islam did not hesitate to do at intervals and in limited areas.

Brahmo Samaj

The first result of the Christian attack on Hinduism was a movement among educated Hindus in favour of a social reform of religion. The leader of this was Ram Mohan Roy (1772-1833), who may be called the father of the Hindu Reformation.

Born in a Brahmin family, Ram Mohan was brought up as a strict Hindu, but educated, as all Hindus who hoped to enter public service had perforce to be at that time, in Islamic culture. He was a deep student of Arabic and Persian when he entered the East India Company's service, where also he rose to some distinction. During this period he took to the study of English, which opened to him the whole range of Western liberal thought.

It was the time when the mellowed glow of the Great European Enlightenment had cast on European intellectual life an amazing serenity and sense of certainty. The light of D'Holbach, Condorcet, Diderot and the great Encyclopaedists had not died down and the dawn of the great nineteenth century thinkers, especially Bentham and the Utilitarians in England, which was destined to have so powerful an influence in the development of ideas in India, had not begun.

What Ram Mohan witnessed around him in India was a scene of utter devastation and ruin. The old order of Muslim rule had disappeared overnight, leaving behind it utter chaos in every walk of life. Hinduism in Bengal, once the centre of a devotional Vaishnava religion of great vitality, had sunk to a very low level of superstition, extravagance and immorality. A seeker after truth, Ram Mohan turned to the new religion which the missionaries were preaching. He studied Hebrew and Greek to understand Christianity better. But his scholarship was taking him at the same time to the well of European liberalism. Ram Mohan Roy was in fact the last of the Encyclopaedists. Thus he came to reject Christ, while accepting the wide humanism of European thought, its ethics and its general approach to the problems of life.

His book, The Precepts of Jesus, the Guide to Peace and Happiness, is an interpretation of Christianity in this new light, a reply to the missionaries rather than a call to Indians.

While Ram Mohan Roy thus rejected the Christian claims, he realized that Hinduism had to be re-interpreted. That interpretation he attempted in the Brahmo Samaj, a new reformed sect of Hinduism, which he founded. The Samaj was not in its essence a Christian dilution of Hinduism, as has often been said, but a synthesis of the doctrines of the European Enlightenment, with the philosophical views of the Upanishads. As a religion Brahmo Samaj was based firmly on the Vedanta of genuine Hindu tradition, but its outlook on life was neither Christian nor Hindu, but European, and derived its inspiration from the intellectual movements of the eighteenth century.

Thus it may be said that as early as 1820 India had come into the direct current of European thought and had begun to participate in the fruits of Europe's intellectual quest. The Brahmo Samaj lived up to this ideal. Its social message was Westernization, to purge Hinduism of the customs and superstitions with which it was overlaid, to raise the status of women, to bridge the yawning gulf between popular and higher Hinduism, to fight relentlessly against caste, social taboo, polygamy and other well entrenched abuses. To the educated

Hindu, who felt unsettled in mind by the attack of the missionaries, the Brahmo Samaj provided the way out.

The Brahmo tradition has become so much a part of the Indian way of life now, that one is inclined to overlook its distinctive contribution. It does not lie primarily in the fact that it enabled Hinduism to withstand the onslaught of the missionaries, but in that it introduced the modern approach to Indian problems. India started on her long adventure in building up a new civilization as a synthesis between the East and the West in the 1820s, and in that sense Ram Mohan is the forerunner of new India.

It has been well stated that 'he embodies the new spirit, its freedom of inquiry, its thirst for science, its large human sympathy, its pure and sifted ethics along with its reverent but not uncritical regard for the past and prudent disinclination towards revolt.'

Macaulay, English Education & Christian Missionaries...

The spirit of reform was entering Hinduism from other sources also. In 1835 the Government of India declared that 'the great object of the British Government ought to be the promotion of European literature and science among the natives of India', and embarked on a policy of Western education...

It was the devout hope of Macaulay, who was the champion of the scheme, and of many others, that the diffusion of the new learning among the higher classes would see the dissolution of Hinduism and the widespread acceptance of Christianity. The missionaries were also of the same view, and; they entered the educational field with enthusiasm, providing schools and colleges in many parts of India, where education in the Christian Bible was compulsory for Hindu students.

The middle classes accepted Western education with avidity and willingly studied Christian scriptures, but neither the dissolution of Hindu society so hopefully predicted nor the conversion of the intellectuals so devoutedly hoped for showed any signs of materialisation.

On the other hand, Hinduism assimilated the new learning, and the effects were soon visible ali over India in a revival of a universalized religion based on the Vedanta. It is necessary to remember that, though the Hindu religion has innumerable cults and sects, the philosophic background of all of them-including Buddhism-is the Vedanta. The doctrine of the Vedanta is contained in three authoritative texts-which are not scriptures-the Brahma Sutras, the Upanishads and the Gita.

Every orthodox sect in India derives its authority directly from these and, as has been state, the protagonists of each new religious sect have had to demonstrate how their own teachings flowed directly from these three sources. Thus it was, that Sankara, the reformer of Hinduism in the eighth century, had to write his commentary on all the three. It is to the doctrines of the Vedanta, as embodied in the Upanishads, that Ram Mohan Roy turned when he also felt the need of a new religious interpretation.

Arya Samaj, Dayananda Saraswati...

The demand of new India was not for a new sect. It was for a universal religion acceptable to all Hindus. The first effort to provide such a basis was by Dayananda Saraswati who saw in the Vedas the revealed Word of God and felt that, as the Vedas were accepted by all who claimed to be Hindus, a religion based on the Vedas should have universal appeal in India.

The Muslims had a revealed book, the Holy Quran. The Christians had the Bible, and Swami Dayananda felt that the amorphous and indefinable nature of Hinduism, which exposed it to so much weakness, could be remedied by providing the Hindus also with a revealed book. This seemed all the more the right path since the Vedas gave no authority to the usages and superstitions that had come to be accepted by the masses as Hinduism.

There was no sanction in the Vedas for caste, for the prohibition of the marriage of widows, for untouchability, for the taboo on food and the other characteristics of popular Hinduism which had been seized upon by the missionaries in their campaign and were being widely rejected by Hindu intelligentsia.

Swami Dayananda in his Satyartha Praksah, or the Light of True Meaning, made a brave and ingenious attempt to see in the Vedas all that the Christians and the Muslims were claiming to be the basis of their religions, universal brotherhood and a direct and non-metaphysical approach to God.

His Arya Samaj, however successful as a militant organization for the protection of Hinduism from the onslaughts of Islam and Christianity, never appealed to the Hindus outside the Punjab. The reasons were simple.

The attempt to go back to the Vedas involved a denial of the Hindu culture of the last three thousand years, a refusal to see any good in the puranic religion, in the variegated traditions which had enriched Hindu thought in the Middle Ages, all of which the Arya Samajists rejected without hesitation and attacked without reservation.

Secondly, the Vedic religion had long ago ceased to be related to the religious experience of Hindus. The Gita had poured scorn on Vedic sacrifices and held up the Veda-vadaratas (those who delight to argue on the basis of the Vedas) to contempt. The exclusiveness of the Arya Samaj, amounting to the intolerance of other religious practices though but a reflection of its prolonged fight against the proselytizing faiths and therefore essentially defensive, was also against the tradition of Hinduism which held firmly to the doctrine that the Gita preached, 'men worship Me in different ways, I give them the fruits appropriate to their worship'.

The Hindu does not deny the truth of any religion, or reject the validity of another's religious experience.

But the Arya Samajists, at least in their polemical days, were rigidly exclusive. The movement, therefore, did not spread to other parts of India and its influence was limited mainly to the Delhi and Punjab areas.

Theosophical Society, Annie Besant...

The urge of educated Hindus to find a common denominator for their various sects, which neither of these movements provided, was for a time fulfilled by the activities of the Theosophical Society, of which Colonel Olcott, the American, and Madame Blavatsky, the Russian, were the founders. Educated Hindus all over the country turned to the Theosophical Society, which introduced into India the organization and propagandist methods of European religious activity. Its interpretation of Hinduism followed the more orthodox lines, and many of its Indian leaders, like Dr. Bhagwan Das, of Benares, and Sir S. Subramania Aiyar, of Madras, were also leaders of Hindu Orthodoxy. Its social doctrines, however, were progressive and more important, and it cut through the sectarian lines of Indian religious organization.

Theosophic Hinduism was an All-India movement and it profoundly affected the outlook of the new generation. When Mrs. Annie Besant, an extremely gifted, persuasive and dynamic personality, became the President of the Society, its propaganda for a reformed universal Hinduism became more marked and was carried on incessantly through schools, colleges and an enormous output of popular literature. Mrs. Besant.had become steeped in Indian culture and her popular approach was Vedantic, as her translation of the Gita would testify.

Swami Vivekananda...

The Vedantic reformation which was thus in the air found its most widely accepted exponent in Swami Vivekananda. Vivekananda was a Western-educated Bengali who came under the influence of Ramakrishna, a mystic whose personality had made a deep impression on the Bengali society of his day. Vivekananda was fired by a desire to revive Hinduism and purify its religious and social teachings. Initiated a Sanyasi, he toured the length and breadth of India spreading the gospel of Vedanta. A prolonged visit to America and a tour in England inflamed his patriotism, his desire to rejuvenate Hindu society and to give Hinduism a social purpose. His fervent declaration that he did not 'believe in a religion that does not wipe out the widow's tears or bring a piece of bread to the orphan's mouth' expresses clearly the changed temper of Hinduism. His own mission he described as follows. Answering the question: 'What do you consider to be the function of your movement as regards India?' the Swami said: 'To find the common bases of Hinduism and to awaken the national consciousness to them.' That common basis he found in the Vedanta which he interpreted in popular phraseology and preached untiringly all over India.

'All the philosophers of India who are orthodox have to acknowledge the authority of the Vedanta and all our present-day religions, however crude some of them may appear to be, however inexplicable some of their purposes may seem, one who understands them and studies them can trace them back to the ideas of the Upanishads. So deeply have these Upanishads sunk into our race that those of you who study the symbology of the crudest religion of the Hindus will be astonished to find sometimes figurative expressions of the Upanishads. Great spiritual and philosophical ideas in the Upanishads are today with us, converted into household worship in the form of symbols. Thus the various symbols now used by us, all come from the Vedanta, because in the Vedanta they are used as figures.'

Again: 'Thus the Vedanta, whether we know it or not, has, penetrated all the sects in India and what we call Hinduism, that mighty banyan tree, with its immense and almost infinite rami fications, has been throughout interpenetrated by the influence J the Vedanta. Whether we are conscious of it or not, we think that Vedanta, we live in the Vedanta, we breathe the Vedanta and we die in the Vedanta, and every Hindu does that.'

He not only preached this gospel, but trained up a body of missionaries, men of education, pure life and religious zeal to carry this message to the villages.

There were innumerable other Sanyasis and learned men who, though belonging to no particular sect, were preaching the same principles all over India. In fact, the revival of Vedanta in Hindu thought at the end of the nineteenth century constitutes a religious movement of national significance. It was at the end of this period that Aurobindo gave what may be called the classic exposition of the entire Vedanta doctrine in his Essays on the Gita and later his Life Divine. By this, Vedanta may be said to have been restored to its place as the common background of all Hindu religious thought.

Vedanta, Popular Hinduism and the Law...

The unifying doctrine was the Vedanta, but the abstract conceptions of this philosophical approach could only appeal to the elite. Popular Hinduism continued in the old way, sectarian, devotional and based on daily rituals. But it also underwent extraordinary changes. The gnarled branches of this ancient tree either fell away by themselves or were chopped off by legislative action promoted by the reformers. Child marriage, which many Hindu communities considered as an essential part of their religion, was abolished by law through the insistence of popular agitation. The remarriage of widows was permitted.

Social disabilities based on caste vanished by themselves, and the occupational basis of caste communities was weakened. Temples were thrown open to the untouchables, and in the most orthodox province of Madras, Hindu religious endowments were placed under the control of public bodies. The movement for the regeneration of the depressed classes assumed a national character, and their participation in social and political life became a major factor in the last days of British rule.

Popular Hinduism had a more vigorous life than it ever had in the immediately preceding times, but it had in the course of a hundred years changed its character and temper, though it had kept much of its form.

The major difficulty of Hinduism which had made it a wild jungle growth of widely varying customs, usages and superstitions was its lack of a machinery of reform and unification. The institutions of Hinduism, which in a large measure got identified with 'the religion itself, were the results of certain historical factors. They were upheld by law and not by religion. Vivekananda put the point well when he wrote:

> *'Beginning from Buddha down to Ram Mohan Roy, everyone made the mistake of holding caste to be a religious institution.... But in spite of all the ravings of the priests, caste is simply a crystallized social institution, which after doing its service is now filling the atmosphere of India with stench.'*

The caste organization, the joint family, the rights of inheritance and the relationships arising out of them, which in the main are the special features of Hindu society, are legal and not religious. They are man-made institutions which do not claim Divine origin or religious sanction, and are upheld by man-made laws and not by any church or priesthood. It is a truism to say that legislation of today meets the social needs of yesterday and, unavoidably, law, as a conservative force, lags one step behind social necessities. When the great codes of Hindu Law were evolved, no doubt they represented the social forces of the time, but soon they had become antiquated. The succession of authoritative commentaries would show that the urge for modifications was widely felt and, in the absence of a legislative authority, the method of a progressive interpretation in each succeeding generation was the only one available to Hindu thinkers.

The immutability of Hindu law and customs was never a principle with the authors of the great codes or their commentators. In fact, the monumental volumes of Dr. Kane's History of Dharma Sastra would demonstrate clearly that in every age social thinkers tried to adjust Hindu institutions to the requirements of the time. If the laws are changeable it follows that the institutions which were based on such laws are equally changeable. The great weakness of Hindu society was not that the laws had remained immutable but that the changes introduced had been spasmodic, local and dependent to a large extent on the ingenuity of individual commentators. They were not in any sense a continuous renovation of legal principles, nor a legislative approximation to changing conditions.

The reason for this lack of direction of social ideas and the failure to prevent the growth of anti-social customs was undoubtedly the loss of political power. Not only was India as a whole never under a single sovereign authority, but even the political unity of North India which existed with occasional breaks from the time of the Mauryas (320 B.C.) to that of Harsha (A.D, 637) was broken up by the political conditions of the eighth century and lost for a period of 700 years with the Muslim invasion of the twelfth century. As a result, the Hindu community continued to be governed by institutions moulded by laws which were codified over 2,000 years ago and which were out of date even when they were codified.

The Muslim State had no legislative machinery, and when for the first time India was united under the British and the entire Hindu community lived under a common administration, the authorities of the East India Company after a first effort at social reform withdrew, under the pretext of religious neutrality, from activities which they thought might cause popular upheaval. Perhaps it was a wise step, as the motive force of large-scale social reforms must come from the people themselves and legislation can only give statutory sanction to principles which have already gained wide acceptance. The reformation of the Hindu religion was therefore an essential prerequisite of social legislation.

It was only after the Great War that the legislating State came into existence in India. Under the scheme of partial self-government introduced in 1921, there was established a central legislative authority with a majority of non-official elected Indians, which; was both competent to change the laws of Hindu society and to enforce obedience to such laws through the length and breadth of India. In the provinces the direction of government passed in a large measure to elected legislatures.

The legislative achievements of the Central and Provincial Governments in the field of social reform have been fundamental, though they did not go anywhere as far as the public demanded. The Civil Marriage Act and the Age of Consent Act (raising the marriageable age of girls to I4) were among the more important pieces of legislation which the Central Indian Legislative Assembly enacted.

The Civil Marriage Act validates marriages between men and women of different castes of Hinduism. It strikes at the very root of the orthodox Brahminical conception of caste, and annuls the laws of Manu and the other orthodox codes of Hinduism.

'The immutable law', prohibiting Varna-Samkara or the mixture of castes, ceased by this single piece of legislation to operate through the length and breadth of India. The Age of Consent Act was equally revolutionary. It was the custom for over two thousand years at least for large sections of people to have girls married before the age of puberty.

There was not only long tradition behind the custom, but it was considered compulsory at least for Brahmins in the light of certain authoritative texts. The Indian legislature made this custom illegal, though it had so much religious authority behind it, and the performance of such marriages became a penal offence.

Thus by the end of the third decade, the Hindu reformation had made enough progress to enable the new society to direct its social forces towards general betterment. The reformation of Hinduism has been treated in some detail, because without an appreciation of its consequences the effects of Western education on Indian society will not be fully clear.

HINDU REFORMERS AND INDIAN NATIONALISM

Brahmo Samaj

In 1828, a man named Raja Ram Mohan Roy (1772-1833) founded an organization called 'Brahmo Samaj'. Indian historians consider this organization forerunner which paved the way for reformation in India and its establisher as the 'father of modern India'. Raja Ram was a Brahman from Bengal. He was a British civil servant in India. He saw in British rule of India the best things that were benefical to India. He adored the west European philosophy of democracy, liberalism and humanism. He had a great interest in non-Indian cultures and religions. He was especially impressed by Christianity and other religions which preached the existence of one Almighty God.

Raja Ram tried to create a new Hindu religion philosophy and enfolded in it the existence of one God and other beliefs, which were then not the predominant features in Hinduism. He attacked some Hindu traditions and features among them caste system, child marriages, Sati-burning of the live wife over her dead husband's pyre, idolatry and other beliefs. He tried to change the popular Hindu traditions and claimed that the popular Hindu traditions were different from the real Hindu beliefs.

Raja Ram and his organization 'Brahmo Samaj' tried to change the social order of India. He established newspapers and schools all around India. He convinced the British in 1829 to outlaw Sati. But during that period there wasn't yet an Indian ethos among the Indians. Indians were never one nation but always a collection of different entities. They were used to different rulers including non-Indians. From their point of view the British were just another ruler over them. But the main contribution of the Brahmo Samaj to the society of India was that it evoked issues that were common to people all around the Indian sub-continent. The notions of this organization were the inspiration for other organizations and various secular political parties, like the Indian National Congress, which were later on created in India.

Sati-The Burning of the Widow

Sati is described as a Hindu custom in India in which the widow was burnt to ashes on her dead husband's pyre. Basically the custom of Sati was believed to be a voluntary Hindu act in which the woman voluntary decides to end her life with her husband after his death. But there were many incidences in which the women were forced to commit Sati, sometimes even dragged against her wish to the lighted pyre.

Though Sati is considered a Hindu custom, the women, known as Sati in Hindu religious literature, did not commit suicide on their dead husband's pyre. The first woman known as Sati was the consort of Lord Shiva. She burnt herself in fire as protest against her father who did not give her consort Shiva the respect she thought he deserved, while burning herself she prayed to reborn again as the new consort of Shiva, which she became and her name in the new incarnation was Parvati. Other famous woman in Hindu literature titled Sati was Savitri. When Savitri's husband Satyavan died, the Lord of death, Yama arrived to take his soul. Savitri begged Yama to restore Satyavan and take her life instead, which he could not do. So Savitri followed Lord Yama a long way. After a long way in which Yama noticed that Savitri was losing strength but was still following him and her dead husband, Yama offered Savitri a boon, anything other than her husband's life. Savitri asked to have children from Satyavan. In order to give Savitri her boon, Lord Yama had no choice but to restore Satyavan to life and so Savitri gained her husband back.

These two women along with other women in Hindu mythology who were exceptionally devoted to their husbands symbolized the truthful Indian wife who would do everything for their husband and they were named Sati. The meaning of the word sati is righteous. But as written earlier the women named Sati, in Hindu religious literature, did not commit suicide on their dead husband's pyre. Therefore the custom of burning the widow on her dead husband's pyre probably did not evolve from religious background but from social background.

There are different theories about the origins of Sati. One theory says that Sati was introduced to prevent wives from poisoning their wealthy husbands and marry their real lovers.

Other theory says that Sati began with a jealous queen who heard that dead kings were welcomed in heaven by hundreds of beautiful women, called Apsaras. And therefore when her husband died, she demanded to be burnt on her dead husband's pyre and so to arrive with him to heaven and this way to prevent the Apsaras from consorting with her husband. There are also other theories about the origins of Sati.

Even though Sati is considered an Indian custom or a Hindu custom it was not practiced all over India by all Hindus but only among certain communities of India. On the other hand, sacrificing the widow in her dead husband's funeral or pyre was not unique only to India. In many ancient communities it was an acceptable feature. This custom was prevalent among Egyptians, Greek, Goths, Scythians and others. Among these communities it was a custom to bury the dead king with his mistresses or wives, servants and other things so that they could continue to serve him in the next world. Another theory claims that Sati was probably brought to India by the Scythians invaders of India. When these Scythians arrived in India, they adopted the Indian system of funeral, which was cremating the dead. And so instead of burying their kings and his servers they started cremating their dead with his surviving lovers. The Scythians were warrior tribes and they were given a status of warrior castes in Hindu religious hierarchy. Many of the Rajput clans are believed to originate from the Scythians. Later on other castes who claimed warrior status or higher also adopted this custom.

This custom was more dominant among the warrior communities in north India, especially in Rajasthan and also among the higher castes in Bengal in east India. Among the Rajputs of Rajasthan, who gave lot of importance to valor and self sacrifice, wives and concubines of the nobles even committed suicide, when they came to know that their beloved died in battlefield. In other parts of India it was comparatively low. And among the majority of Indian communities it did not exist at all.

A few rulers of India tried to ban this custom. The Mughals tried to ban it. The British, due to the efforts of Hindu reformers like Raja Ram Mohan Roy outlawed this custom in 1829.

There aren't exact figures about the number of Sati incidences. In general, before this custom was outlawed in 1829, there were a few hundred officially recorded incidences each year. Even after the custom was outlawed, this custom did not vanish completely. It took few decades before this custom almost vanished.

But still there are rare incidences in which the widow demands to voluntary commit Sati. In 1987 an eighteen years old widow committed Sati in a village of Rajasthan with the blessing of her family members. In this incidence the villagers took part in the ceremony, praising and supporting the widow for her act. In October 1999 a woman hysterically jumped on her husband's pyre surprising everyone. But this incidence was declared suicide and not Sati, because this woman was not compelled, forced or praised to commit this act.

In different communities of India, Sati was performed for different reasons and different manners. In communities where the man was married to one wife, the wife put an end to her life on the pyre. But even in these communities not all widows committed Sati.

Those women who committed Sati were highly honoured and their families were given lot of respect. It was believed that the woman who committed Sati blessed her family for seven generations after her. Temples or other religious shrines were built to honour the Sati.

In communities were the ruler was married to more than one wife; in some cases only one wife was allowed to commit Sati. This wife was normally the preferred wife of the husband. This was some kind of honour for the chosen wife and some kind of disgrace for the other wives. In other communities some or all of the wives and mistresses were immolated with the husband. And in some cases even male servants were immolated with the kings. This kind of Sati in which the wives and servants were treated as the ruler's property intensifies the theory that Sati was introduced to India by the Scythian invaders of India.

In some very rare incidences mothers committed Sati on their son's pyre and in even more rare cases husbands committed Sati on their wives pyres.

RAJ RAM MOHAN ROY VS. DAYANANDA

Hindu Renaissance, which is referred to as a religious and political movement, is closely related to a burgeoning Indian Nationalism. Hindu revivalism is of vital importance in the development of Hinduism as a world religion. The Hindu Renaissance had a tendency to play down the difference between theological traditions and to regulate ritual level, below the ethical spirituality of the Upanishads and the Gita. Hindu reform movement developed to restore the perceived greatness of Hinduism's ancient past, to adopt rationalist elements form within Christianity, and to pay particular attention to social and ethical concerns. The leaders of Hindu renaissance like Raja Ram Mohan Roy and Dayananda Saraswati played an important role in the awakening of social and religious reforms. Raja Ram Mohan Roy (1772-1833) was born of a distinguished Brahmin family in Bengal. He was educated at the Muslim University at Patna where he studied Arabic and Persian philosophical literature. He also studied Sanskrit in Varanasi, as well as English, Hebrew and Greek with a view to translating Bible into Bengali. Because of the Muslim influence, particularly Sufi, Roy was a St...

The main contribution of Brahmo Samaj to the society of India was that it evoked issues that were common to the people all around the Indian sub continent.

They make faith in the doctrines of Karma and Rebirth optional. He wanted to return to the "Sanatana Dharma", the eternal law, which Hindus have moved away from by worshipping icons and reading Epics and Purans. He also supported remarriage of widows, if their previous marriage had not consummated. marriage by choice? the most ancient form of marriage in India-is the best form of marriage. He lost his faith in the Shaiva religion of image worship, when he saw mice climbing over the temple icon, eating the food which had been offered to the deity.

Dayananda Saraswati (1824-1883) was born in Saurashtra in Gujarat to a Shaiva Brahman family.

Raja Ram Mohan Roy, through his services, was considered the true leader of Renaissance and known as the "father of Renaissance". He believed that people should not be discriminating by their birth but by their Karma, actions. It was not a seperate religion but a reform movement within Hinduism.?

Dayananda Saraswati opposed the Varna system. The four Vedas are; Rig Veda, Yajur Veda, Sama Veda, & Atharva Veda.?

Roy founded the Atmiya Sabha in 1815.

BELIEFS OF THE BRAHMO SAMAJ

Fundamental Principles of the Brahmo Religion and Universalism

The fundamental principles of the Brahmo Samaj, founded by Raja Ram Mohan Roy in 1828 are:

1. There is only one God, who is the creator, and the saviour of this world. He is spirit, infinite in power, wisdom, love, justice and holiness, omnipresent, eternal and blissful.
2. The human soul is immortal and capable of infinite progress, and is responsible to God for its doings.
3. Man's happiness in this and the next world consists in worshipping God in spirit and in truth.
4. Loving God, holding communion with Him, and carrying out His will in all the concerns of life, constitute true worship.
5. No created object is to be worshipped as God, and God alone is to be considered as infallible.

To this, Raja Ram Mohan Roy added "The true way of serving God is to do good to man." Since no one person is considered to be infallible, the Brahmos hold all the great religious leaders of the world in respect, and believe that truth is to be gleaned from all the scriptures of the world. To that extent, the Brahmo religion is truly eclectic. Universalist in nature, it is "dogmatically undogmatic". The Brahmo Samaj has a great deal in common with the other free churches of the world, and is one of the founding members of the "The International Association for Religious Freedom". Rationalist in everything, it does not deny the possibility of Divine Revelation, but reserves the right to test the validity of what is supposed to be revelation. The connection between the Brahmo Samaj and the other liberal churches of the world is best understood when we considered the basics of Universalism, which are dealt with in the following paragraphs:

> *Duncan Howlett has aptly described Universalism as a doctrine of "Testing, Questing and never Resting, with Open Mind and Open Heart."*

Each of these items bears detailed examination. The root question is how can we be sure about the truth of our beliefs? After all, there is no doubt that we human beings are fallible. The only way we can surmount our human fallibility is by continually testing the validity of our assumptions. We have to accept that we are prone to making mistakes and deceiving one another all the time. Even in the age of computers, there is always the possibility of mistakes being made in programming or worse still, valuable data being lost on account of viruses deliberately planted by misguided souls. We must therefore check everything by all the means at our disposal. This is true even in the case of religion, where we can no longer be certain of the infallibility of scriptures or prophets.

If our human capacity for error is a severe limitation, then our imagination and probing curiosity are surely among our greatest assets. It is the human spirit of inquiry and questing, in other words, seeking for the truth, which is behind all advances in Philosophy or Religion. The enquiring mind pushes beyond ideas that we already have, in order to discover new perfections. In this process of Questing, we are never really satisfied until we feel that we have gone as far as is humanly possible. This is what is meant by "never Resting". On the path of discovery we are bound to meet like-minded souls also engaged in the same search for truth. We must be open to dialogue with them, and at least listen to them even if we do not agree. The spirit of the "open mind" is a safeguard against dogma, which has no place in Universalism.

While the open mind enlarges our own frontiers, it is not enough to merely be open to other ideas. Acceptance of the other person as a brother and a comrade makes religion truly universal. Merely accepting that "In the Father's house there are many mansions" does not better our human lot the way "Love thy neighbour as thyself" does. True Universalism is based on the "Fatherhood of God and the Brotherhood of Man" more than anything else. Universalists believe that religion should be dynamic and not static. Everything in this world is evolving, and religion too, changes with time. Any religion that adheres to a set of unchanging beliefs is a dead religion. Of course, any change has to be tested for validity by applying our God given powers of logic and reasoning, and must be acceptable to our conscience. The Brahmos believe that God reveals Himself in His own creation, and speaks to man through his conscience. The relationship between God and man is one of loving and giving. Our life is a gift from God. What we do with our life is our gift to God.

HISTORY OF THE BRAHMO SAMAJ

As British rule consolidated in India during the 18th century, two factors contributed to the formation of the Brahmo Samaj in the following century. Firstly the Hindu social system had begun to stagnate and placed too much of an emphasis on traditional rituals. Secondly an English educated class of Indians began to emerge to fulfil the administrative and economic needs of British rule. Raja Ram Mohan Roy, a Bengali, was a product of the latter trend. What made Raja Ram Mohan Roy stand out from his peers was his questioning mind. Apart from knowing several languages he was a Sanskrit and an Arabic scholar, and studied several religions. He campaigned for social reform and women's education. He founded the Brahma Samaj at Calcutta in 1828, which was initially known as the "Brahmo Sabha." Later in 1868 it was changed to the "Adi" (Original) Brahmo Samaj. It rejected idol worship and the worship of multiple gods and goddesses of the traditional Hindu beliefs. Raja Ram Mohan Roy was much influenced by western thought, especially Christianity. He was one of the first Hindus to visit Europe, where he was much admired by the intellectuals. He died in Bristol.

He was friendly with another famous Bengali, Dwarakanath Tagore. Prior to his departure to Europe, Raja Ram Mohan Roy had asked Dwarakanath Tagore's son, Debendranath Tagore, to continue his work in his absence. Debendranath Tagore took an active interest in the Brahmo Samaj, and began to transform the Brahmo Samaj into a spiritual fraternity. He formulated the "Brahmo-upadesa" which were a set of readings from the ancient Hindu book, the "Upanishads."

Debendranath Tagore's successor was Keshab Chandra Sen. He sought to incorporate Christian ideals into the Brahmo Samaj movement. He began the compilation of a scripture including passages from the Holy Books of many religions- Hindu, Buddhist, Christian and Muslim. Gradually, due to differences in certain areas of religious beliefs, three institutions arose:

- The Adi (Original) Brahmo Samaj-founded by Debendranath Tagore
- The Naba-Bidhan (New Dispensation) Samaj-founded by Keshab Chandra Sen
- The Sadharan (Common) Brahmo Samaj-founded by Pandit Shivanath Shastri

The Sadharan Brahmo Samaj sought to provide a more rational and monotheistic interpretation of the Upanishads. A "mandir" (prayer house) was built in Cornwallis Street, (now re-named "Bidhan Sarani") Calcutta. Eventually these three Samajes united to form the "Brahmo Sammilan Samaj," and a "mandir" was built in Bhowanipur, Calcutta. This celebrated its centenary in 1997.

The Brahmo Samajes grew in several Indian cities and abroad. There are records of one being present in Rangoon and in London as far back as 1911.

Social Welfare

Removing the Caste System: The caste system has been a part of Hindu society for hundreds of years. It's inherent divisive nature and social injustices were abhorrent to the early Brahmos. Therefore an important reform that the early Brahmos campaigned for was the removal of the caste system.

Many of the early Brahmos came from the Brahmin caste, who wore a sacred thread around their body to signify their caste superiority. From the 1850's onwards the renunciation of the sacred thread came to symbolise this break with tradition. The equality of all men was fundamental to the Brahmo movement, and to them it did not matter what caste or indeed religion someone was born into. For example even in 1865 there was a case of a Muslim boy being attracted into the religion. Given the polarization of society between Hindus and Muslims at the time, this was revolutionary in those days.

Widow Remarriage: Despite Iswar Chandra Vidyasagar's campaign that led to the legalisation of widow remarriage (1856) in India, Hindu society had many reservations on this issue. The Brahmos campaigned against such pre-judices. To reinforce their commitment to this many young men of the Brahmo movement made a positive point of marrying widows.

Saving of Upper Caste Unmarried Women: It wasn't just the lower castes who suffered in the caste system. Despite their caste status, the girls from the upper caste families suffered because of their position. If a suitable bridegroom could not be found for such a girl in their caste, their options were limited, as marriage to lower caste men was not permitted. These girls often found themselves being married off to very old men who were already married several times over. Or worse still, sometimes these girls would be poisoned to death. Again the Brahmos campaigned against such unjust practices and saved the lives of many such girls.

Women's Education and Status: Traditionally education had been primarily for the men. However during the 1860's and the 1870's the attitude of the Brahmos started to change. Education was encouraged among the Brahmo women. At the same time their equal status in society was emphasised by allowing women to pray with men at the prayer halls. In 1881 the Brahmo Samaj at Barishal (Bengal) appointed the first woman Brahmo preacher (Manorama Mazumdar).

This article was written by Dr. Sumit Chanda, based on source material provided by the Brahmo Sammilan Samaj at Calcutta. The drawings originally formed part of the Poster Exhibition held in August-September, 1997, on the occasion of the Centenary celebration of the Brahmo Sammilan Samaj. These have been reproduced with the kind permission of Mr. P.R. Das Gupta, the Secretary of the Brahmo Sammilan Samaj.

Brahmo Wedding: In a Brahmo wedding, the bride and the groom, as adults, declare in an open house that each is willing to accept the other as a partner for life. Thus a Brahmo wedding has no tradition of "giving away" the daughter by her parents. The bride and the groom pray to God together and take their nuptial vows. The minister and the other fellow Brahmos pray for their welfare and future happiness. The bride and groom typically exchange garlands and rings, and the prayers are complemented by singing of hymns.

Millennium Sermon: On the first Maghotsav of this century and in the new millennium I would like to share with you some thoughts that have crossed my mind.

The word January comes from the Roman God Janus, who had two heads-one pointing to the past, and one pointing to the future.

As we are celebrating Maghotsav in January at the beginning of the century, it is befitting that we first take a look at the past, and then into the future. A look at the past takes us to the Renaissance in India, and in Bengal in particular. In 1828 the Brahmo Samaj was established by Raja Ram Mohan Roy, who was followed by other leaders like Keshab Chandra Sen and Shivanath Shastri. It was a time of great spiritual social reforms against casteism and the emancipation of women. It was a period when superstitious and evil customs like the suttee were abolished. It an era when great educational institutions were established in Calcutta. That era has also seen the birth of men like Ramakrishna and Rabindranath and preachers of a non-violence like Mahatma Gandhi. We have seen the birth of the largest democratic nation when India achieved independence in 1947.

During the last century we have seen tremendous advances in the field of science and medicine. We have made great strides in developing transport-faster cars, trains and planes. Men have landed on the moon and we have watched it sitting in our own homes on TV. The past century has made enormous progress in the field of computers and satellite communication-the mobile phones and telecommunications by way of videoconferences in distant lands has brought the world closer. The world has become smaller and closer. Countries no longer think individually. They take a global view of trade and commerce.

However in spite of all the scientific achievements and material comforts have we made any real progress in moral and human values? Are human hearts and minds now closer to each other than 500 years ago? The 1900s have seen two World Wars-the people of the past century have experienced fighting and bloodshed and the horrific destruction of Nagasaki with the atom bomb. In spite of modern communications systems, communities seem to have grown apart and divided, as we have seen in Bosnia and very recently in the atrocities of Kosovo and now in Chechnya. At present and there are many wars going on in Africa and Asia with the devastating consequences of land mine injuries long afterwards.

Our social structure and family life has also changed. The extended family is on the brink of extinction. The advances in medicine have increased longevity, but are we able to provide a reasonable quality of care? Can we spare a little time for visiting elderly friends? Do we as human beings care for other humans and the plants and animals of this beautiful world? Today at the beginning of the 21st century let us attempt to try to look at the future. We do not know what the future holds for us; but we can hope that the world will be a better place for all of us.

The world, we can hope, will be a peaceful place-not only will there be peace among nations, but also in the hearts all men who will fulfil their duties towards the old, the sick and hungry. Societies and nations will not just think of their own survival but will work for the benefit of others, which is one of the ideals of the promise of the Brahmo Samaj, and that the other principles-"truth, justice and love" shall prevail in the hearts of men and women of the 21st century. We hope that the hearts and the minds of all the people in the world will be united and the century will be a happier place for all of us. It may seem like a dream but it is up to each one of us to make an effort, however small towards achieving this dream-and making this place a better place. May we find the world in the 21st century as Tagore has described in one of his poems.

THEORISING THE DALIT MOVEMENT

The Dalit movement, in the familiar sense of organised resistance of the ex-untouchables to caste oppression, may not be traced beyond colonial times. However, in a wider sense of the struggle of lower castes against the hegemony of Brahminical ideology, it has to coexist with the history of caste itself. The broad framework of caste remaining the same, the Dalit movement could also be seen in a historical continuum with its previous phases. In another sense, it could be taken as the articulation phase of the numerous faceless struggles against the iniquitous socio-economic formation ordained by the caste system, that has occupied vast spaces of Indian history. By any reckoning it seems to have done well in identifying its friends and foes, putting in place its strategies and tactics and more importantly, carving out a space for itself in every sphere. It kept pace with the changes taking place in socio-political sphere during the colonial times and thus displayed significant learning during this phase. However, it could not do so thereafter when it had to consolidate its gains particularly in the context of substantial changes that befell during the post-independence times.

During this period, it appears to have been eclipsed by the shadow of its own past. In an attempt to grasp certain generalities of the Dalit movement, this paper will try to present a hypothesis that all the predominant attributes that the contemporary Dalit movement tends to reflect, are basically acquired from the circumstances that brought it into existence. In corollary, the hypothesis is extended to state that the Dalit movement did not assimilate any significant learning through changes in these circumstances and so allowed itself to degenerate and to be used by the very set of people whom it intended to fight. While wading through the web of Indian reality around the Dalit movement it is expected to throw up issues the clarity on which is considered prerequisite to chalk out a road map for its liberation.

The mythologized history of India does not provide many clues to the direct rebellions of the oppressed masses against their oppression. But it is inconceivable that they did not take place at all over a long period of two millennia that nibbled at their existence every moment with a 'divine' contrivance called caste. The extraordinary success of this contrivance of social stratification is as much attributable to its own design that effectively obviated coalescence of the oppressed castes and facilitated establishment and maintenance of the ideological hegemony as to its purported divine origination. None could ordinarily raise a question as it meant incurring divine wrath and consequent ruination of the prospects of getting a better birth in their next life. Thus the caste system held society in a metaphysical engagement and at the same time in physical alienation with itself. Materially, it provided for the security of every one through caste professions and psychologically an aspirational space for every caste including the non-caste untouchables to feel superior to some other. Since, this superstructure was pivoted on the religio-ideological foundation, the manifestation of resistance to the caste system always used the metaphysical toolkit that contrived its arguments into the religious form. Right from the early revolts like Buddhism and Jainism down to the Bhakti movement in the medieval age, one finds articulation of opposition to the caste system materialising in a religio-ideological idiom. This trend in fact extends well down to modern times that marks a new awakening of the oppressed castes and the birth of the contemporary Dalit movement. All anti-caste movements thus, from the beginning to the present, invariably appear engaged in religious or metaphysical confrontation with Brahminism, either in terms of its denouncement or of adoption of some other religion.

The religious discourse is thus a common feature of all the anti-caste movements. For example, the Satnami movement of the Chamars in the Chhattisgarh plains in Eastern Madhya Pradesh that eventually became an independent religious sect (Russel 1916); the Dravid Kazhagam movement of Periyar EVR Ramaswamy Naicker which created a stir by publicly burning the effigy of Rama and celebrating the virtuousness of Ravana; the Nadar Mahajana Sabha in Tamilnadu (Hardgrave 1969); the Ezhava movement of Narayana Guru which culminated in establishment of a new religious sect called Sree Narayan Dharma Pratipalana Yogam in Kerala (Thomas 1965; Aiyappan 1944; Samuel 1973), and the most pervasive Dalit movement (Zelliot 1969) led by Babasaheb Ambedkar curiously reaching its climax of mass conversion to Buddhism; they all signify an overriding hatred for the religious code of Manu and a proposition of an alternate faith for themselves. It essentially embodied dejection with the Brahminism, which was perceived to be the root cause for their sufferings. The most articulate expression of this dejection is found in Ambedkar's own analyses that holds overthrowing of 'Hindu' religious ideological hegemony as a necessary condition for the liberation of Dalits (Omvedt, 1994).

Notwithstanding the views of some people who contend that the caste system was not a rigid system that had disallowed inter-caste movement of people, the fact remains that it does not have any evidence of having brought in a change in the forces of production or in the relations of production till the advent of British rule. With its quasi-autonomous villages it remained in a fossilised form for centuries. This feature of the Indian society precisely impelled Marx to disdainfully comment that India did not have history and to commend the British colonial rule for waking it up from its slumber to Western modernity. The first cultural shock this Indian society received was through the Moslem invaders. For the first time the Indians got to relate with some other religion and to realise that not only could there be alternative religious systems but also the gods postulating them. Egalitarian Islam initially treated all Indians equally but soon the imperative of their political strategies made them realise the utility of the intrinsic divisions existing in the Indian society and they not only decided to compromise their egalitarian zeal but also allowed adulteration of their cultural broth with the poison of caste.

Bhagawan Das (1983) quotes Ibn Batuta, a Moslem scholar who accompanied Mahmud Ghaznavi stating that the Moslem invaders at first treated all Indians alike but later took advantage of the cleavages existing in Indian society. The compulsions of politics overtook religious spirits, which meant the Brahminic social order, based on castes remained largely unhindered and even influenced the emergent Moslem society with the Hindu converts. Even then this process spelt a sea of opportunity to the untouchables living outside the cities and villages. It was the Moslem invaders who first opened the gates of their cities to these 'Untouchables'. Many 'Untouchables' and low caste people embraced Islam and joined the invaders, partly to avoid persecution and partly in search of better status and fortunes. Those who embraced Islam and joined the armies of Moslem invaders imitated the customs and manners of their new masters. They gradually merged and integrated into Moslem society. Besides those who formally embraced Islam, whether voluntarily or under compulsion, there were millions of those who belonged to the artisan castes like weavers, masons, carpenters, blacksmiths, shoemakers, basket makers, potters, dyers etc., who slowly came to be Moslems.

There were even some high caste Hindus including Brahmins who converted to Islam for various reasons. These converts coming from diverse castes brought in their respective cultural modes of living into the emergent Moslem society and along with it the caste divisions. Thus, although conversions to Islam could not rid the untouchables from their caste status fully, going by the intensity of oppression, they certainly must have experienced a great relief. First of all, the conversion enabled them to come out of their caste professions, which had been the mainstay of their low social status. Secondly, in renouncing their religion they must have had a sense of revenge against the ignominy heaped upon them and a vague sense of belonging to the ruling community. Thirdly, the opportunity to wield the sword in itself meant many things to them: it meant notional raise in their caste status catapulting them from a non-caste untouchable to that of Kshatriya - a penultimate rung in the caste hierarchy; it meant realisation of their manhood for the first time; it meant restoration of their confidence and most importantly, it meant economic betterment.

It is a moot point whether these conversions could be called a social movement insofar as technically the latter insists upon an organisation striving for some collective goal of social change. It certainly reflects a spirit of rebellion at least at the individual level to defy the caste code and embrace a different faith. Insofar as caste society had the intrinsic organisations of castes that governed their respective caste behaviours and managed the community life within the caste framework, it is a difficult proposition to say that this rebellion materialised without any organisational backing. An individual in the caste society was too small an entity to transcend the dictate of his caste organisation. In all probability these kinds of people's choices particularly in large numbers, get exercised only with social connivance. As could be seen from the later instances of conversions (Minakshipuram in Tamilnadu and several conversions of Dalits to Buddhism), the religious conversions never took place in any significant scale without there being a social movement to support it. In this sense, one could surmise the existence of some movement of untouchables that spearheaded the conversion to Islam.

The above overview highlights the following:

- Indian society as a whole never accepted hierarchy as a basic value system.
- The anti-caste movements essentially were against the creed of Brahminism that had ordained the iniquitous social structure.
- They were always articulated in terms of constituting an anti-theses to oppressive aspects of the 'Hindu' religion.
- They invariably materialised in the form of denouncements of these aspects and in corollary, adoption of a different faith, which in their perception was better.
- These movements invariably needed certain extraneous enablers especially the political congeniality.

BIRTH OF AN AUTONOMOUS DALIT MOVEMENT

Unlike the Moslem invaders, who had ruled India on the strength of their developed feudalism, far superior to the priest-ridden Indian system, the British conquest of the country was based on their superior technique of production and social form (the bourgeois), that was much more efficient than the technique of feudalism. The British colonisation with its bourgeois liberal ethos coupled with the imperatives of their ruling strategy, created space for working up subaltern identities, mainly in terms of caste and religion.

The institutional changes (judiciary, civil administration, commodity markets), cultural changes (modernity, western mode of living, English education, exposure to western treasure of knowledge and scholarship), economic changes (zamindari and ryotwari systems in place of jajmani-balutedari), and emergent social changes that came in during the colonial rule gave impetus to the aspirations of the lower castes. The development opportunities that these changes created came into conflict with traditional social relations, which still shackled them through caste bondage.

There appears to be some kind of capability threshold that takes into account a balance of all resources with a social group, below which social movements are not possible. The colonial rule lent various opportunities to the disadvantaged sections and pushed them up past this threshold. It was thus natural that the first of the social resistance movements was by the Shudra castes. Because, as the labouring caste, they constituted an immediate interface with the parasitic upper castes, and in terms of resources they got over the threshold sooner than, say, the more oppressed untouchables. These movements broadly exposed the fraud perpetrated by Brahmins in the name of religion. They denounced their exploitation and praised British rule as an enemy of the enemy. In this formulation Dalits were vaguely bracketed as the co-oppressed ally. But the anti-Brahmin consciousness of these movements could not hold out in the face of the contradictions these castes had with the untouchable castes. Although, the Dalit movement was significantly influenced by the non-Brahmin movement of backward castes, it soon drifted away from the latter. With the advent of Ambedkar, it soon secured national prominence.

Around this time, there was a strong revolutionary movement all across the globe that drew its inspiration from the Bolshevik revolution in Russia in 1917. It claimed its ideological strength from the theories of historical materialism, dialectical materialism and scientific socialism propounded by Karl Marx. The Russian revolution had ignited hope of emancipation in oppressed humanity. In India too, it soon took roots and came to be reckoned as a political force, especially in the urban centres where it had a particular appeal among the workers of various factories. The leadership of this communist movement however came from the middle class educated youth who for historical reasons had to come from the upper castes, the majority being the Brahmin itself. Their comprehension of the philosophy of communism was acutely constrained on one hand by the lack of systematic political education compounded by the non-availability of much of the original literature, and on the other by their class and caste consciousness. It rested on the dictums like class struggle, dictatorship of proletariat and notions of the base and superstructure without the underlying dialectics that lent it its specific meanings. This movement was essentially pitted against British imperialism that brought them nearer some sections of the nationalists and tended to ignore the caste as a superstructural identity. The emergence of autonomous Dalit movement could not therefore be taken kindly by the communist movement, as it saw the Dalit movement to be dividing the workers, diffusing the focus of the anti-imperialist struggle and being non-scientific. On its part, the Dalit movement not only did not find any answer to their specific caste exploitation but on the contrary total apathy about it in the communist movement. In their strategic formulation, the open anti-State stance of the communists moreover did not found favour with the Dalits.

As Gail Omvedt perceptibly observes, the autonomous Dalit movement had to engage with three forces in colonial society:

- It developed in opposition to the socially and culturally pervasive and historically deep-rooted hegemony of Brahminical Hinduism.
- It had to contend with the hegemony of the nationalist movement, which under the leadership of the Congress, strove to take over the agendas of several subaltern movements while restraining their democratic and egalitarian potential.
- It had to face a difficult relationship with the communist movement which otherwise should have been its natural ally.

OPPOSITION TO BRAHMINICAL HEGEMONY

While dealing with Brahminical hegemony, the autonomous Dalit movement naturally perceived an ally in the backward castes. The anti-Brahmin movement launched by the creative and visionary genius of Mahatma Phule in Maharashtra in many ways inspired the Dalit movement (e.g., early proponents of the Dalit movement like Shivram Janaba Kamble were followers of Phule). In spite of the difference in time period marking out different transitory phases in the history of the country; differences in dispositions, equipment and social backgrounds between Phule and Ambedkar, one finds essential similarities in their characterisation of the social structure and the movements they launched and led. Both Phule and

Ambedkar regarded British rule positively for introducing modernity into the moribund Hindu society but simultaneously both showed its limitations; both repudiated the claims of nationalists that India was a nation; both had no faith in the Indian National Congress; both came to characterise and oppose it similarly; both declared their vehement opposition to Brahminism but still did not hate Brahmins; both were rationalist; both had hated the parasitic class of priests, landlords, moneylenders and capitalists and sought to organise their victims; both emphasised the importance of education in the scheme of liberation of Dalits and backward castes; and so on and so forth. The pious formulation of Phule and to a certain degree of Ambedkar hoped to bring together all the Untouchables and the Shudra castes in opposition to Brahminism. Howsoever underestimated or grossly overlooked the contradictions between the Shudra backward castes and the non-caste Dalits may be in the village setting where precisely the caste problem is to be confronted, the Shudra castes came to share the mantle of Brahminism in relation to Dalits. This is basically strengthened by the economic contradictions between these farmer castes and the Dalits who are the farm labourers dependent on them. This legacy of Manu could neither be overcome by the powerful non-Brahmin movement of Mahatma Phule, who had certainly shown how to bring them together during his life time; nor by the Dalit movement despite its significant investment for bringing about a broad unity of all the labouring people during Ambedkar's time. Immediately after the death of Mahatma Phule his Satyashodhak Movement lost its anti-caste zeal. Even the attempts for reviving and revitalising it under the patronage of Shahu Maharaj of Kolhapur could not succeed and by 1920 it completely lost its anti-Brahminism character and degenerated (barring a few who spearheaded leftist struggles) into a political addendum of ruling class.

The majority from the Shudra castes, as marginal or small farmers or artisans labouring in the jajmani-balutedari (client-patron) system, is variously exploited and is poor. A minority of them, as big farmers and middle farmers, were well off. Some of them were vested with the traditional powers of village administrators. These people of the farmer castes came to don the role of exploiter in the village setting. During the post-independence period the imperatives of electoral politics provided the motive force for the consolidation of the middle castes. These castes received disproportionate benefits from the policies and programmes implemented during this period. The most significant have been the land reforms that sought to restore the lands to tenants and later the green revolution that channelled significant investments into agriculture and raised its productivity. The former could not reach real tenants who in most cases were Dalits because the government machinery would not know that there operated a layered tenancy in villages as a Dalit tenant could not be dealt with by the high caste landlord directly. So, by default, it recognised the intermediaries as the legal tenants who invariably belonged to these farmer castes. Many of the benami transfers also went to them, as they were the confidants of the former landlords. The green revolution, as numerous studies concluded, clearly benefited the bigger farmers who again belonged to these castes. The empowerment of a section from these Shudra castes impelled them to create a formidable constituency for themselves in nexus with the capitalist class and to wield significant political power. The contradiction between them and the Brahmins that impelled the non-Brahmin movements during the colonial times were overcome in this process, which enabled them to assume the hegemonic role in the rural setting.

All the castes under this generic Shudra caste-group were not well off economically and equal socially. Many of them, the artisan and service castes, were as poor as Dalits and lay at various rungs in the caste hierarchy. However, they could be bracketed together socially in caste terms and economically as farmers as most of them had land. The caste divisions between them were really imperceptible in hierarchical terms. In relations to Dalits however they were placed socially and culturally clearly apart as the caste Hindus. Their superiority perception in relation to the increasingly assertive Dalits was deliberately worked up by the powerful elements in villages, which thwarted any possibility of their making common cause with Dalits. All these Shudra castes came to pose as a single block in opposition to Dalits for mainly two reasons. One, their superiority in the caste hierarchy to Dalits lent them power over them to extract more and more economic surplus and two, the assertiveness of the majority Dalit caste induced by their political consciousness (through the Dalit movement) and their economic betterment (through reservation policy) made them vulnerable and defensive. These dynamics achieved two things for the rural rich. One, it obfuscated their exploitative relations with their own caste fellows and two, it provided them the requisite mass base to claim political power.

While the caste identity consolidated the middle castes into a powerful block, the same identity was used to catalyse disablement of Dalits by dividing them into various caste groups. Historically, all the Dalit castes were not economically equal. Most of them had a specific caste calling and so had a reason to perceive a stake in the system. But, there was a caste engaged to do low skilled miscellaneous village jobs, by virtue of which it came to be relatively more populous and remained, economically, most vulnerable. Paradoxically, they constituted the interface between the village and town, which enabled them to acquire a self-identity as humans particularly during the alien rule. With nothing to lose, they therefore were the first to rebel against the caste system. There is enough evidence that the other Dalit castes also initially made common cause with this anti-caste movement. But, with the advent of parliamentary electoral politics the ruling class could easily engineer their detachment from the Dalit mainstream movement. Later, the contradiction between the middle caste hegemony and the Dalit struggle accentuated this division and put a cap on the prospects of Dalit unity.

This debacle embodied a larger debate relating to class vs. caste and the concomitant question of how to wage class struggle and also how to annihilate castes. Insofar as the working class in India collectively come from the Dalit and Shudra castes, it is important that they come together to become a class. In the same manner, the question of annihilation of castes is intimately linked to the coming together of the Dalits and lower-rung Shudra castes against the upper caste hegemony in every sphere of power. The class notion subsumes economic exploitation, which cannot be isolated from the notion of social hierarchy in the semi-feudal setting of Indian villages, and is thus essentially intertwined with the notion of caste. But the protagonists of class comprehended it in a restrictive manner and hence failed to tackle caste, which was the tangible and lived reality of the Indian proletariat. They were inevitably led to ignore it till they were compelled to acknowledge its existence by continual blows from concrete reality. It is to be said to the credit of Phule and Ambedkar that they unmistakably understood the crux of the problem, when they took up caste as a comprehensive exploitation-category for their movements and put forth a native agenda for democratisation of Indian society.

Unfortunately, this essentially anti-class, anti-caste agenda got juxtaposed against the class agenda of the communists and unleashed a sterile debate, which refuses to die even today. Caste or class, both these categories, to be workable, need to expand their boundaries to represent the current mode of exploitation in the country. This process would essentially bring out a large interface between them. This ought to happen however through the medium of concrete struggle based on caste or class-consciousness and not through any wishful amalgamation of caste and class conceived in the brains of some intellectual.

Insofar as the Shudra castes largely represent the class of have-nots together with the Dalit castes, and simultaneously functions as the nearest representative of Brahminism and also as the exploiting class, the need to apply a class filter to it cannot be overemphasised. The same principle is applicable to Dalits insofar as there is an evidence of class formation among them. It therefore needs to be understood that mere caste identity is not only going to be inadequate but is also going to prove dysfunctional. The usage of the caste idiom may bring in temporary electoral gains to the parliamentary players but it can never bring the real social change desired by the revolutionists. The prerequisite for this to happen is both, a strong Dalit movement which while fighting the remnant Brahminism is capable of orienting itself as a class assimilating the toiling masses from all the other castes, and a strong communist movement which incorporates into its class struggle the agenda of the struggles against social and cultural discrimination. The struggle shall have to be waged along both the axes of exploitation simultaneously, viz., caste and class.

The Dalits as the most proletarianised people will have to be the vanguard of both these struggles.

The opposition to Brahminical Hinduism led naturally to its rejection by Dalits but not of the religion itself. On the contrary, it gave rise to the Dalit-obsession of religion that curiously refuses to wane even when the organised religions ceased to ordain social affairs as they did many years before. As we know religion is a product of particular socio-economic phase in history that served the purpose to resolve certain crises on the basis of accumulated knowledge available then. The religious resolution invariably took the form of suppression of man's desire to seek a good life by promising him a better after-life (Neusch, 1982). Marx dismissed religion outright as a vestige of superstition and a tool of social control used to enslave the masses. For Marx, religion existed not to console, but to control; it was "the opium of the people,"-a drug that dulled the will to throw off the chains of oppression. When Dalits rejected Hinduism, it might have been necessary to fill the void. But it was not necessary to fill it with some alternate organised religion. Buddhism, howsoever radical in its pristine form, came to be an organised religion with its package of aberrations. In its pure form, it may not even qualify to be a religion but in its popular form, with its own mythology, rituals, and mumbo jumbo, it was no different from any other. The consequence of this change has been in terms disorienting the Dalit masses from the material world where their real problems are rooted.

ISSUES WITH THE HEGEMONY OF NATIONALIST MOVEMENT

The second factor would seem out-of-date as it relates with a specific moment in the past. However, there are a few vital questions that crop up in its conjunction that are still consequential to the discourse of revolutionary change in India and that should impel us to its discussion.

Nation

The first is about what constitutes a nation. The Dalit movement dismissed the premise of the mainstream nationalist movement that India was a nation. Ambedkar, for instance, repudiated the notion of a nation in a caste society and challenged it saying that each caste was a nation. Phule, who was Ambedkar's preceptor, had said that "unless all the people in the Balisthan (his term for India), including the Shudras, Ati-Shudras, Bhill, Koli etc. become educated and are able to think over and unite, they cannot constitute a nation." At some other place, Ambedkar observed, "I am of the opinion that in believing that we are a nation, we are cherishing a great delusion". He questioned," How can people divided into several thousands of castes be a nation?" and said that "these castes were anti-national." At another occasion he had said that, "unless you change your social order you can achieve little by way of progress. You cannot mobilise the community either for defence or for offence. You cannot build up a nation; you cannot build up a morality. Anything that you will build on the foundations of caste will crack and will never be a whole"(Khairmode, 1958). Despite these forewarnings and subsequent nationality movements bloodying the bosom of the country, the ruling classes are yet not awake to India's multi-national character. The vested interests still keep on exhorting the gullible masses to sacrifice for the non-existent nation or dismiss genuine peoples' movements calling them anti-national. Paradoxically, as they do it the nationality problem in India waxes in complexity with the accentuation of inequalities engendered by the capitalist development.

Nation, inasmuch as it is a phenomenon associated with the capitalist development, the pre-capitalist caste has to be antithetical to the concept of nation. Dalit movement by squarely posing this problem has indeed contributed to India's nation building efforts. The Indian National Congress, which spearheaded the national struggle for independence, represented the emerging Indian bourgeoisie's drive for overall political and economic control, whereas the Dalit movement under Ambedkar sought to strengthen the most disadvantaged people in the Indian society and set in the process of internal consolidation of the Indian nation.

With Ambedkar's taking upon a role of a constitution maker and a position in the Nehru cabinet, many of these lofty theoretical standpoints that could provide a framework for the Dalit movement got shifted to background. Although his commitment to his people - the basic propeller for these moves remained undiminished, its expression particularly with reference to the means of its fulfilment suffered from compromise. Notwithstanding his lamentations and exhortations against the post-independence political system, the emergent framework of the Dalit movement could not escape distortion in the powerful vortex of ruling class parliamentary politics. The particularity of the tactics of law-abiding posture of its early phase got universalised into the new constitutionalism that set the parameters of the Dalit movement. Ambedkar's programme for annihilation of caste system thus was completely way laid by the ruling class.

In the context of nation, the question here is what should be the relationship between the Dalit and nationality movements. The nationality struggles invariably land up using certain primordial identities in their anxiety to secure themselves uniqueness but are essentially underscored by the exploitations experienced by a set of people. As Ambedkar argued, Dalit struggle has the characteristics of a nationality struggle. It thus gets linked to the struggles of all the oppressed nationalities the world over. However, the concept of nationality is prone to be abused by a section of ruling classes to settle scores against another and hence warrants a critical examination of the underlying issues and the forces driving it. The alliance of Dalit movement with the genuine struggles of other oppressed nationalities will have a congenial acculturation impact and strengthen the Dalit movement.

Imperialism

The second question is about the struggle against the British imperialism. It is a common feature of anti-caste movements that they did not support the freedom movements and to some extent saw the colonial rule in congenial terms vis-à-vis their objectives of eliminating caste disability and gaining a due share of power. It is a fact that the Dalits and the downtrodden castes had certainly favoured the alien rule to the oppressive Brahmin rule even before they expected anything positive from the former. In most of the decisive battles that established British colonialism in the country, Dalit soldiers had played a heroic role. It is said that while the Brahmins mourned the fall of Peshawa in Koregaon battle, all others celebrated the event as their liberation by distributing sweets all over Pune. It was the spontaneous revelry of the oppressed over the downfall of the oppressor. The British did many positive things: foremost, they admitted Dalits into their army, they made them compulsorily educated, they introduced a modern legal system, which at least in principle disowned caste as the basis for law; they opened up new employment opportunities for the 'Untochables' in the European families, in mills and factories, in the railway and in shipping; and later they introduced political reservation for them. All this opened a new chapter in the lives of the 'Untouchables' (Ellinwood 1978; Galanter 1972; Kananaikil 1981). Phule summarised these sentiments when he said, "We would be grateful to the Britishers because they did not honour the laws of Manu" (Keer, 1965)

It was not for any love for Dalits that the colonial rulers did favourable things to them. Most of it sprang from their strategic imperative and somewhat from a sense of superiority as victors. They did not hesitate reverting them when these reforms proved an impediment in their colonial interests. As for the anti-caste movements, it would be wrong to say that ey were for the continuance of colonial rule. Even Phule who otherwise showered so much praise over the British rulers for having introduced elements of modernity and rule of justice in utter disregard to the demonic caste code of Manu, did not hesitate to highlight the fact that not enough was being done for the have-nots under the colonial rule. They were aware of the limitation of the alien rule. Ambedkar had squarely exposed the exploitative character of the colonial rule not only in his scholarly treatises but also in public. For instance, once he said to Dalits, "..you cannot sit singing the praises of the British bureaucracy for simply giving us improved roads, improved canals, railways, stable administration and new ideas of geography or for stopping internal wars..... I would be the first to agree that the praise given to the British would vanish once we turned our attention to the forcible extraction of profit by big capitalists and landlords from the poor working people of this country..."(Ambedkar 1930). At other time he perceptively said, "we must have a Government in which men in power, knowing where obedience will end and resistance will begin, will not be afraid to amend the social and economic code of life which the dictates of justice and expediency so urgently calls for. This role, the British Government will never be able to play". (Kshirsagar, 1992).

Thus, although the anti-caste movement in general and Dalit movement in particular acknowledged the positive aspects of colonial rule and tactically sought to make use of their contradiction with the bourgeoisie nationalists to exert pressure on the latter to agree for desired reforms and devolution of power to the lower castes, it never was so overwhelmed as not to see its long term interests lying in the demise of alien rule.

Today the menace of imperialism has engulfed the entire world through its credo of globalisation, which is being promoted through its agencies like the IMF and the World Bank. The underlying economic philosophy of these programmes is to rely more on market forces, dismantle controls, reduce the role of State, liberalise prices, and replace the public with private sector. It is going to mean privatisation of government-owned entities, doing away with superfluous labour force, structural changes in the economy aimed at export-led growth, free entry of foreign capital and technology without any let, hindrance or conditions, free entry and exit of foreign firms including financial and services industries, free cross border movement of capital and other funds, legislative safeguards for protection of intellectual property rights, creation of legal climate for enforcement of legal contracts, private property rights; and free entry and exit of business, industrial and financial firms and curbing of peoples' rights to organise and resist. The experience with this package all over the globe is uniformly anti-people and directly proportional to the degree of their marginalisation. Dalits being the most marginalised people in India, their movement ought to have been concerned with these policies. While accepting the proven fact that globalisation hits poor people the hardest, some intellectuals expect that it might do good in terms of removal of social disability of Dalits. The argument though not entirely misfounded, betrays inadequate learning from the experience with the capitalist operations of over a century in this country. As capitalism has made skilful use of caste, globalisation, which is essentially capitalism in the era of information and communication technology, is not going to impact it positively. Rather, in the wake of the increasing hardship of the general mass of people through declining jobs, rising inflation, teasing consumerism, reducing public services and cruel competition, caste, as a divisive instrument, will come in handy for the ruling classes to contain the people's ire. Of particular relevance to Dalits are certain implications of these policies of the free market.

One, the competitive advantage based investment would drive the corporatisation of agriculture and agri-business. The resultant consolidation of farms by the big agro-MNCs to have economies of scale is going to spell doom for the hopes of land reform. In so far the caste question is linked to this material key; it impels one to rethink the consequences. Two, the privatisation of the public sector and reduction of government jobs through the minimalist State that globalisation envisages, will directly hit the job-prospects of Dalits. Even the premature free market ethos unleashed by these policies and so enthusiastically upheld by the high caste bureaucracy, has already impacted Dalit interests adversely. It has many negative implications in terms of exploitation of Dalit women, Dalit culture and most importantly their hopes to struggle out their own emancipation. Dalit movement will have to understand the yawning contradiction between them and the imperialist agenda and devise strategies to counter it in their movement.

State

The third question that could be discerned from this moment is about thc attitude of the Dalit movement towards the State. The Dalit movement reflects distinctly an attitude of one who looks at the State as an impartial, sans caste and class arbiter in the quarrel of classes and castes. Some times, the State is seen as the one genuinely interested in the welfare of downtrodden masses; a benevolent entity. This pro-State attitude could be understood when we see that the very birth of the Dalit movement was attributable to the factors provided by the State. Unless the colonial State had not brought in the western legal framework that treated all Indians equally and had offered certain opportunities of employment and education given to Dalits, the Dalit movement could not have been possible. The Colonial State comes out to be the basic enabler and catalyst of the Dalit movement. One of the first struggles that were launched at Mahad for reclaiming Dalit rights to access the public tank was basically to restore the writ of the State. Even later struggles cared not to violate the legal framework and thus tacitly expected the support of the State.

While contending with the hegemony of the nationalist movement under the nationalist bourgeoisie and while opposing the hegemony of Brahminism, the Dalit movement had essentially to take stock of its resources and opportunities held out by circumstances. In the Mahad Satyagraha, Ambedkar categorically explains his strategic calculation that he could not fight the formidable enemy with his meagre resources on several fronts. He exhorted his people not to violate the law and incur the wrath of the State. As a matter of fact it was the State that had provided them the space to basically raise the issue of violation of their human rights. Their battles were essentially formulated on the strength of the State provision, the strategy being to use the existing law to assert the Dalit rights and expand the former to support the new ones.

Later, with the political reforms the Dalit movement forsook mass struggles and adopted the electoral path to secure political power. Political power was rightly seen as the key to all the problems. However, the concept of political power was acutely constrained by the framework laid down by the State. It was a well thought out strategy, to use the alien State as the bulwark to secure gains for Dalits from the competing camps. But the fact remains that the liberal democratic thought driving the contemporary Dalit movement did neither have any significant variant of this strategy nor any alternate concept of political power in its repertoire. As a result, the Dalit movement, which was conscious of its compulsions during the early days, got stuck in the traps laid out by the ruling classes. It forgot the transition from the colonial rule to the rule of native bourgeois landlord combine in 1947. In its fight for equality, reliance on colonial State as an arbiter could be a strategic decision, but when this State itself represents the adversary power, the continuance of the same behaviour is not only indefensible but also grossly self-defeating.

The Dalit movement linked the concept of State power with its claim of equality. The gamut of reservations basically sprang from this. If Dalits are represented in various parts of State machinery in the ratio of their population then it is assumed that due share of power is enjoyed by Dalits. The flaw in this schema is on account of the State character. The State irrespective of whether it is a welfare State or any other kind of State, admittedly is a coercive organ of the ruling class against the ruled ones. If therefore the ruled classes opted to be the part of such an organ voluntarily, it has to be beneficial to the latter. Generally, when it is difficult to win over an adversarial class in direct confrontation, the ruling class always adopts the strategy of co-opting. It very well knows that the co-opted minority would be submerged by its majority. In simple language, it is a pure bribe to buy-in an opponent. The Dalit strategy of becoming a part of this exploitative mechanism out of their volition in ultimate analysis thus serves the ruling class interest.

There is no denying the fact that following the strategy of sharing State power in the prevailing circumstances certainly brought significant gains to Dalits. Through the mechanism of reservations in education, employment and politics, many Dalits are catapulted to positions which otherwise would have been unthinkable to them. But the buy-ins are always associated with gains.

The truth cannot be denied that this process, instead of strengthening Dalits, has emasculated them politically and caused the creation of a separate class of beneficiaries from amongst them, which if at all, had a very tenuous linkage with the Dalit masses. This class has completely distorted the ideology of Dalit liberation. Dalits as the native proletarian class cannot be liberated by sops granted in a prison. Their liberation is only conceivable in dynamiting this prison and constructing a new shelter in its place as per their own desire.

The profile of a Dalit notwithstanding the changes that has befallen to some due to the post-independence buy-ins is that of an illiterate, half-fed landless labourer utterly dependent upon his high caste patron who is constantly preyed upon by all kinds of vultures. He is the victim of a complex system evolved over several millennia. The Dalit movement may well have taken a tactical approach to make use of the State but they all should be dovetailed to serve its long-term strategy to destroy it and install a Dalit-worker State in its place.

RELATION WITH THE COMMUNIST MOVEMENT

The third factor is about its unsatisfactory relation with the communist movement. This factor will stand as the single most unfortunate paradox of contemporary Indian history. It stemmed from, not so much the ideological differences, which certainly existed in the form of certain unclear theoretical constructs in the mind of Ambedkar - the one who shaped the Dalit movement - as from the attitudes of the communist leaders towards the Dalit movement. These leaders working in Bombay in the Trade Unions dogmatically regarded the caste question as an unimportant superstructural issue, which would automatically disappear when the revolution takes place. The Dalit movement put the question on its head and asked that with the castes intact how would the revolution itself take place. The trade unions (Tus) under these communist leaders were tight-lipped on the discrimination faced by Dalits in not getting jobs in better remunerative departments like weaving in textile mills. The economic condition of Dalits was much worse than their savarna counterparts. Ambedkar observed that the communists used these TUs for their political gains rather than for the welfare of the working class. Whenever they took precipitate action to strike work, the workers tended to suffer differentially, owing to their caste-wise placements.

Ambedkar's objection to this 'irresponsible' TU behaviour was on two counts: (i) they were driven by raw 'economism' to the detriment of prospects of enhancing the political consciousness of the working class, (ii) they were using the working class as cannon fodder in the promotion of their political interests. Ambedkar's writing on communism or Marxism is heavily imbued with his annoyance with the Bombay-Communists. This legacy to identify Marxism with its self-appointed practitioners still appears to be followed by Dalits. They cite examples of the parliamentary communist parties to show the lacuna or inapplicability of Marxism. It is necessary for them to understand that Marxism intrinsically solicits criticism but it presupposes its careful study.

Much of the misunderstanding got reinforced during the course of the petit bourgeoisisation of the Dalit movement. The vested interests used the stray quotations of Ambedkar to denigrate communism. It was a deliberate distortion. For, although Ambedkar could not discuss the philosophy of communism in the manner it deserved, he was never antagonistically disposed towards it. Rather, he acknowledged the beauty of communist philosophy and said that it was closer to his own. Preoccupied with the mission of liberating the Dalits, he insisted, quite like Marx, that the test of the philosophy was in practice, and opined that if communists worked from that perspective, to win success in India would be far easier than in Russia (Janata, 15 January, 1938). He always regarded it (communism) as the ultimate benchmark to assess his highest ideal - Buddhism. With bitter experience with communist dogma and vulgarity of his times, he did sound polemically against Communism and appeared at times even professing its doom but it all underscored his wrath against the dogma that occupied the communist practice. After the collapse of communism in erstwhile Soviet Union and Eastern European countries, the anti-communism argument is gleefully put by certain people to claim Ambedkar right. Indeed, he was right but the kind of attitude embedded in this glee is totally unfortunate. It not only reflects their ignorance of both communism and Ambedkar but also and more importantly, alienates Dalits from the ideology that is specifically dedicated to have-nots of the world. Dalit movement will have to revise its position vis-à-vis its most potential ally.

The Dalit movement has to revisit its stand on the issues of State, Religion, other modes of exploitation and culture. It needs to restate its objective in clearer terms, whether it aims at establishing a society based on liberty, equality, and fraternity or at just reversing the sides in the equation of exploitation. It will have to rethink about its friends and foes in this context. The era of globalisation increasingly demands clearer stands by various classes of people. It already appears sans its vitality and badly stagnated in the past. Its consequent degeneration has already hit the Dalit masses. It needs serious self-criticism.

While there is a need for ruthless self-criticism in the Dalit movement along the above lines it should not mean denying its positive aspects. There are many of them: it implanted positive values of liberty, equality and fraternity; it promoted political consciousness to struggle against exploitation and injustice; it declared its allegiance to scientific rationalism and opposition to humbug of any kind. In terms of its gains, it has created significant resource base for itself in terms of education, organisational experience, and experience of working with the apparatus of its adversary. It is no mean an achievement to have secured this wherewithal in a short time. What is saddening is that it appears to be rapidly losing its grip over these gains and is straying into the channels created by the enemy. It could not consolidate its gains and hold together its constituents to work in a coordinated fashion for its long-term goal. This is possible only if it liberates itself from the grip of petty bourgeois hegemony and orients itself to serve the Dalit masses. The rhetorical aspects of such statements can be easily overcome by establishing certain ground rules, such as fixing priorities as per their salience to the majority Dalit masses; creating the structural space for their participation in decision making; promoting revolutionary culture among them, establishing values of struggle against any act of injustice, and anchoring the vision at achieving liberation of mankind to counter intrusion of any parochial tendencies. It certainly means a complete overhaul of itself. The consciousness and attitude of Dalit movements appears to have been frozen at its birth. It needs to recognise that the post-independence reality presents a far intricate complexity than in the colonial times.

GANDHIAN THOUGHT VIS-À-VIS INDIGENOUS IDEOLOGY

As long as there is violence which threatens the very future of the human race, the relevance of Gandhi would continue. He would remain relevant till this danger of total annihilation of the human race is removed. —J.P. Narayan

Two considerations which require attention at the outset of this paper in the light of the above title are: one, Gandhi did not have direct contact with the indigenous people, nor is there any specific treatment of their problems in his writings; and, two, there is seemingly a dialectical relation between the Gandhian thought and indigenous ideology.

GANDHI AND THE TRIBES

Gandhiji came face to face with the natives of South Africa belonging to various tribes, namely, the Zulus, the Bachuanas, the Basutos and the Swazis, etc. He was shocked to see the plight of about five million natives politically controlled by a meagre 2.5 million Europeans. Gandhi was a witness to the discrimination of the blacks first by the Dutch when they started their colony in South Africa in the middle of the 17th century, and later by the British who overpowered the former in the first half of the 19th century. The basis of the discrimination against the local Blacks was 'color'. Their dignity as human beings took a back seat as Blacks were looked upon as pre-scientific, pre-logical, incapable of any rational thinking. The attitude of the white was that of superiority and ethnocentrism; the rights and privileges of the blacks were insignificant for the white minority. This was apparently the first encounter of Gandhi with an indigenous population who had lost their right of self-assertion. In the context of India we have more than enough sources to show Gandhi's involvement with the low caste whom he called *harijans,* meaning 'children of God', but we hear little about Gandhi's involvement with the aboriginal, the native, the tribal who are the indigenous people of India, though the Indian Government vehemently denies the existence of any 'indigenous' people in the country.

Once, when Gandhi was asked why he paid little attention to the tribals, he said, "I have entrusted that part of our work to A.V. Thakkar". Thakkar was a social worker, who had headed the fact-finding mission to report on the allegation of police brutality in Gujarat. He was sympathetic to Congress without actually being part of it; he was also a friend of the poor, the untouchable and the aborigine. However, the disinterested response of Gandhi regarding tribals is mysterious.

Gandhi did have an impact on the Tana Bhagat movement in Chotanagpur in the sense that the puritanical ideas of Gandhi penetrated the movement. The Oraon Tana Bhagats, who were fighting the British for their socio-economic cause, initiated another element of 'purification' in their sect dividing Oraon tribe itself on the basis of purity-pollution. Thus some would hold Gandhi to some degree responsible for the division and for the Hinduisation of the tribals?

The moral values Gandhi stood for were different from those of the tribals. Gandhi was stern in his dealings with those with moral lapses, and his normal remedy was immediate expulsion from his *ashram*, always with a possibility of a return after real penitence. That may have been one of the reasons why Verrier Elwin was disillusioned with Gandhi.

To say that Gandhi was sympathetic to the tribals would be an exaggeration. In fact, Elwin, though a foreigner, was a real friend of the tribals. No doubt, he has been accused of exploiting tribal women and marrying them for his professional interests as an anthropologist. Nevertheless, if anyone had real love for the tribals of India, it was Elwin and not Gandhi. According to Guha, to Elwin's dismay, the Congress and politicians paid little attention to the needs of the original inhabitants of their country.

It is said that it was Gandhi who gave the term *'adivasi'* to the indigenous people. As far as the Oraons of Bihar are concerned, Gandhi played a significant role either for the better or for the worse. Tribals, especially, the Oraons, Mundas and Kharias of Chotanagpur had united against the atrocities by the British and their unjust laws that were alienating them from their land, society and culture. Rallies organized in Ranchi to oppose the British Government were highly successful. It is alleged that the Congress, under the leadership of the then President of the Congress Party, Dr. Rajendra Prasad, caused division among the non-Christian tribals and the converts by alluring the non-Christians to merge with the Party.

Guha makes some interesting observations about the political developments affecting the tribals in pre-independent India. Congress came to power in the elections of 1937. In the same year the 'Raj Gond' movement began. In August 1937, Elwin visited Gandhi at his new *ashram* at Wardha to acquaint him with the aboriginals' plight. But the latter "did not appear to think that the original inhabitants of India deserved any special consideration." Hence, Elwin thought that the Congress wished only to use tribals as cannon-fodder in their political campaigns and to convert them all to vegetarianism, abstinence and settled cultivation B the plough being the symbol of the Congress-Hindu culture sweeping the tribal areas.

In spite of the fact that Gandhi was relatively passive towards the tribal cause, if one looks into the Gandhian philosophy and indigenous ideology, one cannot but be amazed by the extent to which they shared values, ethos and the spirit.

The effort here is to point out how well intertwined they are. The question of the relevance of Gandhi in the present scenario, let alone the next millennium, has indeed been problematic. Given the rampant corruption, indiscriminate violence and loss of the sense of respect and reverence for human life and dignity, some see the Gandhian model of humanism to be outdated. There was a time during the British rule in India when the Gandhian model of truth and non-violence offered a solution to the existent problems of the day, but times are much different now. At the beginning of the 21st century, there is everywhere an atmosphere of suspicion, insecurity and apprehension. It is appropriate to ask whether Gandhian thought has any significant contribution to make in bringing harmony, peace and prosperity to the third millennium.

What is their relation to the values upheld and cherished by the indigenous community, not only in India but also in many other countries the world over? The present paper attempts to explore objectively the dialectics between Gandhian thought and indigenous ideology for a meaningful inculcation of an integral and holistic humanism in the next millennium.

GANDHIAN AND TRIBAL THOUGHT

Faith: the Basis for Action

Kumar and Kumar treat the Gandhian faith in its full contours, which resonates well with the belief system of the tribes, especially in the tribal belt of Bihar. Gandhi, like the tribals, is a theist. He firmly believes in one God and does not believe in a pantheon of deities. Tribes of Bihar also are basically monotheists, but they believe also in the existence of spirits - some benevolent by nature, others malevolent — who have to be appeased from time to time. Gandhi does not accept God's existence on any scriptural or revelatory authority. For Gandhi, God's existence is a matter of personal faith. According to the tribal world view, the Supreme Being exists very concretely in their midst. It is He who created them and taught them the art of cultivation for self-sustenance. The experience of the Supreme Being is in their Genesis myth which is narrated at every important social activity of the tribe.

In the Gandhian cosmology, there is an orderly world, but the Divine is of a higher order to which the natural order is subordinate. Tribals believe in the hierarchy of beings: there are the natural and the supernatural realms. Whereas in the natural world there is an egalitarian society, the supernatural world is a hierarchy of beings. The Supreme Being is all goodness, the most beneficent one, who can never be wrong. The spirits, on the other hand, are subordinated to Him and depend on human beings for their sustenance.

In Gandhi's philosophy, the divine order is a moral order intrinsically and intuitively realized by every human being. This moral awareness is the basis of the human awareness of God's existence, whose power sustains the moral order. It is Gandhi's conviction that the practice of moral living is possible only for the individual in relation to other human beings. For Gandhi, such cooperation can be based only on genuine love. *Ahimsa* or non-violence is the basic law of love, which, according to Gandhi, should govern all human affairs and all interpersonal relations.

Tribes have a very similar ideology, which notion of the moral order among the tribes is also a foundation of their social order. Their belief system nurtures and nourishes their pattern of Behaviour. Religion thus becomes a way of life for them. Morality is part and parcel of their social framework. All the activities of a good tribesman are governed by his faith in one Supreme Being who is interested in the welfare of the whole of humankind. That is why *Singbonga*, the Great God of the Munda tribe, sent messengers to the Asur, the iron smelters, to stop working on their bellows night and day as it was causing pollution in the entire universe. But when they refused to pay heed to the messengers, as a last resort, He destroyed them, in order to maintain the world order (a popular 'myth of the origin of the evil spirits' in the Munda tribe).

Gandhi's Sarvodaya and the Tribes' Participatory Model for the Community Welfare

Sarvodaya means 'development of all'. Tribal society has evolved a socio-cultural mechanism to take care of the entire tribe. *Gola Dhan,* for instance, is a system of 'grain-bank', contributed by each family. In times of crises, people take loans from the 'grain-bank' and later return it at a low interest rate. Similarly, the tribal villages have a system of *madait* or *sangat* which literally mean 'cooperation'. In case a poor family needs the help of others, the whole village decides to work for it without any remuneration.

The recent trends of planned change have seen many developmental programs not only in India, but also in other developing countries. One of the reasons for the failure of various models of modernization is the insensitivity of the policy-makers the implementation of the policies in local cultures. It was Gandhi, the visionary, who first understood the setbacks of a model where power and power-relations were centralized. Gandhi was a charismatic leader who believed in change not only externally, but also internally. In fact he insisted on the inner change of heart in order to effect an exterior change. According to Midatala Rani, "Gandhi's idea of social change may be described as the ideological combination of two schools of thought, namely, `pacifism' and `social revolution.' Elements of these two traditions converge to produce `non-violent revolution.' Gandhi's concept of social revolution is non-violent his notion of change for the betterment of human life and society is free from violence of all kinds.

His concept of development is *Sarvodaya* through *Antyodaya*, implying the welfare of all through the weakest of the society. The principle of *Sarvodaya* is illustrated in Gandhi's translation of Ruskin's book *Unto This Last.* As a strategy of development *Sarvodaya* emphasizes harmony and ethical virtues of life rather than class struggle or domination. The concept of *Sarvodaya* upholds the moral and human values in economic and social reconstruction. Agriculture is considered by Gandhi to be the most appropriate basis for providing for one's livelihood. Principles of cooperation and collective endeavour are central to society. Education, moral uprightness, non-violence, simplicity, self-restrained life-style, etc., are the values which effect development of the *Antyodaya*, which is the development of the weakest in society.

The Gandhian model of development as a strategy emphasizes *'aparigraha'* or non-acquisition in excess of need.' "Trusteeship" implies that property belongs to all, and the holder manages it and takes care of it only as a socially responsible trustee. The idea of communal holding of property and its participatory management comes very close to the tribal notion of property. Gandhi also advocated anthropo-centered, appropriate technology for development. The dream of Gandhi is of a decentralization of power to the village or locality, based on surplus human labour, small machines and appropriate technology. The Gandhian model also emphasizes decentralization of socio-economic and political systems starting from the village to the highest level.

Gandhi emphasizes consensus to avoid unnecessary confrontation, division and tyranny in the village. The tribal notion of common holding of land and their attitude to the land expresses the solidarity for the tribe. Hence, the tribal worldview has a scope for the human-divine interaction in very concrete terms, even in the holding of property. The village *panchayat* (elders of the village) works on the basis of communal brotherhood, equality and consensus. There is no question of domination. When the *panchayat* is in progress, the *sarpanch* (the President of the elders) is only the president of the meeting; he does not take any decision on his own. He only articulates what the *panchayat* decides. There is consensus in all matters; there is no room for power struggle.

Structural Violence and the Gandhian Ahimsa. The second millennium is marked by violence, violence of all kinds, at all levels. In this century we have seen enough of the violence perpetrated by the state. We have also witnessed the terrorist violence, secessionist-insurgence, ethnic conflicts and caste wars. The phenomenon of violence has been universal: the stripping of women of lower castes or of minority communities; of the rape of nuns; cold-blooded murder of priests; caste conflicts of Jehanabad claiming hundreds of lives; and naxalite attacks on their adversaries. Outside India, we hear of the blood bath in the LTTE attacks, and wars in Croatia, Iraq, Kuwait, East Timor or Kargil that have claimed thousands of lives. Yet, the arms race among various countries goes on. Nuclear experiments continue with a renewed vigour under the pretext of national security. The exploitation, oppression and dehumanization of the tribals continues unabated.

Gandhi's ideology seems dead to some, Gandhi had never been so irrelevant now. Gandhi, they say, has no solution for the present crises. The corresponding traditional tribal values of tolerance, harmony, equality, sharing, humility, honesty, simplicity and symbiosis with nature are being looked upon as irrelevant today, not only by the non-tribals but also by the tribals. The real solution lies in 'tit for tat', in 'an eye for an eye'; 'Might is right' is the slogan of the day.

To serious people concerned about society, however, Gandhi is the prophet of the millennium because he can be relevant only in relation to violence, untruth, corruption and domination. His message makes one's life meaningful only in the struggle to rid the world of the process of dehumanization of the weaker sections of the society. Gandhi is concerned about the structural violence which is perpetuated from one generation to another. According to Dashrath Singh, Gandhi's perception of structural violence was in terms of economics, politics, social systems and the education-system. Evil, according to Gandhi, was a by-product of the social structure. Therefore Gandhi "hated capitalism, not the capitalist; racialism, not the white English men and women; untouchability, not the untouchables; modern civilization, not the Western people living in it. He saw very clearly the evil or violence present in the social structure itself." For Gandhi, economics that is destructive of the moral well-being of any individual or nation is immoral; a political structure bereft of religion and morality cannot bring about the dignity, inner freedom and justice of the citizens. He saw violence in the economic and political systems of India, as well as of the world. Positively, Gandhi was convinced that all societies were held together by non-violence just as is the earth by the law of gravitation. His ideal of social organization was the family: his paradigm of society was in the pattern of family *vasudhaiva kutumbakam* - the idea that the whole world is one family. In such a network of systems, every unit of society is "governed by the principle of interdependence, complementarity, cooperation, dedication towards duty, and enjoys the same respect, social status, and importance." Tribal values resonate with the Gandhian process for making this world a better place in which to live. The tribal's reverence for life can be seen in their myths, ritual practices and entire belief system.

Gandhian Promotion of Human Rights

A closer look at the Gandhi's life and works takes us into the realm of his philosophy of being. What left a lasting mark in Gandhi's life was the suffering of the natives, the workers, the traders, the clerks who were robbed of their human dignity in South Africa. Even before the promulgation of the Indian Constitution underlining the fundamental rights to her citizens, the right to dignity, equality and justice were promoted by Gandhi. In fact, it was precisely this cause that cost him his life.

In a tribal society, egalitarianism is one of the most cherished values. Everybody in the tribe has equal status irrespective of his or her political or economic power. In the Genesis myths of the Oraon, Kharia and Munda tribes, 'pride' and 'disobedience' are said to be the greatest offences. If one is proud, one is sure to disobey or violate the law of the tribe, they argue. Any offence against the tribe is considered an offence against the Supreme Being Himself, which results in *chchilan* or ostracism from the tribe. This excommunication is not for the sake of punishment, but for reconstruction, reparation or reconciliation. Thus the Gandhian model of reconciliation, forgiveness, hatred for the sin and not the sinner, etc., makes a lot of sense in a tribal context. Everybody in the tribe is equal and is treated equally.

The welfare of the tribe is of prime concern. It does not mean that an individual is made a scapegoat. The law of the tribe is to uphold the dignity of each individual, and to facilitate the peaceful and harmonious co-existence of the members of the tribe. The freedom of each individual includes responsibility toward one another. This value was much cherished by Gandhi himself. Thus, Dennis Dalton, on the basis of the Gandhian *sutras* or formulas, draws a link among Gandhi's key ideas of freedom (*Swaraj*), duty (*Dharma*), non-violent action (*Satyagraha*), and self-reliance (Swadeshi).

GANDHIAN THOUGHT AND THE INDIGENOUS QUEST FOR TRUTH

Though Gandhi has not been a crusader for the cause of the tribals, we find in his philosophy a space for an indigenous-Gandhian dialogue. His stress on non-violence and his application of the philosophy of God, world and man is operational in the daily life of the tribals. All life - plant, animal and human - are created by God according to the tribals, which is close to the Gandhian vision of a non-violent society. And in such a society, Gandhi envisages decentralization of power. Village life should arouse a sense of cooperation and fellowship. In such a society the dignity of labour is maintained and is not replaced by the use of machines.

The cherished dream of every tribal is for 'equality,' both economic and social. This finds a central place in the Gandhian philosophy. Humans are all equal and economic equality is the key to non-violence. Land is given to them by the Supreme Being. As humans are his stewards, the land can neither be sold nor misused. Gandhi's idea that man should free himself to serve society is nothing new to the tribals. Their life is an epitome of service and communitarianism. Here Gandhi's position that 'the caste system was to maintain the social order' can be seen as a justification. The equality of man and woman is yet another area of commonality between Gandhi and the indigenous peoples. Gandhi believed in an intimate relation between man and nature.

Times have changed down through the decades. Old values have acquired new meanings or new interpretations, often to suit the convenience of the interpreters. Writing off some great personality's credibility under the pretext of its irrelevance is nothing new. Complacency makes the matter worse. It is difficult, no doubt, to follow the *Mahatma*, 'the great soul,' but not impossible. Similarly, the tribal's own quest for truth is concretized in their signs and symbols, feasts and festivals, rites and rituals, and in the sacraments of their daily life. If they can live a harmonious and an integrated life, why not others?

Gandhi was not a Mahatma by birth, but earned this title because of his magnanimity. In his early days as a student in India and later in South Africa, he was vulnerable to temptations but he developed the moral strength to resist, proving the spirit to be stronger than the flesh. This points to the solution to the problems in the world. Similarly, in their struggle for survival tribals have evolved a way to brave the challenges of violence, untruth, evil and death with fortitude, hard work, truth, benevolence and respect for life.

The problem lies within oneself and not outside, though it has its impact outside. By finding solutions in the inner realms of being, Gandhi drives home the point that only inner freedom can lead one to the ultimate truth. The pre-requisite for inner freedom is openness and disposition of the heart which leads one away from arrogance, pride and disobedience - the vices abhorred in a tribal society. Jayaprakash Narayan, a great Indian leader, rightly said, "As long as there is violence which threatens the very future of the human race, the relevance of Gandhi would continue. He would remain relevant till this danger of total annihilation of the human race is removed." Henry Skolimowski notes that the problems during Gandhi's time, namely, casteism, corruption, violence, exploitation, misery, degradation and poverty, etc., have continued to this day. He calls for a second Gandhian revolution, "a revolution of consciousness, based on high moral values" and a clear realization of the true destiny of man. Such a revolution must be "based on simplifying our life-styles and reducing consumption as a precondition of peace with the poor, with nature, and with and within ourselves." It is no exaggeration to say that Gandhi is a bridge to the 21st century as a symbol of the person who is spiritual, *Satyagrahi* (non-violent) and *Swadeshi* (self-reliant).

SARVODAYA

Sarvodaya is a term meaning 'universal uplift' or 'progress of all'. The term was first coined by Mohandas Gandhi as the title of his 1908 translation of John Ruskin's tract on political economy, *Unto This Last*, and Gandhi came to use the term for the ideal of his own political philosophy. Later Gandhians, like the Indian nonviolence activist Vinoba Bhave, embraced the term as a name for the social movement in post-independence India which strove to ensure that self-determination and equality reached all strata of India society.

Origins and Gandhi's Political Ideal

Gandhi received a copy of Ruskin's *Unto This Last* from a British friend, Mr.Henry Polak, while working as a lawyer in South Africa in 1904. In his *Autobiography*, Gandhi remembers the twenty-four hour train ride to Durban (from when he first read the book, being so in the grip of Ruskin's ideas that he could not sleep at all: "I determined to change my life in accordance with the ideals of the book." As Gandhi construed it, Ruskin's outlook on political-economic life extended from three central tenets:

"1. That the good of the individual is contained in the good of all. 2. That a lawyer's work has the same value as the barber's in as much as all have the same right of earning their livelihood from their work. 3. That a life of labour, i.e., the life of the tiller of the soil and the handicraftsman is the life worth living. The first of these I knew. The second I had dimly realized. The third had never occurred to me. *Unto This Last* made it clear as daylight for me that the second and third were contained in the first. I arose with the dawn, ready to reduce these principles to practice. "

Four years later, in 1908, Gandhi rendered a paraphrased translation of Ruskin's book into his native tongue of Gujarati. He entitled the book *Sarvodaya*, a compound (samasa) he invented from two Sanskrit roots: *sarva* (all) and *udaya* (uplift) — "the uplift of all" (or as Gandhi glossed it in his autobiography, "the welfare of all").

Although inspired by Ruskin, the term would for Gandhi come to stand for a political ideal of his own stamp. (Indeed Gandhi was keen to distance himself from Ruskin's more conservative ideas.) The ideal which Gandhi strove to put into practice in his ashrams was, he hoped, one that he could persuade the whole of India to embrace, becoming a light to the other nations of the world. The Gandhian social ideal encompassed the dignity of labour, an equitable distribution of wealth, communal self-sufficiency and individual freedom.

Sarvodaya movement

Gandhi's ideals have lasted well beyond the achievement of one of his chief projects, Indian independence (*swaraj*). His followers in India (notably, Vinoba Bhave) continued working to promote the kind of society that he envisioned, and their efforts have come to be known as the Sarvodaya Movement. Anima Bose has referred to the movement's philosophy as "a fuller and richer concept of people's democracy than any we have yet known." Sarvodaya workers associated with Vinoba, J. P. Narayan, Dada Dharmadhikari, Dhirendra Mazumdaar, Shankarrao Deo, K. G. Mashruwala undertook various projects aimed at encouraging popular self-organisation during the 1950s and 1960s, including *Bhoodan* and *Gramdan* movements. Many groups descended from these networks continue to function locally in India today.

MAHATMA GANDHI AND INDIAN NATIONALISM

As one who has lived in India - "Hamare Pyare Bharat - Land of my adoption, for 31 years, I am concerned about the present behaviour of radical, religious extremists who seek to violate the principles of the Constitution of the nation by showing intolerant attitudes towards minority groups. It is time that we remind ourselves of the Love, Tolerance and Impartiality the Mahatma manifested even to the lowliest within the community, irrespective of caste, creed, race and gender. May we imbibe the spirit that is enshrined in the life of Gandhiji, the Father of the Nation. Let us dedicate ourselves afresh to the principles for which he gave his life and without which, India could never have become a free nation. It is fitting that the following article be reproduced on the Net and that other articles, such as "Letters from Nehru to his Daughter, Indira", also be made available. Please enjoy the following :-

In his stimulating, polemical journal, "Young India", of 27 May, 1926, Mahatma Gandhi declared - "I am used to misrepresentation all my life. It is the lot of every public worker. He has to bare a tough hide. Life would be burdensome if every misrepresentation had to be answered and cleared. It is a rule of life with me, never to explain misrepresentation, except when the cause requires correction. This rule has saved much time and worry."

So often has Gandhi been misunderstood and misinterpreted that it is now the moral obligation of contemporary historians and exponents of the Gandhian philosophy to disentangle populist Gandhian myths from eternal truths handed down to us as part of our rich legacy.

As the years roll by, the quintessence of Gandhian thought acquires greater clarity and force, which may have escaped the attention of leaders today. In a small band of authentic Gandhian ciceroni, there are a few who have tried to correct warped or falsified exposition of Gandhi's socio-economic and political philosophy in theory and practice. Among them, B.R. Nanda stands out as a balanced, faithful interpreter of the Gandhian moves of 1915 - 1925, the first ten years of his permanent return to India. He provides us with a key to the better understanding of the Gandhian seminal initiatives of that period, which have acquired both urgency and relevance today.

This historic lessons, embedded in the application of Mahatma Gandhi's programme are :- social reform and removal of discriminatory practices; passive, peaceful, determined resistance or "satyagraha" against unjust rules and regulations; abjuration of verbal and other forms of violence; brotherhood and unity of people of all religious denominational, or sectarian orders; self-analysis, self-improvement and self-discipline; avoidance of ostentatious, lavish and wasteful consumerism; austerity in public life; and recognition of individual and national foibles.

These vital principles Gandhi evolved and developed are illustrated in a historical setting of the crusade he launched for removal of chronic social evils and freeing people from political subjugation in the 1920's. But let it be noted carefully; he did not forfeit the respect, friendliness and sympathy of those he justifiably opposed or differed with, because they perpetrated or supported obsolete, undignified or revolting practices and rituals, or served as instruments of alien administration. A trinity of examples, clustered around the broad categories of social service, unity of people and political action, often ignored, misinterpreted or wrongly initiated now, are touched upon here.

For Gandhi, social service implied all-embracing measures for amelioration of human suffering and alleviation of injustice and inequality in society. He denounced the practice of untouchability in the name of religion as a "sin against humanity" and relegation of women to the position of "dolls or slaves" in society. By admitting in 1915 a "Dhed" (or a depressed class) family into his Ahmedabad Ashram, he risked alienation from his wife and many of his followers who protested against it. Referring to this incident, Gandhi wrote to V.S. Srinivasa Sastri that year :- " I have told Mrs. Gandhi she could leave me and we should part as good friends. The step is momentous, because it so links me with the suppressed classes mission that, at no distant time, I might have to carry out the idea of shifting to some "Dhed" quarters and sharing life with the

"Dheds". As we know, Gandhi lived in a Harijan (outcaste) colony in 1947, in New Delhi, cleansing it by his presence. In his Ashram, Gandhi himself, along with others, participated in the household chores. He respected the dignity of labour, not as a ceremonial gesture but as part of his daily routine.

For Gandhi, passive resistance or "satyagraha" was the surest remedy for alien rule, but it had to be absolutely non-violent. The Chauri Chauri mass civil disobedience movement of 1921, leading to the imprisonment of more than 16,000 satyagrahis, and "coming to within an inch of succeeding", to quote the Governor of Bombay, was marred by violence. Shocked beyond measure, Gandhi halted it to the indignation of all his colleagues, particularly the extremists in politics. He wrote at Bardoli, in February 1922:-

" I, personally, can never by party to a movement, half-violent and half non-violent, even though it may result in the attainment of so-called "swaraj" (Independence and national sovereignty), for it will not be real Swaraj, as I have conceived it." After the Chauri Chauri tragedy, he undertook a five-day fast "as a penance and punishment". Later he instituted the unique experiment of individual "satyagraha" by volunteers he selected after testing their moral and spiritual calibre. Thus, "Satyagraha" he hoped, could be free from violence.

Realising the imperative need for Hindu-Muslim harmony, Gandhi befriended the Khilafat leaders, Mohommad and Shaukat Ali, in the 1920's. With him, in South Africa, were Hindus, Muslims, Christians and Parsis, fighting against Apartheid and racial discrimination. He cautioned people against "selfish and false religious teachers". And told Mahadev Desai, in March 1918, that "deep within him, was a feeling that, through Satyagraha, he could transform the British relationship with India so as to transmute hatred into love and friendship." The same thing, he said, was true of Hindu-Muslim relationships. "Hinduism, with its essentially liberal and broad-minded streak, could captivate Muslims by the power of its compassion which is its very essence. ...We (Hindus) can win over the Muslims this very day, if we are sufficiently imbued with that spirit of brotherly love." The orthodox Hindu leadership accused Gandhi of unduly favouring the Muslims. But his affection for the Ali brothers did not dissuade him from rebuking

Mohammad Ali in May 1919, for indulging in verbal violence:- "I consider your memorial was too undignified for the great cause (of Khilafat) you are espousing and of which I have felt you are pre-eminently the embodiment. Your language was inflammatory and too full of declamation for a memorial. Your statement of the Mohammedan claim, instead of representing irreducible minimum is an exaggeration. I am sure you do not propose to raise questions affecting issues that were, rightly or wrongly, settled long before the war. I would like you, even now, to redraft your memorial. Make a seasoned and logical statement that must arrest and command the attention of the world." Though Gandhi was fighting against British colonialists, he did not hate them. In May 1921, Lord Reading, the then Viceroy of India, wrote to Edwin Montague, the Secretary of State for India at the time, in London:-

"Gandhi came to visit me in a white dhoti and cap, woven on a spinning wheel, with bare feet and legs, and my first impression was that I should have passed him by in the street without a second look at him. When he talks, the impression is different. He is direct and expressed himself well in excellent English, with a fine appreciation of the value of the words he uses. His religious views are, I believe, genuinely held, and he is convinced to a point almost bordering on fanaticism that non-violence and love will give India its independence and enable it to withstand the British Government. His religious and moral views are admirable. Our conversations were of the frankest; he was supremely courteous with manners of distinction. He held in every way to his word in the various discussions we had... Altogether you will judge that I liked him, and I believe there are possibilities in the future ..."

INDIAN NATIONALISM

Indian nationalism refers to the many underlying forces that molded the Indian independence movement, and strongly continue to influence the politics of India, as well as being the heart of many contrasting ideologies that have caused ethnic and religious conflict in Indian society. Indian nationalism often imbibes the consciousness of Indians that prior to 1947, India embodied the broader Indian subcontinent and influenced a part of Asia, known as Greater India.

National Consciousness in India

India has been unified under many emperors and governments in history. Ancient texts mention India under emperor Bharata and Akhand Bharat, these regions roughly form the entities of modern day greater India. Mauryan Empire was the first to unite all of India, South Asia, and much of Persia. In addition, much of India has also been unified under a central government by empires, such as the Gupta Empire, Rashtrakuta Empire, Pala Empire, Mughal Empire, Indian Empire etc.

Conception of Pan-South Asianism

India's concept of nationhood is based not merely on territorial extent of its sovereignty. Nationalistic sentiments and expression encompass that India's ancient history, as the birthplace of the Indus Valley Civilization and Vedic Civilization, as well as four major world religions - Hinduism, Buddhism, Jainism and Sikhism. Indian nationalists see India stretching along these lines across the Indian Subcontinent.

The Gandhian Era

Mohandas Gandhi pioneered the art of *Satyagraha*, typified with a strict adherence to ahimsa (non-violence), and civil disobedience. This permitted common individuals to engage the British in revolution, without employing violence or other distasteful means. Gandhi's equally strict adherence to democracy, religious and ethnic equality and brotherhood, as well as activist rejection of caste-based discrimination and untouchability united people across these demographic lines for the first time in India's history. The masses could participate in India's freedom struggle for the first time, and the membership of the Congress grew over tens of millions by the 1930s. In addition, Gandhi's victories in the Champaran and Kheda Satyagraha in 1918-19, gave confidence to a rising younger generation of Indians that the British hegemony could be defeated. National leaders like Sardar Vallabhbhai Patel, Jawaharlal Nehru, Maulana Azad, Chakravarti Rajagopalachari, Mohandas Gandhi, Rajendra Prasad and Badshah Khan brought together generations of Indians across regions and demographics, and provided a strong leadership base giving the country political direction.

6

Social Work Education in India

SOCIAL WORK EDUCATION

Are you a person who really wants to serve the society or lend your service to the needy? Do you have enough compassion or consideration for the needy to put them first than your own lucrative development? If so, here is an apt career for you which is challenging and at the same time provides great mental satisfaction... It is the career in Social Service, in other words, pure charity work that has gradually grown into a profession. People who were involved in charity work understood the drawbacks of the lack of scientific approach to their work and so gradually it was developed into a profession scientifically by applying theoretical and practical knowledge. Social work is all about improving the lives of people by helping them to deal with their problems such as personal issues, diseases, unemployment etc. It is an exciting, demanding and immensely rewarding profession which requires exceptional dedication to strive for social reform. Social work is a profession for those with a strong desire to improve people's lives.

Social workers are the helping hands for needy people who are suffering from homelessness, poverty, violence, abuses and diseases like cancer, AIDS etc. They work towards the solutions of people's social, economic and emotional problems through counseling, arranging conferences, increasing resources, spreading public awareness and starting social programs and health services. The area of service for a social worker is wide, which can range from working in various developmental projects of the government to working for NGOs. The work of a social worker can be related to an educational programme, health, environment or forest and water management. It is the duty of the social worker to answer their client's specific needs and to do the follow up for providing apt service to them.

As a practical oriented course, Social Work deals with the study of methods and techniques used in developmental activities. Emerging in the 19th century, it has now become a major career choice with the increasing number of social organizations. Professional social work education began in India in 1936 with the establishment of TATA Institute of Social Sciences.

SPORTS AND PHYSICAL EDUCATION

Sports in India are as popular as in many other parts of the world. Nevertheless, physical education and organized recreational activities do not take a high priority in most government schools. Sports activities and facilities are not formally integrated into the curriculum of most schools.

Where physical education programs do exist, the activities and facilities are not adequately supported by resources or instruction. As a result, most rural Indian children lack the regular joyful exercise that promotes health, stimulates their motor function abilities, and teaches teamwork and cooperation. And as importantly, the children are deprived of teachers that through physical education act as role models and teach positive behaviour.

How Volunteers Help

Article 31 of the UN Convention on the Rights of the Child states that: "Every child has the right to rest and leisure, to engage in play and recreational activities" In the spirit of the UN Convention, volunteers promote leisure, play, and recreational activities to communities that do not have the adequate resources to provide these services.

Physical education volunteers' primary role is to act as sports teachers and promoters of organized recreational activities within a particular community. Volunteers set up recreational clubs in the evenings, arrange sports tournaments and organized activities in schools, and introduce foreign sports and games, all while promoting health, cooperation, and fun.

DEVELOPMENT INTERNSHIP INDIA

Idex offers a wide range of Volunteer Programs in several areas throughout India. Rajasthan, Delhi, Bangalore, Punjab, South India, Uttar Pradesh, etc.! For development internship India Idex provides programs require extremely committed and self- motivated participants who are willing and able to work and live outside of their comfort zone. Maturity and independence are crucial and the ability to help out wherever needed. Flexibility is important as you may be asked to fulfil a variety of responsibilities. All Volunteers must be at least 18 years of age and in good physical and strong mental health. Some programs are suitable for volunteers up to 65 years of age. Final program eligibility is up to individual project leaders. Idex want to take part in developing internship in India.

Volunteer Social Work Education in India

For a developing country literacy is very important. So, Volunteer Social Work Education in India play an important role in raising awareness about the need for regular schooling and offer much needed support to local teachers. Working in local schools gives volunteers a chance to meet regularly with local children and their families and for those volunteers with a professional interest in education, teaching gives them a chance to hone their skills in a very different environment. The most commonly requested subject of teaching is English; however you are also invited to teach math, science, geography or other subjects covered by the curriculum. Idex encourage volunteers to create their own lesson plans and teaching materials are available for this purpose. You may also bring your own teaching materials such as reading and picture books and flash cards. Interacting with them is extremely valuable for children's confidence and also for your learning of the local culture.

THE CHALLENGES FOR INDIA'S EDUCATION SYSTEM

India's education system turns out millions of graduates each year, many skilled in IT and engineering. This manpower advantage underpins India's recent economic advances, but masks deep- seated problems within India's education system. While India's demographics are generally perceived to give it an edge over other countries' economies (India will have a youthful population when other countries have ageing populations), if this advantage is restricted to a small, highly educated elite, the domestic political ramifications could be severe.

With 35 per cent of the population under the age of 15, India's education system faces numerous challenges. Successive governments have pledged to increase spending on education to 6 per cent of GDP, but actual spending has hovered around 4 per cent for the last few years. While, at the top end, India's business schools, Indian Institutes of Technology (IITs), Indian Institutes of Management (IIMs) and universities produce globally competitive graduates, primary and secondary schools, particularly in rural areas, struggle to find staff.

Indian governments have seen education as a crucial development tool. The first part of this paper provides a historical perspective on the development of the education system in India, highlighting the changing emphases within government policy. Since Independence, the education policies of successive governments have built on the substantial legacies of the Nehruvian period, targeting the core themes of plurality and secularism, with a focus on excellence in higher education, and inclusiveness at all levels. In reaching these goals, the issue of funding has become problematic; governments have promised to increase state spending while realizing the economic potential of bringing in private-sector financial support.

The second part of this paper examines how recent governments have responded to these challenges, which have remained largely unchanged since Nehru's era, despite the efforts of past governments and commissions to reform the Indian education system. Attention will be paid to more recent policy initiatives, both those of the previous BJP-led administration and the proposals of the current Congress-led United Progressive Alliance. It will become clear that the same difficulties that existed nearly sixty years ago remain largely unsolved today – for example, the need to safeguard access to education for the poorest and most disenfranchised communities of India.

THE EVOLUTION OF INDIA'S EDUCATION POLICY

Elitism, Nehruvianism and Development

Traditional Hindu education served the needs of Brahmin families: Brahmin teachers would teach boys to read and write. Under the Moguls, education was similarly elitist, favouring the rich rather than those from high-caste backgrounds. These pre-existing elitist tendencies were reinforced under British rule.

British colonial rule brought with it the concept of a modern state, a modern economy and a modern education system. The education system was first developed in the three presidencies (Bombay, Calcutta and Madras). By linking entrance and advancement in government service to academic education, colonial rule contributed to the legacy of an education system geared to preserving the position and prerogatives of the more privileged. In the early 1900s, the Indian National Congress called for national education, placing an emphasis on technical and vocational training. In 1920 Congress initiated a boycott of government-aided and government-controlled schools and founded several 'national' schools and colleges. These failed, as the rewards of British-style education were so great that the boycott was largely ignored. Local elites benefited from the British education system and eventually used it expel the colonizers.

Nehru envisaged India as a secular democracy with a state-led command economy. Education for all and industrial development were seen as crucial tools to unite a country divided on the basis of wealth, caste and religion, and formed the cornerstones of the anti- imperial struggle. Following Independence, school curricula were thus imbued with the twin themes of inclusiveness and national pride, placing emphasis on the fact that India's different communities could live peacefully side by side as one nation.

The legacies of this Nehruvian approach to education are considerable; perhaps most notable is the entrenchment of the pluralist/secularist perspective in the minds of the Indian people. Subsidized quality higher education through institutions such as the IITs and IIMs formed a major contribution to the Nehruvian vision of a self-reliant and modern Indian state, and they now rank amongst the best higher education institutions in the world. In addition, policies of positive discrimination in education and employment furthered the case for access by hitherto unprivileged social groups to quality education. It has been argued that while access for some marginalized communities continues to be limited, the upward mobility of a few Dalit and tribal households resulting from positive discrimination in educational institutions and state patronage has created role models that help democracy survive in India.

The Kothari Commission

Drawing on Nehru's vision, and articulating most of his key themes, the Kothari Commission (1964–6) was set up to formulate a coherent education policy for India. According to the commission, education was intended to increase productivity, develop social and national unity, consolidate democracy, modernize the country and develop social, moral and spiritual values. To achieve this, the main pillar of Indian education policy was to be free and compulsory education for all children up to the age of 14. Other features included the development of languages (Hindi, Sanskrit, regional languages and the three-language formula), equality of educational opportunities (regional, tribal and gender imbalances to be addressed) and the development and prioritization of scientific education and research. The commission also emphasized the need to eradicate illiteracy and provide adult education. India's curriculum has historically prioritized the study of mathematics and science rather than social sciences or arts. This has been actively promoted since the Kothari Commission, which argued that India's development needs were better met by engineers and scientists than historians. The perception has remained that students only study social science or arts subjects as a last resort, though recently commerce and economics have risen in stature.

The National Policy on Education

In 1986, Rajiv Gandhi announced a new education policy, the National Policy on Education (NPE), which was intended to prepare India for the 21st century. The policy emphasized the need for change: 'Education in India stands at the crossroads today. Neither normal linear expansion nor the existing pace and nature of improvement can meet the needs of the situation.' According to the new policy, the 1968 policy goals had largely been achieved: more than 90 per cent of the country's rural population were within a kilometre of schooling facilities and most states had adopted a common education structure. The prioritization of science and mathematics had also been effective.

However, change was required to increase financial and organizational support for the education system to tackle problems of access and quality. Other problems also needed addressing: India's political and social life is passing through a phase which poses the danger of erosion to long accepted values. The goals of secularism, socialism, democracy and professional ethics are coming under increasing strain.

The new policy was intended to raise education standards and increase access to education. At the same time, it would safeguard the values of secularism, socialism and equality which had been promoted since Independence. To this end, the government would seek financial support from the private sector to complement government funds. The central government also declared that it would accept a wider responsibility to enforce 'the national and integrative character of education, to maintain quality and standards'. The states, however, retained a significant role, particularly in relation to the curriculum.

The central government committed itself to financing a portion of development expenditure, and around 10 per cent of primary education is now funded under a centrally sponsored scheme. The key legacies of the 1986 policy were the promotion of privatization and the continued emphasis on secularism and science. Another consequence of the NPE was that the quality of education in India was increasingly seen as a problem, and several initiatives have been developed since in an attempt to counter this:

- Operation Blackboard (1987–8) aimed to improve the human and physical resources available in primary schools.
- Restructuring and Reorganization of Teacher Education (1987) created a resource for the continuous upgrading of teachers' knowledge and competence.

- Minimum Levels of Learning (1991) laid down levels of achievement at various stages and revised textbooks.
- National Programme for Nutritional Support to Primary Education (1995) provided a cooked meal every day for children in Classes 1–5 of all government, government-aided and local body schools. In some cases grain was distributed on a monthly basis, subject to a minimum attendance.
- District Primary Education Programme (DPEP) (1993) emphasized decentralized planning and management, improved teaching and learning materials, and school effectiveness.
- Movement to Educate All (2000) aimed to achieve universal primary education by 2010 through micro-planning and school-mapping exercises, bridging gender and social gaps.
- Fundamental Right (2001) involved the provision of free and compulsory education, declared to be a basic right for children aged between 6 and 14 years.

Other schemes specifically targeted at marginalized groups, such as disabled children, and special incentives targeting the parents within scheduled castes and scheduled tribes have also been introduced.

In 1992, when education policy was re-examined, the NPE was found to be a sound way forward for India's education system, although some targets were recast and some re-formulations were undertaken in relation to adult and elementary education. The new emphasis was on the expansion of secondary education, while the focus on education for minorities and women continued.

THE DEVELOPMENT OF NON-FORMAL EDUCATION

Despite Nehru's visions of universal education, and the intentions of the Kothari Commission to provide all young children with free and compulsory schooling, a significant proportion of India's young population remained uneducated by the 1970s. To address this problem, the Centrally Sponsored Scheme of Non Formal Education was set up to educate school dropouts, working children and children from areas without schools. It started on a pilot basis in 1979 and expanded over the next few years to cover ten educationally backward states. In the 1980s, 75 per cent of those children not enrolled in school resided in these states.

The 1986 National Policy on Education built upon this scheme and recognized that a large and systematic programme of non-formal education was required to ensure access to elementary education. The NPE developed the system of non-formal education, and expanded it to urban slums and other areas beyond the initial ten states. It also revised the system, involved voluntary organizations and offered training to local men and women to become instructors. For instance, the Non-formal Adult Education for Women based in Lucknow (UP) opened 300 centres in rural areas with financial support from UNESCO. As a result of many such local programmes, literacy rates improved significantly between 1981 and 1991: male literacy increased from 56.5 per cent to 64.2 per cent while female literacy increased from 29.9 per cent to 39.2 per cent.

Primary and Secondary Education: Access, Quality and Literacy

Despite efforts to incorporate all sections of the population into the Indian education system, through mechanisms such as positive discrimination and non- formal education, large numbers of young people are still without schooling. Although enrolment in primary education has increased, it is estimated that at least 35 million, and possibly as many as 60 million, children aged 6–14 years are not in school. Severe gender, regional, and caste disparities also exist. The main problems are the high drop-out rate, especially after Class 10, low levels of learning and achievement, inadequate school infrastructure, poorly functioning schools, high teacher absenteeism, the large number of teacher vacancies, poor quality of education and inadequate funds. Other groups of children 'at risk', such as orphans, child-labourers, street children and victims of riots and natural disasters, do not necessarily have access to schools.

Furthermore, there is no common school system; instead children are channelled into private, government-aided and government schools on the basis of ability to pay and social class. At the top end are English-language schools affiliated to the upscale CBSE (Central Board of Secondary Education), CISCE (Council for the Indian Schools Certificates Examination) and IB (International Baccalaureate) examination boards, offering globally recognized syllabuses and curricula. Those who cannot afford private schooling attend English-language government-aided schools, affiliated to state-level examination boards. And on the bottom rung are poorly managed government or municipal schools, which cater for the children of the poor majority. Therefore, while education for all is safeguarded by the Constitution, and a majority of people can now access educational resources, the quality of the education that young people in Indian receive varies widely according to their means and background, which is a worrying and problematic trend. In India's 600,000 villages and multiplying urban slum habitats, 'free and compulsory education' is in fact basic literacy instruction dispensed by barely qualified 'para teachers'.

The thrust on elementary education over the last two decades and the growing aspirations of poor communities resulting from their participation in a political democracy have already led to a situation where most children at age six are enrolling in schools/learning centres and residential bridge courses. However, the poor quality of these schools and their rudimentary physical and human infrastructure often lead to children dropping out of the school system without learning or continuing in it with limited learning. An emphasis on food, livelihood and health guarantees is therefore simultaneously required to level out the initial disadvantages of the poor in the educational sphere stemming from malnourishment, poverty, and health-related debility.

The present Indian government, the United Progressive Alliance, appears to be committed to confronting these challenges, as reflected in their Common Minimum Programme. The introduction of a 2 per cent education cess (surcharge) on tax, a stress on employment guarantees and the establishment of a National Rural Health Mission are thus welcome developments in this respect. India's aim of providing basic education for all stems from the empowering and redistributive impact of education. Until recently, literacy, and the related issue of access to schooling, have taken precedence over curricular content. J. Dreze and A. Sen argue:

Literacy is an essential tool for self-defence in a society where social interactions include the written media. An illiterate person is significantly less equipped to defend herself in court, to obtain a bank loan, to enforce inheritance rights, to take advantage of new technology, to compete for secure employment, to get onto the right bus, to take part in political activity – in short, to participate successfully in the modern economy and society.

Dreze and Sen argue that the 1991 census indicated that about half of the adult population were unable to read or write. Unsurprisingly, literacy rates vary widely between states, and between genders. The northern Hindi-belt states, whose economic performance has been worse than that of western and southern states, have lower literacy rates. Female literacy varies from around 34 per cent in Bihar to 88 per cent in Kerala; male literacy varies between 60 per cent in Bihar and 94 per cent in Kerala. Rajasthan suffers the widest gender difference: female literacy stands at 44 per cent; male at 77 per cent. One of the main aims of education policy in the 1990s was to accelerate the progress of literacy and school attendance and to create an equitable system for girls, as had been planned by the Kothari Commission in 1964.

In recent years, however, attention has shifted away from the provision of basic literacy skills and towards debates surrounding the content of school curricula. These debates have been particularly concerned with the traditionally secular emphasis within education, which has become vulnerable since the successes of avowedly Hindu political parties.

Curricula Content

The BJP, which dominated coalition governments from 1998 until 2004, initially came to power with an agenda heavily influenced by Hindutva, including the introduction of a uniform civil code under Hindu law and the construction of the Ram temple in Ayodhya. Since a significant proportion of the BJP's electoral constituency comes from right-wing Hindu organizations, such as the Rashtriya Swayamsevak Sangh (RSS) and the Vishwa Hindu Parishad (VHP), it was expected that the government would further the rather chauvinist aspirations of these groups. However, in most policy fields it took a moderate stance, since it needed to maintain the support of its coalition partners, many of which were regional and secular in nature.

But the reverse occurred in the field of education. The 1999 election manifesto of the National Democratic Alliance (NDA) included a section entitled 'Education for all', which appeared in harmony with the reforms implemented under Rajiv Gandhi. The preamble stated that 'State support for education has been wholly inadequate. Quality education is fast becoming the preserve of the social and economic elite of the country.'

When the NDA came to power in 1999, the BJP kept control of the two most senior positions in the Ministry of Human Resource Development, which included education policy. Two party hardliners, Murli Manohar Joshi and Uma Bharti, took the positions of Union Minister and Minister of State respectively. The former oversaw the expansion of the network of RSS schools and the appointment of RSS members or sympathizers to top national education bodies. In 2000/01, the National Council of Educational Research and Training (NCERT) issued a National Curriculum Framework for school education under the slogan of 'Indianize, nationalize and spiritualize'. The framework called for the purging of all foreign elements from the curriculum in state schools. These included the British legacy as well as aspects of Indian culture which were seen as having been introduced by the Mogul invaders.

The new policy involved a massive textbook revision. The revisions were contested by a petition to the Supreme Court brought by three activists who argued that the NCERT had not followed the correct procedures of consultation with the states and that it had tried to introduce religious teaching, which is forbidden by the Constitution. However, the Supreme Court rejected this petition.

The new history and social science textbooks were accused of promoting an anti-minority outlook through flaws and omissions. The BJP argued that it was correcting formerly one-sided interpretations of history. Sixteen pages in three history textbooks in years 6, 7 and 11 were removed. These included a paragraph suggesting that there was no archaeological evidence of settlements in and around Ayodhya around 2000 BC. In an interview Murli Manohar Joshi explained that the changes were made following complaints from Jains, Sikhs, Jats and others who felt aggrieved by the events depicted in the old textbooks:

We examined them and the NCERT made a decision to delete them. (...) Certain authors of history have tried to distort history. They have given it a purely leftist colour. They say that India had no history of its own because they are guided by Marx. They teach the history of a nation that was mainly defeated and conquered by foreign powers. It's a travesty of facts and an attempt to kill the morale of a nation.

Aside from accusing India's historians of an underhand communist agenda, Joshi also denied that the RSS had been involved in the process, arguing that, in science books, discoveries were falsely credited to the Western world: 'Was the invention of computers possible without the invention of the Indian binary system, zero and one?'

The changes were an attempt to increase pride in being Indian, but concerns were raised that Indian culture was presented as Hindu culture, ignoring India's pluralistic roots and the contributions of Muslim and other minorities. This was a reversal of the Nehruvian view of the roots of India's education system. The Human Resource Development Minister responded to the widespread criticism from the historical profession by calling the criticism 'intellectual terrorism unleashed by the left ... more dangerous than cross border terrorism'. The press described the moves as the 'saffronization' of education, and it became a national issue in 2001 when non-BJP parties within the NDA said that even if the Human Resource Development Ministry insisted on the new curriculum, they would not accept the changes in the states they ruled. There were two main criticisms of the new education policy: first, that they were directed by the communal agenda of the Sangh Parivar and were contrary to the principles enshrined in the Constitution; and, second, that education was the responsibility of the states and changes could not be centrally imposed.

In Delhi, the Congress chief minister, Sheila Dikshit, said she had no problems with the old textbooks and would happily have reprinted them. However the NCERT refused permission and insisted that the new textbooks with the historical revisions be used. So, instead, the Delhi state government created its own books.

Aside from what was happening in state schools, the RSS started to expand its influence in education and health. The first RSS-backed school had been established in 1952 by some RSS members whose aim was to contribute to 'nation-building' through education. There are now more than 50 state and regional committees affiliated to Vidya Bharati, the largest voluntary association in the country. These coordinate around 13,000 institutions with 74,000 teachers and 1.7 million students. The expansion of RSS schools was a major pillar in this strategy, essentially circumventing the traditional separation of education and religion. This expansion has been funded in various ways, including through charities operating in the West. According to a recent report published by Awaaz, a London-based secular network, almost a quarter of Sewa International earthquake funds raised from the UK to help Gujarat were used to build RSS schools.

RSS teaching is centred on knowledge of culture or Sanskrit Gyan. The RSS, however, also sponsored an agenda paper on education that the central government tried to present before the Conference of State Education Ministers in October 1998, suggesting that these and similar texts could in the future be made compulsory for all schools.

RSS schools teach a Hindu-centric world view, which works both to highlight the difference between Hindus and non-Hindus and at the same time to emphasize the role of Hinduism as the source of all human wisdom. The proposed legislation to legalize RSS schools, enabling them to receive state funding, would be a significant policy change for a country so traditionally committed to the provision of secular education. As Nalini Taneja observes:

Through a directive that makes all schools running for 10 years automatically entitled to affiliation and recognition, the BJP govt. has ensured large transfers of state funds to RSS schools in the states of BJP govt., especially if it can be easily shown that govt. schools are not functioning well.

While there is doubt about the impact of the 'saffronization' of the education system, nonetheless it was this issue that the

UPA government tackled first. Only a few weeks after the elections, on 12 June 2004, the government ordered a panel of historians to be constituted to advise on the issues of communalization and inadequacies of the history textbooks of the NCERT. The three history professors, S. Settar, J.S. Grewal and Barun De, submitted a report which concluded that 'the textbooks prepared since 2000 are so full of errors and sub-standard that we find it impossible to recommend their continuation'. The panel acknowledged that though there are different interpretations with regard to historical facts, at school level history teaching should reflect a consensus. The Executive Committee of the NCERT subsequently issued a note to all schools, explaining that the report had been accepted, but that because the academic session 2004/05 was too advanced the books would not be withdrawn until the 2005/06 academic year. The note also gave some advice on how to cope with flaws in the history books, detailing errors and page numbers and promising to reprint and make available the old textbooks. It also emphasized that history was not to be used for political purposes:

> The past has a value of its own and distinctive fact of its own, not to be twisted for present purposes, either of the state or regional predilections of that element of the past as it was, distinct from the past as we would like it to be today.

The Minister of Human Resource Development made a statement in parliament on 20 July 2004, promising to restore the earlier books in the next academic session. However the exercise has flagged up the flaws in the old textbooks, which were seen as too dry, and lacking narrative and emotion. While the government will try to address this in the medium term, in the short term it will focus on restoring pedagogy 'which helps raise questions and prevents indoctrination'. The curricula changes introduced by recent BJP-led governments indicated a shift from the Nehruvian tenet of secular education and diverted attention from more deep-seated structural problems in India's education system, such as the need for universal access to quality education. But for non-BJP parties, the development of a Hindu-centric education system presents a major political concern and, as is inevitable in a representative democracy, political issues take precendence over more substantive issues. The challenge for the present government will be to move past this political obstacle and push through more comprehensive reforms, rather than simply undoing the policies of its predecessor.

Funding and Higher Education

Under the Constitution, responsibility for education is shared between central and state governments. The central government sets policy, stimulates innovation and plans frameworks. The state governments are responsible for running the education system on the ground. This has exacerbated problems since states have differing resources to allocate to education. It is the inadequacy of resources that has recently become the most pressing and central issue. Allocation is another issue. When resources are scarce, what are the state's priorities? In general southern, richer states do better than the poorer, northern ones. According to India Together reporter Summiya Yasmeen:

> The Central and state governments are hard put to mobilise 4 per cent of GDP for education. (...) With 59 million children out-of-school and another 90 million in school learning very little, the common school system is not a utopian ideal dug out from the archives of the Kothari Commission, but an imperative that will decide India's place in the comity of nations.

The standard of educational facilities, and the quality of education, are generally higher in primary and secondary schools in richer states than poorer ones, such as Bihar and Jharkhand. In higher education, differing availability has itself contributed to the economic differences. The IT-based success of southern states owes much to their higher number of engineering colleges, and consequent greater pool of graduates.

The number of engineering colleges demonstrates incredible diversity, and has helped contribute to the concentration of high-technology industry in southern India. But the disparity between these states and northern states is dramatic; Bihar, for instance, has less than one engineering college for every 10 million people in the state; Tamil Nadu has almost four colleges for every million people. The growth of the IT and BPO (Business Process Outsourcing) industries and the concomitant spread of computer use and application in the private sector has had a significant impact on the expansion of the highly skilled labour market, and thus on higher education. In fact, private- sector education is a growing field in itself, estimated to make up nearly 2 per cent of GDP. Unfortunately, this top-quality education is restricted not only geographically to those areas where the IT industries are based (as we have already seen), but also according to ability to pay, as the private-sector educational institutions charge prohibitive fees.

Negotiating the need to share the burden of funding higher education between the public and private sectors has been a continual problem for the Indian government. For example, the 1986 reforms reinforced the independent status of higher education institutions, but led to a gradual decline in government expenditure in this area. The government faced a serious resource crunch and decided to reduce the subsidization of higher education by around 50 per cent. Two committees were set up to mobilize additional resources for universities and technical education institutions. Universities were encouraged to raise fees and to turn to the private sector for additional funding. Consequently, the balance between the public and private sectors becomes almost synonymous with a balance between excellence and access. While it is important for India to produce top- quality graduates, it is equally important that the opportunity to gain a degree is not restricted to privileged communities.

The University Grants Commission (UGC) holds a large measure of responsibility for negotiating this excellence/equity dilemma. It does not simply provide grants to universities and colleges, it also maintains, and tries to raise, academic standards in higher education, frames policies to this end and advises the central and state governments on the subject of expanding and improving higher education. However, the proportion of the education budget allocated to higher education has gradually decreased from 24 per cent in the 1970s to around 9 per cent today. This is posing a problem as Indian universities and colleges are of varying quality. Widening access is also an issue – only 6 per cent of those aged between 18 and 23 enter tertiary education. Dilip Thakore asserts in India Together:

With the annual outflow of students fleeing India's second rate tertiary education institutions showing no signs of abating and a growing number of foreign universities clamouring to establish campuses in India even as government budgetary allocations for higher education are shrinking rapidly, UGC top brass have no option but to focus on their mandate to raise teaching and learning standards in academia and also to teach business illiterate college and university managements to gradually become financially independent.

In the light of these recent trends and difficulties, the NDA manifesto pledged to ensure the independence of higher education institutions, but in fact control was centralized in the past few years. The party's proposals represented a tip in the balance away from public funding towards the private sector, but at the same time displayed a commitment to controlling the upper echelons of higher education institutions by appointing party sympathizers (including RSS members) to the top posts. In addition, pro-Hindutva policies were to have a notable impact on universities, colleges and other academic bodies, which critics argue amounted to a centralization of control over the education system.

Critics claimed that vice chancellors of various universities were appointed on the sole criterion of their sympathy with the new policies: In Delhi University, while the BJP was holding the State Government, all democratic norms were flouted and the functioning and role of the statutory bodies such as the Academic Council completely undermined. Governing Bodies of Delhi Administration and other colleges were filled with known sympathisers of no academic achievements or interest in education with a view to ensuring appointment of affiliated persons as Principals for the colleges. Appointments to teaching posts were similarly ensured through this process. These RSS filled Governing bodies were openly used for undermining the autonomy of the University, and giving support to corruption and goondaism [hooliganism] on the campus. In flouting and withdrawing many aspects of the agreement arrived at with the teachers last year, the BJP government is devaluing education itself.

The personnel changes were not confined to universities. New appointees to the Indian Council of Historical Research (ICHR) supported the VHP campaign on Ayodhya, while RSS supporters or sympathizers have been appointed to the Indian

Council of Social Science Research (ICSSR), the Indian Institute of Advanced Studies in Simla, the Indian Institute of Mass Communication and the All India Council for Technical Education. Moreover, the National Museum galleries have been renamed and the choice of items displayed reflects the Sangh Parivar's view of Indian history. As mentioned above, the authority and autonomy of the University Grants Commission was undermined with regard to teachers' salaries, promotion and working conditions. The UGC was being used to commercialize education and to cut state funding. Personnel at the National Institute of Planning (NIEPA) and the NCERT were also changed.

The BJP's policies in this area have extended beyond educational institutions alone, and have had a considerable impact on academia as a whole. These events have led to concern within academia. Sharad Pawar, leader of the Nationalist Congress Party, observed: 'Research scholars should not tarnish the image of inspiring personalities.'

The greatest success of the BJP's education policy has been neither the introduction of new textbooks nor the emergence of RSS activists at the helm of national education institutions. It is that the discriminatory discourse appears to have been accepted by the public, many of whom grew up with Nehru's secular ideals of constructing an inclusive Indian national identity. On top of the existing problems in the education system, the BJP added a further concern – that through education India's inclusive identity would be directly eroded.

Recent statistics on the expansion of tertiary-sector education highlight the scale of the problem faced by the new government for creating and implementing policy in this area. The number of colleges and universities across the country has risen from 565 and 25 in 1953 to 15,600 and 311 respectively in 2004. Simultaneously the number of students in higher education has risen from 230,000 to 9.28 million and the number of staff from 15,000 to 462,000. India produces over 2.5 million university graduates per year.

The commission for the Tenth Plan (2002–7) has set itself the target of identifying and designating 25 universities 'with potential for excellence' across the country. These institutions will be 'funded at a higher level to enable them to attain excellence in teaching and research', according to the UGC concept paper. Along with a few hundred colleges, they will be given full academic freedom to experiment with the curriculum, introduce innovations in teaching, conduct their own examinations and award joint degrees with affiliating universities. In addition, quality control issues resulted in the creation of the National Assessment and Accreditation Council of India (NAAC) in 1994 with the objective of assessing and grading institutions of Higher Education on a scale from 1 to 5. These proposals appear to reflect the need to invest in higher education to attain the high quality now demanded by the growing economy. The role of the NAAC is particularly important for achieving increased accountability for publicly funded institutions. Clearly, the current government understands the need for university subsidies, but it is not yet certain whether these subsidies will be directed so as to widen access to those communities traditionally excluded from tertiary education.

WOMEN'S EDUCATION: PROSPECTS AND CHALLENGES

In spite of the forceful intervention by a bastion of female privilege, feminist critics, constitutional guarantees, protecting laws and sincere efforts by the state governments and central government through various schemes and programmes over the last 62 years and above all, the United Nation's enormous pressure with regard to the uplift of the plight of women in terms education is still in the state of an enigma in India for several reasons. The 2001 Census report indicates that literacy among women as only 54 percent It is virtually disheartening to observe that the literacy rate of women India is even much lower to national average i.e. 65.38. The growth of women's education in rural areas is very slow. This obviously means that still large womenfolk of our country are illiterate, the weak, backward and exploited. Moreover education is also not available to all equally. Gender inequality is reinforced in education which is proved by the fact that the literacy rate for the women is only 54% against 76% of men as per 2001 Census.

The pre-Independence time literacy rate for women had a very poor spurt in comparison to literacy rate of men. This is witnessed from the fact that literacy rate of women has risen from 0.7 % to 7.3 % where as the literacy rate of men has risen from 9.8 % to 24.9 % during these four decades. During the post-independence period literacy rates have shown a substantial increase in general. However the literacy rate of male has almost tripled over the period e.g 25% in 1951 and 76 % in 2001. Surprisingly the female literacy rate has increased at a faster pace than the male literacy during the decade 1981 -2001. The growth is almost 6 times e.g. 7.9 % in 1951 and 54 % in 2001. From this analyse one can infer that still the female literacy rate (only half of the female population are literates) is wadding behind male literacy rate (three fourth of the male population are literates). The rate of school drop outs is also found to be comparatively higher in case of women. This higher rate of illiteracy of women is undoubtedly attributing for women dependence on men and to play a subordinate role. The lack of education is the root cause for women' exploitation and negligence. Only literacy can help women to understand the Indian's constitutional and legislative provisions that are made to strengthen them. Thus promoting education among women is of great important in empowering them to accomplish their goals in par with men in different spheres of life.

THE ROOT CAUSES FOR LOW LITERACY AMONG WOMEN IN INDIA

Women education is a multi-dimensional phenomenon. No single factor or cause can be held responsible for very low literacy rate of women in India. Subsequently it is associated with combination of many factors including social, cultural, economic, educational, demographic, political and administrative and so on. The following are the some of the important factors which could be attributed for the present poor state of affairs of womenfolk in education.

The Lower Enrolment: The lower enrolment of girls in schools is one of the foundational factors which stand as stumbling block for women empowerment in India. Reliable sources indicate that more than 50 % of the Non-Starters (those who have never been to school) are girls. According to the latest statistics, two out of every ten girls in the age group of 6-11 are still not enrolled in schools.

Higher drop-out rate among girls from schools: The incidence and prevalence of drop –outs among girls especially in rural, tribal and slums areas seem to be quite high. According to available sources, occurrence of drop-out and stagnation amongst girls is nearly twice that of boys all over India.

Girl Child as Second Mother: In many families girl children play the role of second mother by shouldering the responsibilities of household work such as looking after the sibling, fetching water, collecting firewood, bringing fodder for cattle, cleaning and cooking etc. In rural India especially in poor families this traditional sex role makes girl child handicapped and conditioned by the attitude of mother and the family and discourages girl child to go school as it becomes secondary.

Bonded Labour System: This social evil is a quite discouraging phenomena which stand as barrier for girl's education in rural areas for the underprivileged families of washer men and agricultural labour, scheduled caste and scheduled tribes.

Cast System as a Barrier; Children belonging to low caste families are forced to learn skills and work ways and not encouraged to go to school due to various factors in the sphere of strict instruction/threat from high caste communities for their selfish motives of keeping them as domestic servants and child labourers in the farms or factory.

Dowry as cordon: Dowry system and other social practices act as main causes of the neglect of the girl child and discrimination against girl child including the deprivation of right of education. In many families especially poor and down-trodden think that if their daughters are educated more, they have to accumulate more assets and properties to provide as dowry in large proportion at the time of marriage, so prefer rather to either stop their children with average education and so on but never higher education. This prevails more in underprivileged families and communities.

Child Labour Practice: A large segment of child population in India is engaged in child labour practices. According to UN sources India is the most child labour populous nation in the globe with more than 50 million child labourers indulged in beedi works, carpet making, bricks, mining, quarrying, glass, bangles, match and fireworks, gem polishing, handloom works, zari, embroidery, coir industry, domestic works, construction etc. In most of these industries girl children are preferred for high productivity and low cost.

Poor School Environment for girls: In general the school environment for girls in India is not really interesting and encouraging. The subjects taught in schools are also not related to the environment of girl children. The methods of teaching are mostly out – dated, rigid and uninteresting. There are still hundreds of schools with poor basic amenities such as drinking water, latrine and toilet facilities, improper building, and inadequate number of teachers' especially female teachers preferable for any parents for safety of their girl children from different types of exploitation and abuse.

Female age at marriage: There is high association of female literacy with female age at marriage. By and large the female age at marriage of 18 (recently 21 years) as prescribed by various legislations not at all followed in India. It is very much ignored and neglected by the families of parents with low literacy and illiteracy background. This obnoxious practice discourages female children to continue their schooling and higher education as they enter into family life at the early age which is not advisable from the physical and mental health point of view and also of social development.

Inferiority, subservience and domesticity: The female child in Indian culture especially in rural, tribal and poor families is expected to develop the qualities of inferiority; subservience and domesticity which place sever limitations on her education and development.

Poverty as a Barrier: In many poverty stricken families, children especially girls are considered as economic assets as they bring income for livelihood as well to save from economic crises due to death or incapacity of parents (sick/handicapped/ aged).

Ineffective Law Enforcing Machinery: Indian constitution and various legislations pertaining to education to children assure free and compulsory education all children of this nation but unfortunately the enforcement machinery fail to discharge its duties and responsibilities to the satisfaction of the public interest and welfare of women.

Demographic Factors: The high population growth rate, rapid urbanisation, migration etc. also attribute immensely for the poor literacy level of women and girls in India.

Poor Political Will and Conviction: Government officials, policy makers, politicians etc. of our country have neither political will nor conviction for the empowerment of women in general.

REMEDIAL MEASURES FOR IMPROVING THE LITERACY LEVEL OF WOMEN IN INDIA

The following measures can be considered for bringing phenomenal change in the plight women's education and empowerment in India

Since the prevailing situation of poor or less enrolment of girls in schools closes the doors for development and prosperity of future generation of women, concerted efforts must be initiated jointly by the government, parents and civil society to achieve universal enrolment for girls without any compromise. The enrolment can be made even mandatory for every girls by the government in the realm of compulsory education.

The Ministry of Education both at Centre and State level should work out strategic steps to stop firmly the ongoing high drop –outs among girls especially in rural, tribal and slums areas with the serious involvement of voluntary organisations in every locality to realize zero drop-out among girls. The poverty stricken families can be identified through proper research and necessary poverty alleviation services be provided to strengthen the income thereby to enable the families to send their children to schools and colleges without much financial difficulties Bonded Child labour and Child labour practice must be abolished with strict administrative measures and the relieved children form bondage should be integratedinto schools with suitable defence social mechanism. Appropriate steps should be taken by the educational authorities with the participation of communities in order to bring the girl children to the main stream of education and development at every level including family and community.

The female child in every Indian family irrespective of socio-economic status should be moulded to overcome the challenges of inferiority; subservience and domesticity which place sever limitations on her education and development. Every family irrespective its socio-cultural and economic background can take it a challenge to bring up their girl children as dignified human being with empowerment in physical, mental, economic and social dimensions of life.

The Midday meal scheme and other educational supportive services like free text books, Note books, Fee uniforms, Free Bicycles, Free bus, scholarships Free bus pass and so on as done in the state of Tamil Nadu can be provided in all states and union territories to lift up the literacy level among girls As social evils like dowry, child marriage, caste system and other practices deprive rights of education for children belonging to poor and underprivileged families and communities, they should eliminated through well-designed packages of mass awareness programmes and social welfare measures with full support of public, political parties, NGOs and government agencies. The electronic and print media can play significant role in building a good and positive image about girls and women in general in the society by giving no focus for such advertisements and news fetching commercial gain at the cost of depicting women as an object. This would help in changing the society's attitudes towards girls and their roles to treat every girl or woman as human being with self respect and dignity.

Government, voluntary sector and philanthropic organisations and individuals should come forward to provide free education for poor girls and provide free hostel facilities for girls studying in schools and colleges in every state of India. This will certainly encourage children of poor families to pursue good and higher education without much impediments The schools of social work, departments of women studies, Women Universities and other educational institutions in hand with NGOs and social service organisations such as Rotary Clubs, Lions Clubs, women lib organisations associations can work together to improve the educational status of the womenfolk in this country on mutual respect and understanding. The parents of children belonging to poor, underprivileged families must be specially educated with proper social formula to help them to understand the significance of education for their girl children as foundation for empowerment Government, NGOs and public should work hand in hand to implement the minimum age at marriage (21 and above) Awareness should be created to institutionalise it as a traditional practice cut acrossing castes, religions, community etc. Government officials, policy makers, political parties and others should have adequate political will and conviction to empower women in India without double standard mind The law enforcing machinery should be made really effective with efficient monitoring vigilant system to implement the constitutional and legislative provisions and administrative measures to assure free and compulsory education for all children of this nation without any gender discrimination.

G.I.A. TO VOLUNTARY ORGANIZATIONS

Under various schemes of Delhi Govt. Department provides Grant-in-aid to voluntary organization & under various schemes of Govt. of India. Department recommends the applications for grant-in-aid of voluntary organization. Apart from this Dept. also gives license to run residential institutions for the welfare of women & children.

The Dept. of Social Welfare, Govt. of NCT of Delhi through its Voluntary Action Cell situated at Canning Lane deals with the following GIA schemes of the following bodies detailed as follows:-

1. Deptt. of Social Welfare, Govt of Delhi.

a) Delhi Grants to Social Welfare Institutions/ Organizations Rules, 1975

b) Scheme for the Welfare of Children in Need of Care & Protection.

Ministry of Social Justice & Empowerment, Govt. of India.

a) Deen Dayal Disabled Rehabilitation Scheme(Scheme to Promote Voluntary Action for Persons with Disabilities) (DDRS)

b) Assistance to Disable Persons for Purchase/fitting of Aids & Appliances. (ADIP)

c) An Integrated Program for Street Children.

d) Assistance to Homes for Infants & Young Children for Promoting In-Country Adoption.

e) An Integrated Program for Older Persons.

f) Scheme of Assistance to Panchayati Raj Institutions/ Voluntary organizations/Self help Groups for construction of Age Homes/Multi Service Centres for Older Persons.

g) Scheme for Prevention of Alcoholism & Substance (Drugs) Abuse.

h) Scheme for the Welfare of Working Children in Need of Care and Protection.

i) General GIA Program for Assistance in the field of Social Defence.

Ministry of Women & Child Development, Govt. of India.

a) Support to Training & Employment Program (STEP)

b) SWADHAR- A scheme for Women in Difficult circumstanes.

c) Construction/Expansion of Hostel building for working women with a Day Care Centre.

d) Short Stay Homes for Women & Girls.

e) Education Work for Prevention of Atrocities on Women.

f) General Grant In Aid for Voluntary Organizations in the Field of Women & Child Development.

g) Organizational Assistance to Voluntary Organizations for Women & Child Development.

h) Grant In Aid for Research & Publications,.

General Check-List of Documents Required Along with the Application for Grant-In-Aid

1. Application in prescribed Performa of the relevant GIA scheme under which the organization seeks to obtain GIA, with all the columns satisfactorily filled in.
2. Valid proof of legal entity/personality of the organization (e.g. copy of registration certificate under Societies Registration Act, 1860, Trust Deed etc.)
3. Memorandum of Association.
4. Rules & Regulations of the organization.

5. List of Members of Executive Committee/Governing Body etc. alongwith their names, father's name, age, address, qualification, profession etc.
6. Budget estimates for the project with proper detailed justification for all cost items.
7. Audited statements of accounts for he last three financial year (i.e. 2005-06,2004-05,&2003-04).
8. Annual activity/progress reports for the last three years, showing the range of activities, corresponding achievements of the organization etc.
9. List of identified/proposed beneficiaries' alongwith all the details about them like name, father's name, age, gender, address, and reason for his/her identification.
10. List of beneficiaries with details as mentioned in previous columns, benefited by the organization during the last years.
11. Details of staff/employees alongwith their names, designation, complete address, date of appointment, educational qualification, salary per month, total salary paid during the previous year etc.
12. Valid registration under Section 52 of the PWD Act. (if applicable)
13. Copy of the minutes of the last meeting geld of the Executive Committee.
14. List of staff registered under Rehabilitation Council of India alongwith the copy of their certificates (if applicable).
15. Utilization certificate of any grant-in-aid from any other sources during the last year.
16. Copy of sanction letter the GIA received, if any, from any other sources during the last financial year.
17. Proof of authorized construction of the project site or Rent Deed, if applicable for the project.
18. Proof of linkages/networking of the organization with other profession agencies.
19. Any other document relevant to the scheme.

VOLUNTARY WORK

Opportunities for voluntary work may be available with statutory bodies such as local authority social services departments and, more commonly, voluntary agencies. For people whose full time jobs and/or financial commitments prevent them from spending long periods in unpaid employment, the most effective way of gaining relevant experience may be to undertake voluntary work in the evenings or weekends. After several months, it is possible to gain paid employment in social care using the experience and reference from that period of voluntary work.

The addresses of local volunteer bureaux or councils for voluntary service are listed in telephone directories, public libraries and citizens advice bureaux. Newspapers such as The Guardian on a Wednesday, magazines like Community Care, and this website and local and community newspapers also advertise voluntary work vacancies. Large public libraries and town halls usually have a notice board advertising local voluntary work opportunities.

Working as a volunteer can be extremely satisfying and rewarding. It is also a great way of finding out more about different kinds of social work and social care and helping you to think about your future career. Voluntary experience will be an advantage when applying for courses and jobs in social services as it demonstrates an insight into the work involved and a level of commitment to the sector.

For people whose full time jobs and/or financial commitments prevent them from spending long periods in unpaid employment, the most effective way of gaining relevant experience may be to undertake voluntary work in the evenings and/or weekends. After several months, it is possible to gain paid employment in social care using the experience and reference from that period of voluntary work.

VOLUNTARY WORK AND BENEFITS

If you are unemployed you can undertake unpaid voluntary work and continue to claim unemployment benefit or income support provided you are free to attend interviews and take up a job if offered one.

Employment as an Assistant or Ancillary

Many social service and voluntary agencies employ staff at assistant level with job titles such as care assistant, support worker, residential social worker or ancillary worker.

Care assistant/support worker/ancillary worker posts are reasonably common if not very well paid and can provide people with enough relevant experience to apply for the Diploma in Social Work (DipSW). However you will be expected to have reflected on and learnt from your experience and to have received good references.

The Guardian on Wednesday, Community Care Magazine and this website and the local press all advertise vacancies for unqualified social workers. Details may also be available from local job centres and employment agencies. Local authority social services/social work departments and voluntary agencies may also be able to provide details of current or forthcoming vacancies.

Private Social Care/social Work Agencies

For those people with considerable paid relevant experience, there are employment agencies specialising in the recruitment and placement of unqualified and qualified social workers. These can be found in telephone directories and in advertisements in the social care press. It is advisable where possible to select long-term placements so that you can build up working relationships and demonstrate your competence with both service users and managers.

VOLUNTARY ACTION

A voluntary action is produced by conscious choice of an organism. The organism, would in turn also be aware of the action while it is executed. This is the opposite of an involuntary action. When involuntary actions occur in response to a specific stimulus that may arise outside the body (e.g., sudden glare that would result in closing of the pupil) or inside the body (e.g., or widening of the pupil that might occur with excitement or anxiety). Thus, an involuntary action need not be a reflex if it is not a direct response to a stimulus, e.g., alternate contraction and relaxation of skeletal muscles during a "fit" (seizure). Another distinction is that reflexes tend to have a protective value for the organism, and are seen in all members of a species, but involuntary movements may not be.

VOLUNTARY ASSOCIATION

A voluntary association or union (also sometimes called a voluntary organization, unincorporated association, or just an association) is a group of individuals who enter into an agreement as volunteers to form a body (or organization) to accomplish a purpose.

Strictly speaking in many jurisdictions no formalities are necessary to start an association. In some jurisdictions, there is a minimum for the number of persons starting an association. Some jurisdictions require that the association register with the police or other official body to inform the public of the association's existence. This is not necessarily a tool of political control but much more a way of protecting the economy from fraud. In many such jurisdictions, only a registered association is a juristic person whose membership is not responsible for the financial acts of the association. Any group of persons may, of course, work as an association but in such case, the persons making a transaction in the name of the association are all responsible for it.

Legal Status

An unincorporated association has been defined as existing:

> *"...where two or more persons are bound together for one or more common purposes by mutual undertakings, each having mutual duties and obligations, in an organisation which has rules identifying in whom control of the organization and its funds are vested, and which can be joined or left at will."*

In most countries, an unincorporated association does not have separate legal personality, and few members of the association usually enjoy limited liability. However, in some countries they are treated as having separate legal personality for tax purposes. However, because of their lack of legal personality, legacies to unincorporated associations sometimes fall foul of the general common law prohibitions against purpose trusts. Associations that are organized for profit or financial gain are usually called partnerships. A special kind of partnership is a co-operative which is usually founded on one person—one vote principle and distributes its profits according to the amount of goods produced or bought by the members. Associations may take the form of a non-profit organization or they may be not-for-profit corporations; this does not mean that the association cannot make benefits from its activity, but all the benefits must be reinvested. Most associations have some kind of document or documents that regulate the way in which the body meets and operates. Such an instrument is often called the organization's bylaws, regulations, or agreement of association.

Civil Law

In some civil law systems, an association is considered a special form of contract. In the Civil Code of Quebec this is a type of nominate contract. The association can be a body corporate, and can thus open a bank account, make contracts (rent premises, hire employees, take out an insurance policy), lodge a complaint etc. In France, conventional associations are regulated by the Waldeck-Rousseau law of July 1, 1901 and are thus called *Association loi 1901*, except in Alsace and Moselle where the law of April 19, 1908 applies (these countries were German in 1901). The Civil Code of Germany contains different regulations for registered non-profit and for-profit associations regarded as juristic persons ("Vereine", articles 21-79) on the one hand and for not necessarily registered associations by contract ("Gesellschaften", articles 705-740) on the other hand. In Texas, state law has statutes concerning unincorporated nonprofit associations that allow unincorporated associations that meet certain criteria to operate as entities independent of their members, with the right to own property, make contracts, sue and be sued, with limited liability for their officers and members.

EDUCATION AND CULTURE

Straight to the Education

Education is the generational transmission of the knowledge of scientific and social rank for the development of the personality, and the forms customary established to facilitate the relations of coexistence in the community. The ethical foundation of the education is in the respect due to the human being, so that the ways of performance in the interpersonal relation do not hurt the sensitivity of the contenders. The education must constitute the substratum of all social relation because it supposes the first approach to justice.

The next norm of education is intuitive in the man and consists of dealing to the other part with the same particularitity whereupon one same one pleases to be treated. As in the society cultural habits are created that determine rooted tastes of politeness, these must be taught to the following generations to facilitate the relations. In this education the familiar group implies itself specially.

The knowledge derived from the intellectual penetration in the nature have come to denominate scientists. The generational transmission of such constitutes the social patrimony par excellence and to which all subject person as of the humanity must right to accede. A fundamental part of the education consists of the education systematized of all that knowledge scientist. In addition to science and its technical applications the education takes care of the development of the artistic creativity of the man by means of the creative models of our predecessors who conform the humanistic patrimony.

The right to participate in the collective knowledge of the humanity generates the right to the education. Since education demands an educative specialization is reason why -in the distribution of the allocation of tasks in the social group- the professor have constituted. It originates the one that the education, in this facet of intellectual knowledge, has been constituted with rank of collective responsibility to take care of this right social. The difference of capacity and personality of the individuals is what originates the one that in everyone embodies in greater or smaller measurement the educative influence equally trasmitido within a social group. Although in the right of know all the citizen are equaled, in the yield of the acquired knowledge that will facilitate the labour development the application is very different. For that reason the equality of opportunities is preached of justice to learn.

The education constitutes the basic element of development of a community, because being the human creativity the motor of any progress will be in the full dependency of the knowledge acquired like elaborated material content on which to project the creative capacity. The essential difference of development between the different towns is based more in its education than in its accessibility to the natural resources. From this perspective, the implication of all the humanity in harnessing the education would have to be constituted like one of the high-priority necessities to tend.

The right in himself to the education is one of the essential contents that must contain education when it approaches the communication of the relations of the individual with the community. This is understood so much for the familiar community, in that duties in the greater ones with respect to the education of prole are created, like in the superior structures to which on the suitable corporation it falls the obligation of the education of the people until his qualification sufficient to act responsibly in the social framework.

The right to the education, like fundamental right of the person, is of universal scope, reason why it must be exerted in all situation. Of some way also this responsibility from which the education arrives at all the human beings implies all the society, that through the suitable international organisms must cause the one that are a reality anywhere in the world. For it it is precise to second plans of promotion and aid for the less sensitized towns with this social good of first necessity.

This right must specially be taken care of when by circumstances of displacement, migration, physical handicap, unjust segregation, etc. special difficulties could appear to be taken care. As soon as it supposes a fundamey right for the formation of the personality is of vital importance of taking care of the psychological complicated individualities.

THE FREEDOM IN THE EDUCATION

To educate taking care of the right fundamental of each individual first of all demands to educate in the truth. As well as the right to the education is universal, also a universal obligation of all the citizens exists for, in its scope of participation in the society, to assume a directed Behaviour to serve to the others by means of the transmission of the knowledge acquired judged according to the experience like positive or negative. Specially each man is it jeopardize socially to the education of the good. As the obligation of the education implies to all the social estates, each one of them will exert a more important influence according to its suitable capacity with respect to the contents to communicate in each phase of the education. This way: the family, the school, the university, the sport community, the circle social, the religious community, the communications groups, the international organisms, and any other association of social initiative must guard by the respect to its educative influence by means of the transmission of contents fit to the truth. Since the consideration of the truth can contain many subjective influences, it is reason why before nothing must notice that all the education is sustained on the forge of an other people's personality, individual and frees, and that therefore all education must focus to inform a rational mind with object to forge a free and independent personality.

One of the great temptations of the humanity is to form beings in who the own personality projects, they already are of the parents, the tutors, the educators, the politicians, the ministers. That should not prevent him for that everyone assumes the responsibility of really to trasmit all those true contents that a good for educating considers, but always saving the freedom of conscience of the formed personality. The greater danger to project the own personality is directly proportional to the magnitude of the relation; very specially in the maternity and the paternity is confused the affection that moves to try permanently the best good inculcating the experienced ideas of good Behaviour with educating to the children according to the tastes and preferences of the own personality. In this dimension one is due to try to aim what the own formation is really a good for the children improving the own educations if accessible means exist, and always counting on the advising of the experts who can share tasks in the education of the boy, as they are the professors and tutors.

The obligation to educate that it is incumbent on to the community with respect to his members is exerted of more direct way by the professors on those who the task is incumbent of teaching with respect to the truth that makes possible the freedom of its students. It is this task of special responsibility and extreme gentleness. Here he is possible to make a distinction between the objectives which they identify scientific knowledge, whose objectivity contributes the forcefulness to it of its experimentation, and the humanistic contents, whose subjectivity is influenced much for the thought or ideology that all time, fashion and man has. To educate in the freedom represents therefore to really teach to the contents scientists like scientists, and the matter of opinion like of opinion, really sustained in all the justifications that can help to educating to form their better criterion. Based on the age he is essential that is educated in the progressive freedom of judgment, that is that the own criteria must vary based on the information which they can contribute to new experiences or studies.

IDENTITY OF THE CULTURE

The culture is formed by the collection of knowledges and ways to interpret the life that the human people have purified in each community; trasmiting that wisdom of generation in generation, and being left certainty of the same one through traditions that articulate the relation forms, which they determine a particular language like communication vehicle, which they are expressed in artistic manifestations, as in use as compiled in the urbanism, museums, libraries, etc. whose influence extends and altogether determines the historical personality of a colectvidad.

According to the social scope that is limited it can speak from a culture of the humanity to the culture of a certain town. The essential characteristic of the culture is its social reality, that is that corresponds to which that way of knowing on the life it shares in a colectivity and from the same one it spreads like own characterization of the same one, so that somehow it is possible to be said that the culture identifies to the group in its projection sociohistorical. The culture is made in each community in two slopes:

1. The one that corresponds to the communitarian global conception of its cultural reality.
2. The one that each person internalizes like experience of relation with the outer world.

From the collective perspective the culture constitutes like a set of wisdom and sensitivities harmonized from subgroups that can be understood of way diachronic or made in the time, or synchronous according to the different creative facets from the human perception. In the diachronic axis the tendencies are pronounced that at every time social sensitivity has taken like references of its creativity, and serves to study their influence in the vitality of that group at every historical moment and the influence on the later stages and the present time.

The valuation of the cultural heap of a society can be measured so much in the values that project on the present moment, like also in the value that supposed for the relations of the society in every time. First it analyzes sociology in the study of the social Behaviours, the second belongs properly to historical science. The influence of the historical culture remains of more or less explicit way on every moment of the society because it is in the customs and because beyond his study it goes to the conscience of the citizens as exemplary forms that can be pronounced in the individual or collective Behaviours of each social group.

The one is east cultural influence diachronic that of a clearer way shows the cultural patrimony of a community and influences determining in its conception of nation. The conformation of a subgroup division of the culture in the synchronous axis is made from the contemplation of each one of the diverse manifestations in which cultural contents are made such: social language, literature, painting, music, cinema, events, forms of leisure, etc. Although the mutual influence and the common dependency to contemporary forms of thought and operative habits cause that common existencial denominators exist that they constitute the cultural essence of the moment and who they are pronounced like the own cultural values of the time.

The synchrony of the diverse cultural manifestations not prevent so that at every moment the preeminence of aspects on others is transcendental, so that when the diversity is eclipsed towards the monopolismo of few manifestations the universalidad of the creative possibilities suffers and generates spaces and times of cultural blackouts. To pronounce creative depends much on which the formativo surroundings and the vital surroundings find an animation cultural that it moves to wake up the spirit of the material lethargy. For that reason the diachronic influence of the cultural conscience of a town is a factor entertainer of the culture and also of the personal inner freedom, as soon as that as the creation is a projection of the spiritual intuition on the intellect its possibility of accomplishment will be greater if the person perceives her capacity of transforming influence.

The culture also has a personal slope defined by the affinity with the sensitivity of each person towards the experimentation of the creative contents. In relation to the knowledge the culture is distinguished of the erudition in which this one is characterized by the accumulation of knowledge; and of the wisdom, of which the same one consists of the interpretative capacity of the contents of the knowledge; whereas the personal culture is perfected in the sensible experience of the contents of the knowledge and the forms of manifestation of the creativity. The culture therefore estimates the knowledge, but it is only defined as so when it enters to integrate itself in the world of the personality.

The culture contains a very important social value well by its content appears like an element of relation between the people. The culture contributes a space important to share experiences, and although he is inferior in the nature essence of the bonds to the one of the family relations or work it promote the same ones by the increase of contents that favor the transmission and interchange to seem. A intellectual exercise exists combined to compendium cultural that boosts the perception of the own personal accomplishment. The man in his cultural experience knows itself like being spiritual sensible, beyond the mere physical sensitivity, interpreting the meaning of the creativity in which the expression of the received knowledge has been pronounced. The culture is interpreted thus intellectually like a value that allows us to enjoy and to progress in our relation with the nature. It would be possible to be said that the experience of the cultural content is something that differentiates from the other species animals, because the essential contents of our experience move from those of survival to those of intelectiva perfection.

Although to a large extent sensitivity by the culture is in the degree of the propitious disposition of each personality to be interested in that perspective of creativity in its relation with the nature, also it is certain that the inner motivation is increased with the education that allows a greater interaction with the knowledge and for that reason the possible scope of cultural speculation is extended. The motivation acquires the function of a catalyst for the cultural development, that is born from the society to the person and reverts later in a superior stage for the same society. The projection that has perceived between the culture and the individual freedom is born of which the culture contributes to the human being an important vision on the matter that reduces the dependency sense. Although also it would be necessary to review that the culture involves a certain dose of agreement when inserting to the individual in a space cultural partner who determines his experiences to a great extent. That's why a diversity of contact of cultural sources is considered beneficial for the freedom of the person to favor its free enrichment. From this perspective the societies opened to the cultural interchange with other groups will be those more favor the freedom of their citizens. It would be possible to be gotten to even conclude that the world will be freer as soon as more increases the cultural development of its towns and more favours the interchange between the different cultures.

CULTURAL RELATIONS

History demonstrates us that the cultural relations have not always represented a positive frame of coexistence between the different towns because the different interpretation from the intellectual reality has fomented the envy, the hatreds and the resentments trying to impose by the force the criterion of the own group. The difference between social levels of culture has been also a cause of the stratification of the societies in compatible groups with habitual scorn or marginalization of the inferior groups.

Although in himself the culture would have to involve the intellectual opening to the compression between the people, and therefore from the most favored to the less, the social reality sample that it is not thus; so that he is very habitual that the culture degree supposes an attraction of the relations towards the superior groups and a scorn of the inferior ones, which is an indicator of how much still the culture represents a material value more than intellectual. The social relations so that they are healthy must involve a respect between the respective cultures and a taking in consideration of the enrichment that contributes the one that in the relation affects diverse cultures.

In himself relations exist that generate conflict by the different approach that occurs in the culture of the parts. Among them they deserve to stand out:

1. The generational relations.
2. The relations between stratums.
3. The conflicts of genus distinction.
4. The marginalizations.
5. The conflicts of race or state.

Generational Relations

The different perspective that grant to the interpretation of the life tend to vary the culture of each generation adapting the received one in the education to the new ways to think, almost always in an opened sense more of the freedom, which originates that conflicts between the people arise frequently which they comprise of successive generations, very specially if coexistence in common exists, because usually it essentially considers the new cultural form like rupturista, without taking in consideration that the evolution of the culture is an unquestionable diachronic fact. The cultural conflict between generations hits between not yet mature yearnings of freedom and a tendency to the conservadurismo that is dissuaded to accept cultural changes. At heart all preservative tendency contains a certain dose of conformismo and a inplicit judgment of which by coming it is worse than the present thing. This situation is psychological consequence of which it is considered that the optimal thing always corresponds to the modified thing in the previous process of generational relief and that it, therefore, must be armoured like permanent value.

The generational conflicts mark to the familiar, scholastic relations and a nondespicable part of the relations of the coexistence community. The youthful culture tends to affirm in the change as the standard of the own generational identity. The change is as much more accusing as soon as than the community it has a developed cultural baggage more, which generates a vindication of the freedom in rupture terms or progress. Although the influence of the generational confrontation is let mark in the culture in the axis of its synchronous dynamics, in the one of the diachronic influence is smaller, because its social importance is diluted, partly, because the influence of the young people is adjusted in the age of the incorporation to the productive life, the one that extends more on the culture. However, a part consolidates in the new forms of thought and is the one that assumes the generational cultural relief.

RELATIONS BETWEEN ESTATES

The estamentaria division of the society is a reality with different imposition according to the cultures, but that even though it does not acquire a determining social relevance in the communities for that reason does not let exert its influence on the related parts. The consistency of the classement culturally societies shows it in the relations social of work, political participation, concerning the marriage, access to goods, inheritancc, etc.

The classement division affects the culture of the relations of coexistence of the daily life in so common aspects of expression as they can be: the greeting, the submission, the presence in certain social events, the assumption of fault, the access to the education, etc. A society established on estates is an inclined society to the distinction of the culture opportunities and education for its citizens, because the favored estates more, than usually do not agree to integration, demand in name of the freedom the opportunity to dedicate the own rcsources for the formation of his, being left the access diversity institutionalized to equal means of opportunity at the formation of the young people. This aspect originates a confrontation in the social relations between the estates, because most inferior they demand, by virtue of the equal contribution that make to the society with their work, conditions of promotion for its children in order progressively to palliate the differentiation generated between the resources which you have yourself and the promotion that the culture facilitates. As soon as more integrated are the class of a society, greater is the cultural coherence of the society. The culture of the distinction of people is trasmited in the social scope with such force that hardly is surpassed in the individual scope. Except for a reduced group animated by a privileged social conscience, most of the citizens becomes aware from group and its mental scheme dreams up on the categorization of the people based on its hereditary estate. This conception displays a generalized exception, and is the one to attribute condition of cultural class based on the rent level that is pronounced. With enough frequency the relation between estates suffers from lack of intermediation means that facilitate the mutual knowledge and the establishment of political resources that favor integration. In the democratic societies this is palliated partly by the popular representation, but the experience comes demonstrating how the projects of integration of many processes by the inconsistency or the irresponsibility of the chosen politicians are weakened.

An aspect where cultural integration continues being very deficient is the one of the relations between the national groups or social stratas that look down for their assimilation to the members of other cultures. The affirmation of the own culture must be so of integration that it becomes attractive favoring the assimilation. Neither the national conscience, nor the religion, nor the conception of the family or the economy must constitute ties closed for integration, on the contrary dependy of its internal coherence those realities will prevail or in opposite case they will be perfected with the outer contributions.

THE CONFLICTS OF GENUS DISTINCTION

The relations between people of different genus have in the society a substantial load in which it extends to the reproduction and consolidation of the species. The fertilization of new human beings follows a process ordered from the conjunction of two people of different genus who enter a specific relation that has like main aim the concurrence of the respective personal resources for the correct raising and development of the children. The one that the relations of reproduction of the species are in the nature trusted to the sexual distinction of the people does not determine that they are these only or the main ones in the relations between genus, since the affective necessities of the individuals, in a very important determination, are also subject to the diverse form to be of the respective genus. It seems that between the two more specific causes of the relations between genus, the affectivity and the procreation, a common element exists that it formalizes them that is the sexuality. The sexual distinction and the mutual attraction to the intimate accomplishment have the double aim of the generation of the species and the affective culmination. Therefore, one of the components of the genus relations is made orienting the purpose for which it settles down. Being the human people free creatures, correspond to them in the genus relations to settle down the priority of their aims, without the acts in pair can acquire irrational tendencies. The intelligence is the one who must as much assume the governing role of the relational acts of genus in its formal agreement as in its accomplishment during the time in the relation lasts. The different culture that each part can have of which involves a genus relation must be put under the mutual consensus, because as any interpersonal relation is based on the mutual agreement, without they are accepted to impose particular cultural values. The culture of the freedom must prevail over any other than in his application it implied a dominion situation.

A characteristic of the genus relations establishes the one that the physical nature and psychological of the people of different sex they have specific peculiarities that cause that in the relation exist predeterminations of peculiar positions of power. The generic relation must assume that the differences of rolls between sexes do not consolidate dominion positions, for that reason must be oriented from a frame that assumes the difference of characters but the equality of right. Like any human act, the genus relations, from the social perspective that studies the relations in its essence, are subject to the free will of the people that contract them, which does not exclude the ethical responsibilities with respect to the scopes of protection from prole and social integration of the pair.

In search of the common good, the social group, out of danger leaving the freedom of those who personal relations of genus contract, can regulate the frame of duties and rights that must be protected in the group so that each member is also considered according to the indirect labour cost that the customs impose to him. The equality of right in the relation must progressively be persecuted within the framework legal of the society although the customs or the cultural surroundings have accepted forms of dominion of members on others. The right to the equality between genus comes from the same nature of person and -no matter how hard at last times it was interpreted according to other values- the projection of the modern legal systems must go to its consolidation. It is not justifiable the resource to the violence to impose the own criteria of culture in the interpersonal relations. Of very special way it is not it in the relations of genus by the privacy degree in which they are developed, where the same one could degenerate in serious consequences for the freedom and the stability of the familiar group. To this aim, in the same concert of the relation, he is positive to fix Behaviour guidelines to explain the internal conflicts. To heft the mutual offences in a frame of stimulus of the coexistence must lead back the aggressive Behaviours towards a tolerance that facilitates the coexistence preserving the rights. If the concord of the relation is not possible is due to sink the assumption of the inconsistency of the same one and to formalize the rupture of the bows, without he is acceptable in no case the resource of the violence.

The legal orderings must prevail over the cultural tendencies and serve as models for modification of the customs fitting them the greater fairness of the defence of the freedom. The cultural rooting of these tendencies facilitates the culture of the peaceful coexistence.

THE MARGINALIZATIONS

The cultural forms of each community involve possible layers of marginalization, are at personal level or of group, by the lack of integration of those people in which it is the common culture. They are elements that to cut oneself off because they present psychological characters by which tend to the social isolation, or because their personality or forms of Behaviour entails a social exclusion, or because of ideological reasons a cultural segregation is followed. In all the cases the marginalization is pronounced in a tangencial life with respect to the cultural scope established by the social group. It is necessary to differentiate what corresponds to different cultural structures between chaste or estates, and the individuals exist that do not integrate themselves culturally in the own group, being in a marginality situation that determines to a large extent its social relations. The causes can come from the cultural rigidity of the group or the personality of the individual. Also a marginalization cause exists that is born of physical handicap to share the cultural habits of the community.

The nature of the marginalization usually is followed of an accumulation of circumstances as individuals as much social that they hit with the culture with roots in the society. Normally protocols cultural comdemn the marginalization, because they hit the integrating nature that supposes the culture, but in fact are the conventions of these cultural forms cause to a large extent the marginal fact.

To work to construct from the heart of the culture bridges for integration is obtained by means of the consolidation of the same one in universal principles of social philosophy, that by their same condition can serve as common control to converge the tendencies of the different cultures. To base the cultural realizations on common principles favours the general interest and the acceptance and integration by the deprived minorities. The culture has to be an instrument of integration and not of disintegration, reason why it has to favor itself that they can reach his different manifestations from the greater percentage of individuals of the community, this principle demands the imagination of resources to adapt to the language of the children, the diminished ones, the immigrants, the older, etc. A culture socially is excellent when it enjoys implantation in the society. Valid the exemplary forms are whatever do not determine for themselves but that they dream up with influence spirit. When the culture establishes confrontation of the parts within a society really must to the deficient foundations on the criteria of the truth. For that reason it is necessary that the social people in charge of the cultural involution are sensible to the critic.

According to the progressive intercultural contact that is generated from the globalization of the social relations, the same culture must evolve from a paper of doctrinal essence towards the relativity of its contents as multipurpose forms able to adapt to the very different considerations from the life. In that amplitude of the forms the intercultural dialogue is favoured; and the one is that dialogue that can deepen towards the common essences that they must inform all cultural fact.

CONFLICTS OF RACE AND STATE

To particularize the political life on a ideario of part comfronts the citizens so that sometimes the same idea of democracy or respect to the majority option of freedom is even questioned. This side division of the society supposes a serious risk of unstructuring that denies the same essences of the social concert for the communal property. Diverse interpretations exist on if a society unstructures by the intolerance of the parts, or if the society is divided in sides by structuring defects. This question, that concerns to the sociological studies, which leaves patent is that a society faced from intransigent positions the dialogue is a fractured society that generates citizens induced to the violence like means of reaffirmation of the own criteria.

The State, as form of arrangement of the social life, must favor the freedom of its citizens so that they are by themselves who identify the values on which they want to seat his personality. For favoured this freedom must promote the cultural diffusion that is sustained on the double performance of which all the groups have right to the free expression and communication, and watch over so that under the cultural appearance radical forms of dominion of the consciences are not created. The maximum negation of this doctrine is that it is the own State that, from the social group that structure like administration and government, directs the cultural uniformity of the citizens towards predetermined values.

The supreme value of the social arrangement he is the fundamental right to the freedom of the human person, and therefore any sphere of communitarian order must guard not to do violence to that right in his more intimate relation; this valid from the family and the her insertion in the clan, the political parties respect to the political order, the religious confessions with respect to the dictation of the moral, to the roll of the nations in the international order. For the promotion of that right against the effective power of chaste, estates and governments, are reason why the legal formulation of the essential rights of the person are contained in the Constitutions of the States and the emergent international institutions while the legal mechanisms for impose them within the framework them of the social relations.

7

Fields of Social Work

SOCIAL WORKER FIELDS

Social workers take on the awesome responsibility of helping those who struggle in the world to stay afloat. As a social worker, you will be a vital bridge for someone in need to accessing services and support for the provision of basic needs. This article is a look at the various areas of social work and the educational requirements for going into a career as a social worker.

What is a Social Worker?

Broadly speaking, social work is for people who want to help people, by giving them access to the resources they need to improve their lives and build brighter futures. Social workers try to help people make the most of their surroundings, their relationships, and their struggles with money or family. Many social workers deal with people who face life-threatening situations, such as criminal activity or substance abuse. Other issues that social workers try to address are inadequate housing, unemployment, illness, disability, or difficulties around childbirth.

There are various social work specializations, but the larger categories include child, family, and school social workers, who provide social services and assistance to children and their families; medical and public health social workers who provide support for people with illnesses, such as Alzheimer's disease, cancer, or AIDS; mental health and substance abuse social workers who deal with people who struggle with psychological issues; and social workers who deal with the intricacies of social policy and planning.

SOCIAL WORK, CORRECTIONS, AND THE STRENGTHS APPROACH

The theoretical framework for this paper is the strengths/ empowerment perspective, the approach which most closely parallels the rehabilitation model of correction. Both authors have worked in various capacities in the criminal justice system; the first author published a monograph on women in prison and later counselled offenders with chemical dependency problems; the second author worked as a probation officer for seven years in Oregon and Pennsylvania. Our purpose in writing this article is to present the case for the strengths approach in corrections, an approach which has been a recurrent theme in social work history and which is receiving increasing attention today.

Central to the profession of social work is a concern with social justice. According to the CASW Code of Ethics (1991 Preamble), "social workers are dedicated to the welfare and self realization of human beings... and to the achievement of social justice for all." And to the U.S. NASW Code of Ethics (1996:V1:6) similarly, "the social worker should advocate changes in policy and legislation...to promote social justice." The values of contemporary society, however, are sometimes clearly at odds with the ideals and principles of the profession. A politically popular and increasingly widespread reaction on both sides of the Canadian/U.S. border has been a "lock 'em up; throw away the key" mentality. Punishment comes first and treatment last under the modern political agenda, an agenda at sharp variance with the humanitarian and egalitarian ideals, which Robert Mullaly (1993) delineates as the cornerstone of social work's ideal society.

Social work has been promoting social justice for some time, all the way back to the settlement houses and children's aid societies. And until the mid-1920s, a substantial amount of social work effort, as Jerome Miller (1995) informs us, was directed at institutional wards of state — individuals confined to prisons, reform schools and the like. And long before that, the first days in the late 1800s in England, the charities and corrections movement regulated the poor by depriving the "undeserving" of aid. The two words, charity and corrections, in fact, were once used almost interchangeably (van Wormer, 1997). In later years, the mantle of professionalism, however, geared them away from authoritarian thinking and authoritarian institutions into work with troubled individuals in a variety of less coercive settings, namely, community mental health centres and child welfare. In the U.K. and Canada, and to a lesser extent in the U.S., social workers are becoming increasingly involved in working with offenders. Given the tremendous upsurge in drug related prosecutions, a heightened focus on substance abuse treatment is only logical. Treatment of sexual offenders, battering men, and their victims are other areas in need of enhanced social work services. Mental health counseling should be a high priority as well. An underlying assumption of this paper is that social workers, with their strengths, ethnic-centred awareness, have a major contribution to make to the field of criminal justice. Social workers have a contribution to make in terms of one-on-one counselling and in shaping policy.

The Contemporary Scene

The globalization and privatization of society are reflected in the homogenization of news stories: The aftermath of shootings in a schoolyard which would once have been merely regional news is beamed onto TV screens across the world. Meanwhile, newspaper headlines from Dallas to Winnipeg report on the urgency to crack down on crime, crime which according to the federal sources in both the U.S. and Canada, is actually on the decrease In Canada, according to a speech by the solicitor general, crime rates are down for the sixth year in a row (Scott, 1998). On May 13, 1998, banner headlines in the Winnipeg Free Press proclaimed, "War on Youth Crime." The Liberal Party proposes lowering the age limit to 14 from 16 for serving adult sentences and publishing the names of youths convicted of crimes among other harsh proposals (Samyn, 1998). Still, according to Turpin (1997) writing in Corrections Today, in the most recent Canadian election, crime was not a major campaign issue. This was in sharp contrast to elections in Britain and the U.S., however, where even the left wing parties came out on the offensive, calling for more police, tougher prosecutions and more law and order in general. Reflecting an Americanization of penal approaches, Britain recently has appointed its first drug czar.

Although Turpin correctly perceives Canada as much more subdued regarding criminality than the U.S. or Britain, it seems likely that there is a trend toward less compassion here too. The hype in international mass media, the impact of the global economy, the appeal of right wing zealotry to people who feel economically powerless, and contagion from events south of the 48th and 49th border—all bode ill for progressive criminal justice policies.

Ultimately, the current set of global economic and political forces that are driving countries to reduce their federal budget deficit combined with increased health care expenditures will lead to similar solutions. A study of U.S. and Canadian newspaper and Internet services reveals the following parallel political developments with special relevance to women: - Budget cuts to women's shelters; reduction in welfare benefits that would enhance battered women's escape from dangerous situations;

- A social climate in which the welfare state is seen as the problem rather than the solution that is especially hard on woman who as caregivers are more dependent than men on aid by the state;
- Gender-blind policies that often work against women as mothers are pushed into a low-paying labour market;
- As more men are getting custody of their children, women increasingly are required to pay child support; harsh punishments are meted out for women who break the law and keep their children after visitation;
- Rapidly increasing incarceration rates for women especially in connection with the international war on drugs; the U.S. saw the execution of two women in 1998; - Impact of racism and classism reflected in high percentage of convicted women who are aboriginal or of African or Hispanic descent;
- Recent scandals in women's prisons involving extreme brutality, especially in Georgia in the U.S. and in the Federal Prison for Women in Kingston, Ontario.

On the bright side, in Canada, as we shall see, the correctional system is being redesigned and decentralized for federally sentenced women; a wealth of innovative proposals has emerged following a spate of highly publicized reports of female inmate mistreatment, especially at the hands of male guards. In Canada, furthermore, there is a strong move toward the restoring of balance between offender and victim. This concept, which has become known as *restorative justice*, has been widely practiced in work with Native offenders and journals of all ethnic backgrounds.

A society's treatment of those who break its laws is widely regarded as a barometer of its social climate. Violent societies tend to mete out severe and often violent punishments as well as to provide conditions of oppressions ripe for the criminalization of citizens in the first place. Conditions of oppression are the breeding grounds of resentment and hatred associated with crime (Gilligan, 1986). In moralistic societies such as the U.S., a nation which has never been able to cast off the shackles of its Puritan heritage, and which has almost prided itself on demeaning work environments, dire poverty in the midst of plenty, a steady diet of horrible violence in the mass media, and high availability of guns, the climate is conducive to violent crime as well as to harsh punishment. Even when the crime rate is not particularly high in a given area, moreover, mass media highlighting of horrifying events from far away serves to incite fear in the general public and perpetuate crics for revenge. Kinder and gentler societies such as Sweden and Norway, in contrast, have much lower crime rates and much more humane treatment of criminals.

This is the law and order setting, then, in which the practice of social work makes its entrance. Social work, as we are all aware, is the profession dedicated to maximizing the dignity and worth of individuals and of reinforcing their strengths and resources. It is immediately obvious that these ideals of empowerment and empathy may create some conflicts for the worker in a system constrained by punitive legislation. And yet, for women under the jurisdiction of the courts, in circumstances of extreme disempowerment, the need for an empathic connection, an affirming voice, is paramount.

THE STRENGTHS PERSPECTIVE

At the heart of the strengths perspective is a belief in the basic goodness of humankind, a faith that individuals, however downtrodden or debilitated, can discover strengths in themselves that they never knew existed. The strengths or empowerment approach is a crucial part of effective therapy and increasingly articulated in the social work literature (Mullaly, 1993). No matter how little or how much may be expressed at one time, as Weick, Rapp, Sullivan, and Kisthardt (1989) explain, people often have a potential that is not commonly realized. A belief in human potential is tied to the notion that people have untapped, undetermined reservoirs of mental, physical, emotional, social and spiritual abilities which can be mobilized in times of need. This is where professional helping comes into play — in tapping into the possibilities, tapping into not what is but what can be.

Deficit, disease, and dysfunction metaphors permeate treatment at every stage of the process, from intake to termination (Cowger, 1994). In the criminal justice system, clients often find their very selfhood defined by their crimes. For such persons, whose views of therapy and of all authority figures are apt to be decidedly negative, a positive approach is essential to establish the one crucial ingredient of effective treatment — trust. Sometimes one encounter or one supportive relationship — whether with a teacher, social worker, or priest — can offer a turning point in a life of crime.

The most poignant example of a reversal of a life of crime, of a seemingly miraculous turnabout, was revealed to the world in the case of 35 year old Karla Faye Tucker, the first woman put to death in Texas since the Civil War. It is not her execution, however, but the loss of what could have been, that makes her case tragic. Here was a drug-addicted axe-murderer, turned born-again Christian, who helped fellow inmates and moved the hearts of compassionate people all over the world. " I'll be face to face with Jesus now," she said as she went to her untimely death.

Another murderer, Jean Harris, a high school principal at an exclusive girls' school, also committed murder in a drug-affected state, and she also found repentance and even a humility of sorts in prison. During her term at Bedford Hills Correctional

Facility in New York state, Harris was credited with setting up a thriving model Children's Centre operated by prisoners (Faith, 1993). During Harris's confinement and personal suffering, her attitude changed from bitterness and denial to love for her fellow human beings.

Let us briefly consider the relevance of the strengths approach for working with female offenders. These two examples — one of a woman born into the most miserable of circumstances, the other, a socialite — illuminate a theme we see expanded upon in this paper, the theme of personal empowerment. One of the major tasks of the professional helper is to facilitate such change. Within the justice context, the challenge consists of promoting personal power in people whose lives have become circumscribed to a varying degrees and whose very existence has been devalued and even criminalized.

Of special relevance to criminal Behaviour, and without which change is unlikely, is the taking of personal responsibility for one's actions and for one's life. The treatment relationship can serve as a powerful tool for helping the client change cognitive misconceptions that result in self destructive thoughts and Behaviour. Even in a life most crushed by circumstances of time and place, there nevertheless exists the potential for actions other than those (for example, heavy drinking, violent outbursts, etc.) that have become problematic. This belief in the human potential is at the core of the therapeutic relationship.

Brief Literature Review

We are dealing here with the literatures of two separate enterprises — criminal justice and mental health counselling. Whereas the criminal justice emphasis is largely on the state enterprise and legal prerogatives, social work, in its mental health component, has as its focal point, the individual within the system. And yet the two literatures share a commonality : Both are applied as opposed to strictly academic fields; both are closely bound up with the social and political forces of the day. Prison reform, innovative rehabilitation programs, and generous social services tend to go together. Preparation for war, mandatory sentencing laws, and spending cutbacks tend to go together also. The way criminals are treated in a society, in short, reflects the ethos of the culture.

Criminal Justice Literature and Rehabilitative Goals

To Theodore Zeldin, (1994) the most insidious impediment to compassion is a cynical or despairing view of humanity. This phenomenon, as Zeldin further states, can be illustrated by the experience of the U.S.: Disillusioned by mass media sensationalism in crime reporting, high criminal recidivism rates, debates over treatment effectiveness, and general political conservatism, legislators have turned to a punitive, severe sentencing approach that is immensely popular with the general public. In Canada, likewise, a public outcry against the leniency of the courts has tempered expansion of the kind of therapeutic programming that once was very much in vogue (Evans, 1995). Most of the vast expenditures in the U.S. criminal justice system, accordingly, are for law enforcement, punishment and custody, not for prevention or treatment. The predominant treatment modality utilized in correctional treatment programming today is the innocuously sounding Cognitive Skills Program.

Developed in Canada, the Correctional Program Assessment Inventory is currently in its sixth edition (Gendreau and Andrews, 1996). What Gendreau and Ross (1980) heralded as the cognitive revolution in corrections was inspired by Yochelson and Samenow's (1976) voluminous writings and popular workshops on the criminal personality. Based on their work exclusively with male antisocial offenders at St. Elizabeth's Hospital for the criminally insane in Washington, D.C., the "revolutionary" framework was designed to tear down criminals' defenses, the tendency, for example, of rapists and robbers to blame their victims for the crimes inflicted upon them. Van Voorhis, Baswell, and Lester (1997) praise Yochelson and Samenow's work as especially useful to counselors and custodial staff in correcting inmates' errors in thinking. Institutional staff are taught the following correctional techniques:

- Accept no excuses for irresponsible attitudes or Behaviours.
- Point out ways in which the offender may be refusing to accept responsibility.
- Call attention to, and do not accept "power thrusts."

- Teach offenders that trust must be earned, and call attention to other instances when the offender is betraying the trust of others.

These concepts are used with incarcerated DWI (driving while intoxicated) offenders in Iowa and also at the women's prison in Mitchellville, Iowa. In sharp contrast to the strengths perspective, this approach is exclusively negative. And yet the focus on cognitive errors is one which can easily be adapted (but from a positive rather than a negative perspective) to help women believe in themselves and in their potential.

One goal of what Bayse (1996) terms the moral-cognitive approach serves to encourage male inmates' awareness of how they described their victims so as to arouse feelings of guilt and self-disgust. Perhaps this focus may be warranted with the type of person for whom they were designed, the diagnosable psychopath or man without a conscious, no called the person with antisocial personality. Citing Yochelson and Samenow's work, Bayse (1996) further asserts that narcissism or self-centeredness is the central theme of the criminal's psychological makeup. The criminal views life, friendships, and even love with the thought of, "What's in it for me?" Helping victimizers to empathize with their victims, to stop devaluing them, is instrumental in helping them mature ethically and to quit using people.

Many men in trouble with the law, however, are non-violent offenders, and even many of the violent offenders are putting on an act of bravado for survival within prison walls. (Psychological testing, such as the Minnesota Multiphasic Personality Inventory [MMPI], can fairly effectively differentiate among various types of criminal mentalities.) The overwhelming majority of women caught in the throes of the criminal justice system have been convicted of drug offences or crimes of passion. Still others have been merely "in the wrong place at the wrong time" or are taking the rap for somebody else. Some have been convicted more because of poor legal defence than their own criminal Behaviour. Many of female offenders' problems most likely stem from addictive tendencies and/or relationship issues. They are in trouble with the law because essentially a public health problem has been criminalized. The narrow, one-size-fits-all approach can be downright detrimental to persons who do not fit the criminal blaming mold. Rarely is the strengths or empowerment perspective articulated as such in the criminal justice literature. A computer search of the criminal justice abstracts index (as of February 1998) reveals no listing for articles with the heading strengths approach or strengths perspective. A search through the criminal justice journals themselves, however, revealed a notable exception, a strengths-based practice article for work with adolescents (Clark, 1998). Writing in Federal Probation, Clark points us in the direction of a focus on solutions rather than problems, and a focus on youth capabilities rather than liabilities. Elsewhere, the empowerment concept, however, is used as a descriptive term for progressive work with juveniles, female victims, and occasionally female offenders according to the computer index. The gender difference in the use of an empowerment approach is striking.

Despite the absence of a comprehensive strengths formulation, several works on correctional counselling do infuse principles of a positive, client-oriented treatment philosophy throughout the chapters. As for example, Paul Haun's (1998), Emerging Criminal Justice: Three Pillars for a Proactive Justice System. Calling for reinforced community corrections and punishments for crimes that allow for non-restrictive environments, Haun proposes a restorative approach to criminal justice, one built on the concepts of community healing, social support, and innovative community based programming.

The American Correctional Association (ACA), a professional organization which advocates for the professional interests of workers in jails, prisons, and the community maintains a focus on rehabilitation and treatment as proper correctional goals. During the annual Congress of Correction, The ACA (1997) adopted the following policies for correctional professionals and agencies recommending substance abuse treatment and parent training programs to break the cross-generational "cycle of violence."

Paradoxically, the ACA also passed a resolution in support of more funding for jails and prisons. One would think that a moratorium in a new prison construction would be more to the point. On the other hand, continuing expansion of the prison industry guarantees unprecedented job opportunities for correctional personnel, so this perhaps explains the seeming inconsistency in professional policies. The ACA opposition to legislation barring color television or college courses or weightlifting options, in part, is an opposition to the loss of discretion by correctional authorities to exercise their best professional judgement to make rules for their facilities (Alexander, 1996).

The Correctional Service of Canada, similarly, seeks to maintain a balance between the stress on control of offenders and an awareness of the importance of assisting offenders to become law-abiding citizens (Griffiths and Verdun-Jones, 1994). Within the custodial facilities, accordingly, a wide variety of programs and services are provided, including inmate employment and vocational training programs. Consistent with the North American stress on individual responsibility, inmates must seek out their own rehabilitative programs; the responsibility for participation has shifted away from the providers to the offenders for maximum effectiveness.

A major criticism of the Canadian system of justice is the overcrowding of facilities related to the ever increasing portion of the population that is incarcerated. (Canada ranks third in the world in the number of adults incarcerated although a long way behind Russia and the U.S., each of which has almost three times the Canadian percentage. Canada's rate of locking up children is excessively high as well [Cayley, 1999]).

Descriptive studies of recent programming in the Canadian correctional system are provided by Kerr (1998) and Hannah-Moffat (1999). In Canada, as Kerr reveals, women's correctional programs are informed by five basic principles: empowerment; meaningful and responsible choices; respect and dignity; a supportive environment; and shared responsibility. The system, notes Kerr, is moving away from the old punishment paradigm into a healing paradigm. This programming, as we learn from Hannah-Moffat, can be traced to the reform strategies of the 1990s which culminated in a new woman-centred model of punishment. The Canadian concern with addressing the uniqueness of women's needs marks a sharp contrast to the U.S. feminist focus on equality — equalization of male/female prison opportunities, especially in the educational/vocational realm (van Wormer and Bartollas, in press).

As rates of imprisonment have soared in Canada, criticism of the situation has increased coupled with a search for new directions (Scott, 1998). A vision of justice as peacemaking rather than punishment is an encouraging development. Emanating from Mennonite church conflict resolution teachings and Aboriginal practices, this new but not new vision of justice has spread into the mainstream. The Correctional Service of Canada, in partnership with First Nation communities, has established federal healing facilities for Aboriginal offenders (Scott, 1998). The challenge, according to Scott, is to explore restorative justice options in all communities. Typically, the procedure involves the convening of family group conferences moderated by a state official to reach agreements on restitution when a wrong has been committed; the emphasis is on restoration and concensus rather than conflict. The reoffense rate for young offenders participating in this formality has been shown to be far below that of traditional approaches (Cayley, 1999).

Literature from the Helping Professions

Within the social work practice literature, a focus on client strengths has received increasing attention in recent years. The strengths perspective, as Kirst-Ashman and Hull (1997) note, assumes that power resides in people and that we should do our best to promote power by refusing to label clients, avoiding paternalistic treatment, and trusting clients to make appropriate decisions. Two popular textbooks, for example, Generalist Social Work Practice: Empowering Approach (Miley, O'Melia and Dubois, 1998) and The Empowerment Approach to Social Work Practice (Lee, 1994) incorporate the principle of strengths into every phase of the helping process. Although the literature consistently articulates the importance of a stress on clients' strengths and competencies, however, we must all be cognizant of the reality of standard clinical practice built on a treatment problem/deficit orientation, a reality shaped by agency accountability and the dictates of managed care. Third party payment schemes mandate a diagnosis based on relatively serious disturbances in a person's functioning (e.g., organic depression or suicide attempts) and short-term therapy to correct the presenting problem. Furthermore, the legal and political mandates of many agencies, the elements of social control embodied in both the institution and ethos of the agency, may strike a further blow to the possibility of partnership and collaboration between client and helper (Saleebey, 1997).

The strengths perspective has been applied to a wide variety of client situations: work with the mentally ill, child welfare clients, homeless women in emergency rooms, the elderly, and African American families. The concept of strength is also part and parcel of the growing literature on empowerment, feminist therapy, narrative therapy, client/person centred approach, and the ethnic-sensitive model. In his comprehensive overview of social work theory, Francis Turner (1996) perceives two common threads unifying contemporary theory. These are the person-in-the-situation conceptualization and a holistic understanding of clients in terms of their strengths and available resources.

In their article, "Empowering Female Offenders: Removing Barriers to Community Based Practice," Wilson and Anderson (1997) provide a prime illustration of strengths-based approach to correctional treatment. A key component of their practice model is the placement of competence and coping within a sociopolitical context. Empowerment practice with female inmates entails intervention directed at the economic, educational, social, and political structures of society in addition to strengths-focused individual and group therapy with women.

Effectiveness Studies

The Cognitive Skills Program, developed in Canada, has been held up as an exemplary, effective, and properly evaluated program (Matthews and Pitts, 1998; and Scott, 1998). A critical examination of the program and its evaluation, however, reveals serious flaws, according to Matthews and Pitts. The major failing of the evaluation is that it tells us very little about what works and what doesn't. Scott, in his position as solicitor general, declares that the Correctional Service of Canada is committed to a research-based approach. While recidivism rates for inmates in cognitive skill and sex offender programs have been reduced, according to Scott, we also know that programs offered in the community are more effective than programs behind bars.

Research on the effectiveness of female inmate programs are scarce (Loucks and Zamble, 1999). Research based on the strengths model in work with female offenders is even more scarce. Impressive results are being reported from New Zealand in correctional workers' use of family group conferences to address youth crimes; such conferences which resolve conflict through restorative justice avoid the negatives that accompany traditional sentencing practices. Costs have fallen dramatically and the reoffending rate significantly reduced (Cayley, 1999).

In his review of all the research to date on the strengths model of case management, Rapp (1998) concluded that although research is limited to two experimental (involving a control group), one quasi-experimental, and three non-experimental studies, results have been consistently positive.

The focus of the studies was persons with severe mental disorders, and the success rate was measured in terms of a reduction in the need for hospitalization and an unanticipated generalization of success in other areas such as sociability and community involvement. These positive results, although limited in scope, augur well for clients who are involved in a close treatment relationship for emotional problems, a relationship characterized, as Rapp terms it, by trust, friendliness, reciprocity, and purpose.

In a small scale program evaluation of therapeutic services at the Canadian Prison for Women, Kathleen Kendall (1993) confirmed the findings of previous reports which identified mental health and substance abuse services as critical programming areas for incarcerated women. The prison where the program evaluation was conducted had suffered the loss of seven inmates to suicide in a five year period; six of the victims were aboriginal. The program evaluation involved qualitative interviews with the 40 inmates and 20 staff members.

Because the perception among staff was that grueling therapy sessions with inmates had pushed them into dealing with disturbing aspects of the past, and over the brink into suicide, inmate perceptions were very important. Prisoners reported overwhelming support for the counselors at the prison. Kendall attributes the warm response to the feminist therapy approach and trauma expertise of the therapists. Identified as most helpful to the inmates were: assistance in taking control over their own lives, the opportunity to value and be valued by others, and the existence of mutually respectful relationships.

The feminist approach provided at the Canadian federal prison for women parallels the empowerment approach advocated in this article. Kendall describes the framework as consisting of the following components:

- A recognition of the close connection between women's marginalized status (e.g. poverty, abuse, sexism, racism) and their criminal activity;
- Stress on women's ability to resist violence in its various forms and to find creative ways of coping;
- The belief that as women develop a deeper awareness of their own strengths they will take greater control over their own lives;
- An awareness of the paradox that prisons generally remove whatever autonomy women have left, yet expect mature Behaviour from them, an experience reminiscent of earlier abusive experiences.

Kendall summarizes her findings by noting that although the therapeutic services provided by the prison were helpful, the creation of real choices for women lies in developing genuine alternatives to incarceration. Since her report was completed, the federal prison for women is being decentralized into regional centres for maximum community involvement. Further research is needed into the long term effectiveness of a strengths/ empowerment approach with adult female offenders.

MEDICAL AND PSYCHIATRIC SOCIAL WORKERS

Job Description

In the medical field a Social Worker may be involved in rehabilitating critically ill patients or those who face permanent disability. They are trained to help people to come in terms with their disabilities and also in counselling and giving practical assistance to such patients and their families.

Psychiatric Social Workers work in child guidance clinics or psychiatric unit of hospitals. They work with children and adolescents having behavioral problems, phobias, withdrawal symptoms etc. In hospitals they work with various kinds of patients like those suffering with chronic depression or drug addiction and help the Psychiatrist in finding out the root cause of the problem and thereafter continue to work as facilitators in the treatment process.

CHILD WELFARE

Demographic Situation

Children constitute principle assets of any country. Children's Development is as important as the development of material resources and the best way to develop national human resources is to take care of children. India has the largest child population in the world. All out efforts are being made by India for the development and welfare of children. Significant progress has been made in many fields in assuring children their basic rights. However, much remains to be done. The country renews its commitment and determination to give the highest priority to the basic needs and rights of all children. Children are most vulnerable to exploitation and abuse. A lot more has to be done for the health, nutrition and education of children. It is unfortunate that girls in particular face debilitating discrimination at all stages. Therefore, specific concentration is being given to the efforts to improve the life and opportunities of the Girl Child.

Constitutional Provisions

There are several constitutional provisions for children. These include the following.

- *Article 14* provides that the State shall not deny to any person equality before the law or the equal protection of the laws within the territory of India.
- *Article 15(3)* provides that, "Nothing in this article shall prevent the State for making any special provision for women and children."
- *Article 21* provide that no person shall be deprived of his life or personal liberty except according to procedure established by law.
- *Article 21A* directs the State shall provide free and compulsory education to all children of the age of six to fourteen years in such manner as the State may, by law, determine.

- *Article 23* prohibits trafficking of human beings and forced labour.
- *Article 24* prohibits employment of children below the age of fourteen years in factories, mines or any other hazardous occupation.
- *Article 25-28* provides freedom of conscience, and free profession, practice and propagation of religion.
- *Article 39(e) and (f)* provide that the State shall, in particular, direct its policy towards securing to ensure that the health and strength of workers, men and women and the tender age of children are not abused and that the citizens are not forced by economic necessity to enter avocations unsuited to their age or strength and that the children are given opportunities and facilities to develop in a healthy manner and in conditions of freedom and dignity and that the childhood and youth are protected against exploitation and against moral and material abandonment.
- *Article 45* envisages that the State shall endeavour to provide early childhood care and education for all children until they complete the age of six years.

Legislations

There are several Legislations pertaining to children. These include the following.

1. The Child Marriage Restraint Act, 1929.
2. The Child Labour (Prohibition and Regulation) Act, 1986.
3. The Juvenile Justice (Care and Protection of Children) Act, 2000.
4. The Infant Milk Substitutes, Feeding Bottles and Infant Foods (Regulation of Production, Supply and Distribution) Act, 1992.
5. The Pre-Conception and Pre-natal Diagnostic Technique(Prohibition of Sex Selection) Act, 1994.
6. The Persons with Disabilities (Equal Opportunities, Protection of Rights and Full Participation) Act, 1995.
7. The Immoral Traffic (Prevention) Act, 1956.

8. The Guardian and Wards Act, 1890.
9. The Young Persons (Harmful Publications) Act, 1956.
10. The Commissions for Protection of Child Rights Act, 2005

POLICIES

The National Policy for Children was adopted on 22nd Aug.,1974. This Policy lays down that the State shall provide adequate services towards children, both before and after birth and during the growing stages for their full physical, mental and social development. The measures suggested include amongst others, a comprehensive health programme, supplementary nutrition for mothers and children, free and compulsory education for all children up to the age of 14 years, promotion of physical education and recreational activities, special consideration for children of weaker sections like SCs and STs, prevention of exploitation of children, etc.

The Government of India adopted the *National Charter for Children* which has been prepared after obtaining the views/ comments and suggestions of the State Governments/UT Administrations, concerned Ministries and Departments and experts in the field. The National Charter is a statement of intent embodying the Government's agenda for Children. The document emphasizes Government of India's commitment to children's rights to survival, health and nutrition, standard of living, play and leisure, early childhood care, education, protection of the girl child, empowering adolescents, equality, life and liberty, name and nationality, freedom of expression, freedom of association and peaceful assembly, the right to a family and the right to be protected from economic exploitation and all forms of abuse. The document also provides for protection of children in difficult circumstances, children with disabilities, children from marginalised and disadvantaged communities, and child victims. The document while stipulating the duties of the State and the Community towards children also emphasizes the duties of children towards family, society and the Nation. The National Charter for Children was notified in the Gazette of India on 9th Feb., 2004.

India acceded to the UN Convention on the Rights of the Child on 11th Dec., 1992 to reiterate its commitment to the cause of children. The objective of the Convention is to give every child the right to survival and development in a healthy and congenial environment.

India is also party to the Millennium Development Goals and the SAARC Conventions on Child Welfare and Combating Trafficking of Women and Children in SAARC Region.

National Plan of Action for Children 2005 M/o of Women and Child Development has prepared a National Plan of Action for Children 2005 after harmonizing the goals for children set in the UN General Assembly Special Session on Children held in 2002 and the monitorable targets set in the Tenth Five Year Plan, and goals for children in related Ministries/Departments. The Action Plan has been prepared in consultation with concerned Ministries and Departments, States/Union territory Governments, Non Governmental Organizations and experts. The National Plan of Action includes goals, objectives, strategies and activities for improving nutritional status of children, reducing IMR and MMR, increasing enrolment ratio and reducing drop out rates, universalization of primary education, increasing coverage for immunization etc. The Prime Minister's Office is quarterly monitoring the National Plan of Action for Children 2005 on the basis of eight parameters. These are as under:

1. Reduce IMR to below 30 per 1000 live births by 2010.
2. Reduce Child Mortality Rate to below 31 per 1000 live births by 2010.
3. To reduce Maternal Mortality Rate to below 100 per 100,000 live births by 2010.
4. Universal equitable access and use of safe drinking water and improved access to sanitary means of excreta disposal by 2010.
5. 100% rural population to have access to basic sanitation by 2012.
6. To eliminate child marriages by 2010
7. To eliminate disability due to poliomyelitis by 2007
8. To reduce the proportion of infants infected with HIV by 20 percent by 2007 and by 50 percent by 2010, by ensuring that 80 per cent of pregnant women have

access to ante natal care, and 95 per cent of men and women aged 15-24 have access to care, counselling and other HIV and prevention services.

SCHEMES/PROJECTS

Several Ministries and Departments of the Government of India are implementing various schemes and programmes for the benefit of children. Some of the Schemes and Programmes being implemented by the Ministry of Women and Child Development are as under:

Integrated Child Development Services (ICDS) Scheme

Rajiv Gandhi National Creche Scheme for the children of working mothers: The Ministry of Women and Child Development has launched a *new Creche Scheme w.e.f. 1.1.2006 by merging the National Creche Fund with the Scheme of Assistance to Voluntary Organisations for Creche for Working and Ailing Women's Children* and also to revise the *financial norms from Rs.18,480/- to Rs. 42,384/- per crèche per annum.* The Scheme provides crèche services to the children of age group of 0 to 6 year, which includes supplementary nutrition, emergency medicines and contingency. The Scheme has been named as *Rajiv Gandhi National Creche Scheme for the Children of Working Mothers.* These crèches will be allocated to the Central Social Welfare Board, Indian Council for Child Welfare and Bhartiya Adim Jati Sevak Sangh in the ratio of 80:11:9. The priority will be given to uncovered districts/areas and tribal areas while extending the scheme to maintain balance regional coverage. Eligibility criteria under the Revised Scheme has also been enhanced from Rs 1800/- to Rs.12,000/- per month per family. So far about 25605 creches have been sanctioned including 5137 creches sanctioned under erstwhile National Creche Scheme upto 20th Nov., 2006

Nutrition Component of Prime Minister *Gramodya Yojana* and *Nutrition Programme for Adolescent Girls in 51 Districts* being implemented with additional central assistance given by the Planning Commission, directly and indirectly contribute to promoting nutrition of children. A National Nutrition Mission has been set up under the chairpersonship of Hon'ble Prime

Minister vide notification dated 31st July 2003 with a view to enable policy direction to concerned Departments of the Government for addressing the problem of malnutrition in a mission mode.

An Integrated Programme for Street Children is being implemented by the Ministry of Women and Child Development specifically for those children who are on streets and homeless and include the ragpicking and vagabond children. The Scheme aims at providing full and wholesome development of children without homes and family ties. The children without homes and family ties and children especially vulnerable to abuse and exploitation such as children of sex workers and children of pavement dwellers are the target group for this Programme. Financial assistance is provided to the NGOs who are eligible and working for the welfare of the street children, for Formal & Non-formal Education, Shelter Home, Vocational Training to Children, Nutrition, health care, sanitation and hygiene, safe drinking water, education and recreational facilities and protection against abuse and exploitation.

Integrated Programme for Juvenile Justice

The programme is being implemented by the Ministry of Social Justice and Empowerment with a view to providing care to children in difficult circumstances and children in conflict with the law through Government institutions and through NGOs. Some special features of the scheme areas:

- Establishment of a National Advisory Board on Juvenile Justice
- Creation of a Juvenile Justice Fund.
- Training, orientation and sensitization of Judicial, administrative police and NGOs responsible for implementation of JJ Act.
- Institutional care shall be used but only as a last measure by enlarging the range of suitable alternatives.
- Financial assistance to bring about a qualitative improvement in the existing infrastructure.
- Expansion of non-institutional services such as sponsorship, foster care, probation etc. as and an alternate to institutional care.

Childline India Foundation (CIF) has been set up as a nodal organization, supported by Government of India, to monitor and ensure the qualitative development of the Childline service across the country. Childline is a toll free telephone service(1098) which anyone can call for assistance in the interest of children. It has prescribed minimum quality standards for the services to be provided by its partner organizations that are implementing Childline programmes in various cities of the country. It initiates preparatory activity that precedes the initiation of Childline service in any city. CIF is also involved in awareness and advocacy in order to strengthen the efforts relating to child welfare.

The objective of the Shishu Greh Scheme is to promote adoptions within the country and to ensure minimum standards in the care of abandoned/orphaned/destitute children. Grant-in-Aid upto a ceiling of *Rs.6 lakh has been provided per unit of 10 children in a Shishu Greh.*

RECENT INITIATIVES

The Commissions for Protection of the Child Rights Act 2005 The Government has recently notified the Commissions for Protection of Child Rights Act 2005 in the Gazette of India on 20th Jan., 2006 as Act No.4 of 2006. The Act envisages setting up a National Commission at the National level and the State Commissions at the State level. The proposed Commission would be set up for proper enforcement of children's rights and effective implementation of laws and programmes relating to children.

The National Commission for Protection of Child Rights will be a statutory body to be set up under the Commissions for Protection of Child Rights Act. The proposed Commission will have a Chairperson and six other Members, including two women members, a Member Secretary and other supporting staff. The Chairperson would be a person of eminence in the field of child development. The members would be the experts in the field of child health, education, child care and development, juvenile justice, children with disabilities, elimination of child labour, child psychology or sociology and laws relating to children. The officers and the staff of the Commission will be provided by the Central Government. The proposed Commission would be set up for proper enforcement of children's rights and effective implementation of laws and programmes relating to children.

The Functions of the Commissions are:

- Examine and review the safeguards provided by Constitution or any law for the protection of child rights and recommend measures for their effective implementation
- Present to the Central Government, annually reports upon the working of those safeguards.
- Examine all factors that inhibit the enjoyment of rights of most vulnerable children and children in need of special care and protection
- Study treaties and other international instruments and undertake periodical review of existing policies, programmes and other activities on child rights and make recommendation for their effective implementation in the best interest of children.
- Undertake and promote research in the field of child rights
- Spread child rights literacy among various sections of the society and promote awareness
- inspect any juvenile custodial home, or any other place of residence or institution meant for children for the purpose of treatment, reformation or protection and take up with these authorities for remedial action
- inquire into complaints and take *suo motu* notice of matters relating to,-
  - (i) deprivation of child's rights;
  - (ii) non-implementation of laws for protection and development of children;
  - (iii) non-compliance of policy decisions, guidelines or and to provide relief to such children,
- or take up the issues arising out of such matters with appropriate authorities; and
- Such other functions as it may consider necessary for the promotion of child rights.

The Powers of the Commission include the following:

(a) summoning and enforcing the attendance of any person and examining him on oath;

(b) requiring the discovery and production of any document;

(c) receiving evidence on affidavits;

(d) requisitioning any public record or copy thereof from any court or office; and

(e) issuing commissions for the examination of witnesses and documents.

(f) forwarding any case to a Magistrate having jurisdiction to try the same and the Magistrate to whom any such case is forwarded shall proceed to hear the complaint against the accused

(g) recommending to the concerned Government or authority the initiation of proceedings for prosecution or such other action as deem fit against the concerned person/s

(h) approaching the Supreme Court or the High Court concerned for such directions, orders or writs as that Court may deem necessary;

(i) recommending to the concerned Government or authority for the grant of such interim relief to the victim or the members of his family as the Commission consider necessary.

State Commissions for Protection of Child Rights

- The Bill also provides that State Governments may constitute State Commissions for Protection of Child Rights in their State and designate a State level and other district level children's Court in their respective State.
- The Bill has similar provisions for State Commissions in respect of their constitution, reporting, functions and powers.

With the alleviation of the status of Department of Women and Child Development to an independent Ministry headed by the Minister of State having independent charge it was necessary to change the above provision to make the Minister in charge of the Ministry or Department of Women and Child

Development as the Chairperson of the Selection Committee for the selection of the Chairperson of the National Commission for Protection of Child Rights. Hence, the Commissions for Protection of Child Rights (Amendment) Bill 2006 was prepared which has been passed by both the Houses of Parliament in the Winter Session. The Commission will be set up once the above Amendment Bill is assented to by the President which would enable the Ministry of Women and Child Development to select the Chairperson and Members of the Commission for its constitution.

The initiatives are being taken for constitution of the National Commission for Protection of Child Rights. The Rules for implementation of the provisions of the Act in respect for National Commission for Protection of Child Rights have been notified on 31.7.2006. Ministry of Finance have also approved certain number of posts for the National Commission. Initiatives have been taken for appointment of Member Secretary and staff for the National Commission.

Offences Against Children (Prevention) Bill

Child abuse involves several aspects, such as, sexual exploitation, economic exploitation, domestic violence, trafficking for prostitution, corporal punishment at school, and others. Therefore, the Ministry felt a need to have a dialogue on the issue so as to ascertain the views from all quarters and to formulate a consensus in order to address the issue more adequately and effectively. Accordingly few consultations have been made with voluntary organizations and experts dealing with the subject. It has been decided after consultation to constitute a small group consisting of representative from Government, NGOs, legal experts and social workers which will go into all aspects of the subject and after considering all existing legal provisions and others available on the subject and formulate a draft legislation to address all issues pertaining to child abuse. After wide consultations a draft Bill for Offences Against Children was prepared and circulated to the State Governments for their comments and views. After obtaining the comments of concerned Ministries and Departments a draft Cabinet Note has been referred to Law Ministry for their vetting. The proposal will be placed before the Cabinet shortly.

Child Budgeting

The key objectives of the endeavour would be to analyse budgetary provisions on social sector, to identify the magnitude of budgetary allocations made by the Centre/State Governments on schemes meant for addressing specific needs of children, to examine the trend in child specific expenditure etc. The main agenda for the exercise of child budgeting is to review resource allocations related to children; explore ways to increase budgetary allocations for children; assess budget utilization rates for social sector and child specific programmes, identify blockages and constraints to effective utilization; identify methods for tracking expenditure and monitoring performance to ensure that outlays translate into outcomes for children

Proposed Integrated Programme for Child Services. As per the 2001 Census, there were 427 million children in the country. There are millions of children living in the difficult circumstances. The child protection programme in India is shared between various Ministries, which have been implementing the schemes and programmes to reach out to varied groups of vulnerable children with complex and diverse needs. The important schemes and programmes for such children include *Programme for Juvenile Justice, Integrated Programme for Street Children, Shishu Grih Scheme, Scheme for Working Children in Need of Care and Protection, General Grant-in-Aid Scheme, CHILDLINE Service, Rajiv Gandhi National crèche scheme for the children of working mothers, Pilot Project to Combat the Trafficking of women and Children for Commercial Sexual Exploitation in Destination Areas*, etc. However, experiences with the implementation of existing programmes and polices has brought out a large number of shortcomings in the system.

In view of the gaps identified and recommendations and suggestions received from various quarters it has decided to combine the existing child protection schemes under one integrated scheme titled "Integrated Child Protection Scheme". The proposed scheme aims to provide for care and protection of all the children in conflict with law and children in need of care and protection. It would involve steps to strengthen families and prevent them to breakup leading children to become homeless and without care and protection. At the same time, children already outside the mainstream need to be provided support beginning from emergency outreach services to final rehabilitation with their families/society. Details of the Scheme are being worked out which is proposed to be implemented in the Eleventh Plan.

OTHER ACTIVITIES OF CHILD WELFARE

Cooperation with UNICEF

UNICEF projects are being implemented in India through Master Plan of Operations, which is an agreement prepared after mutual consultation and consensus within the framework of Basic Agreement signed between India and UNICEF in 1978. India is the largest Country Programme of UNICEF in the world.

The Programmes are being implemented through various Ministries and Departments dealing with children which includes Ministry of Women and Child Development, Department of Elementary Education and Literacy, Department of Family Welfare and NACO, Ministry of Social Justice & Empowerment, Ministry of Labour, Ministry of Information & Broadcasting, Ministry of Youth Affairs & Sports, and Department of Drinking Water Supply (Rajiv Gandhi National Drinking Water Mission).

The Ministry of Women Child Development is the nodal Ministry for coordinating the implementation of the Master Plan of Operations. The Ministry of Women and Child Development conducts periodic review meetings to coordinate and monitor the implementation and expenditure of the UNICEF programmes in India.

The total allocation for the last UNICEF-GOI Programme of Co-Operation for the period 2003-2007 is US$ 400 million. An additional funds of US $ 100 million has also been approved by UNICEF for utilization in the current MPO period.

The current Master Plan of Operations for the period 2003-07 was signed by GOI & UNICEF on 13th January, 2003.

The MPO aims to achieve the following objectives: - (a) to empower families and communities with appropriate knowledge and skills to improve the care and protection of children (b) to expand partnerships as a way to leverage resources for children and scale up interventions (c) to strengthen the evaluation and knowledge base of best practices on children.

The programme contribute towards (a) reduction in infant and maternal mortality (b) improvements in levels of child nutrition (c) ensuring universal elementary education (d) enhancing child protection (e) protection of children and adolescents from HIV/AIDS.

The major activities included in different sectoral programmes are given below:

- Education
- Child Development and Nutrition
- Child Protection
- Reproductive and Child Health
- Child's Environment: Water, Environment and Sanitation
- HIV/AIDS
- Advocacy and Partnerships.

India is annually contributing an amount of Rs. 3.80 crore to UNICEF

Children's Day/Vatsalaya Mela

The Ministry of Women and Child Development organized a festival for women and children, Vatsalya Mela, from 14 to 19 Nov., 2006 at Cricket Grounds Taalkatora Gardens. The inaugural function on 14th Nov., 2006 was held at Vigyan Bhawan, in the presence of Hon'ble Prime Minister. The National Child Awards for Exceptional Achievements were presented to the 29 Awardee children on the occasion. A list of the Awardees is enclosed. About 600 children participated in the function which were brought by the voluntary organisation working for children. These organizations were ICCW, Prayas, YWCA, Salaam Balak Trust, Arushi Salaam Balak Trust, Deepalaya, Bal Sehyog, Anubhav, Don Bosco, Ashyalayam, Asha Deep, Angaja Foundation and Butterflies. Two organizations, namely, Amarjyoti and Akshaya Pratishthan brought the disabled children of the function.

The Vatsalaya Mela was subsequently opened by Smt. Renuka Chowdhury, MOS(WCD) in the evening of 14th Nov.,

2006 for public. MOS(WCD), an exhibition on issues pertaining to women and children was also inaugurated on the occasion which was organized by the Ministry in collaboration with NIPCCD, UNICEF and UNIFEM which was one of the attraction of the Vatsalaya Mela. The exhibition depicted various initiatives taken by the Ministry for upliftment of women and children and objectives and activities of institutions/ Departments working under the Ministry such as FNB, RMK, NIPCCD and CSWB.

There were nearly 40 panels which displayed the working of the Ministry and various themes relating to women and children like young child, child protection, girl child, women's empowerment, nutrition, security for all, etc. The Mela remained open from 9 am to 12 noon for school children and from 2 pm to 8 pm for public for 6 days from 14th November to 19th November, 2006. About 300 children from Government Schools run by the Department of Education, Delhi Government participated on each day from 15th to 17th Nov., 2006.

In addition on 18th Nov., 2006 children from two Government run Children Home namely, Ujjawal Children Home and Nirmal Chaya and five NGOs, namely, Angaja Foudation, YWCA, Butterflies, Salaam Balak Trust and Bal Sehyog participated in the Mela. There were 150 children from children homes and 150 from five NGOs.

These children were basically the street and working children supported by these NGOs. During this period there were cultural programmes and other performances for children. At the same time the children had opportunities for participation in various activities such as on the spot painting, essay and story writing, GK and aptitude test, debates and quiz, athletic and sports activities. There were competitions for the disabled children as well. Various competitions were organized for children who showed interest in essay competitions, drawing/ painting competitions, etc. The topics like child labour, national integration, education for women, street children, importance of education for girls, my mother, etc. were given in the essay competitions while themes like mother and child, a village – nature scenery, condition of women in villages, etc. were given for drawing and painting competitions. For undertaking these competitions children were provided with stationery items.

There were talent hunt competitions which included dance, singing, general knowledge, etc. The mela had facilities like music system and a dance floor. Children were encouraged to come forward and show their talent in these competitions. On the basis of the performances of the children prizes were distributed which were selected by a group of Judges.

The evening hours, from 2 pm to 8 pm, of the festival were devoted to women activities like cookery demonstration, mehendi, rangoli, street play, pottery, talk show, counselling, quiz, health check up, skill development, cultural programmes and others. All activities were enjoyed by women folk. It was an opportunity for them to move out of their houses and involve themselves in any of the activities of their choice out of the variety of activities organized by the Ministry for them. Exposure of Self Help Group Members towards potential items which can be made at a low cost and with ease was made feasible through this Mela. Women were also sensitized towards creative and skill development activities, healthy living as also enhancing leadership and capacity building qualities. The Mela facilitated the aim of increased participation and promotion of positive portrayal of women.

In addition to above there were food stalls, stalls of SHGs with their products for sale and exhibition, FNB exhibition, MWCD exhibition, health checkups, counselling, Bioscope, Long stick men, jokers, clowns,, mehendi kiosks, street play, folk dance, balloons, kite flying, women helpline, childline, Giant wheel, joy rides, etc. There were stalls by Child Line Foundation, Butterflies and Salaam Balak Trust displaying information about their activities and products made by children. The Child Line stall had a telephone line available throughout the period of Mela on which one could access to toll free helpline 1098 for immediate help of a child in need of care and protection. Lot of public attention was attracted at the stall by playing Child Line Song on a regular basis. The entry to the Mela was free for all. The festival was organized to raise the profile of the Ministry and dissemination of schemes and programmes of Ministry for women and children.

Ina function held in the Mela in the evening of 15th Nov., 2006 National Awards for Child Welfare and Rajiv Gandhi Manav Sewa Awards were presented by Shri Janardhan Divedi,

Chairperson, Parliamentary Standing Committee. A list of Awardees is attached. Shri Raghuvansh Prasad, Minister for Rural Development and Smt. Kanti Singh, MOS for Industries also visited the Mela on 16th Nov., 2006. Hon'ble Speaker for Lok Sabha also paid a visit to Mela to encourage the children on 16th Nov., 2006. Celebrities like Mr. Vivek Oberoi and Shri Kapil Dev also visited the Mela. On 19th Nov., 2006 the Stree Shakti Awards were presented by MOS(WCD) in the concluding event.

The mela was a grand success.

INDIA'S FAMILY WELFARE PROGRAM

At the outset it must be stated that 'family welfare' as a title is highly misleading because the entire effort of the concerned department is family planning, and that too mostly tubectomies. Other concerns of this department like child immunisation, ante-natal care, abortions, deliveries, post-natal care etc.. are only marginal; occasional spurts of activity like universal immunisation using a mission approach did change things temporarily but as routine set in, it could not be sustained and has again been marginalised. One doesn't have to give the gory details of statistics to show how miserable health care in general and specifically for women and children is. It should suffice to mention that access to basic services like basic medical care, facilities for child birth, abortion services, contraceptive services, pregnancy care, immunisation etc. are just not there when clients visit the primary health centres or other provider units.

While in the fifties, the state did put in efforts at building an infrastructure to deliver basic health care, these were abandoned sometime in the sixties when population control started to become the cornerstone of India's health policy. The first casualty of this new approach was the maternal and child health program with which the family planning program was integrated on the advise of a United Nations Advisory Mission to accomodate the loop program (the first ever IUCD program). The mch program had at that time just taken off in the rural areas with the setting up of subcentres and a large scale appointment of auxiallary nurse-midwives but both were hijacked by the newly created family planning department.

From then on there was no looking back and population control kept getting an ever-increasing share of attention of health policy, planning and resource allocations. This might appear to be an exaggeration because 'only' about 15% of the budget of the ministries of health goes to family planning, and hospitals and medical care get about 'as much as' 40% of the budget share. But it is not, because 80% of the 15% on family planning is spent in the rural areas and 85% of the 40% on medical services goes to the urban areas, which have only one-fourth of the country's population. Further, the entire health team working in the rural health infrastructure (as also those from other government departments who have FP targets to fulfil) spend an overwhelming proportion of their time on family planning related activities - this means they are forced to encroach on their time for other health care tasks.

The fate of all subsequent programs, like the minimum needs program and integration of health workers under the multipurpose worker scheme, the child survival and safe motherhood program, the community health volunteer scheme, universal immunisation program etc. was the same - all ended up serving more the interests of the population control program than adhering to its own objectives. And it is this that makes up the misery and tragedy of health care, and specifically women's' health, in India. If each of these programs had been implemented genuinely as vertical programs like the small pox eradication program or the malaria control program of the sixties (even though I am against the concept of vertical programs) some significant achievements in women and child health care would have taken place. I fear that the fate of the proposed reproductive and child health approach will not be different and it will end up being a mere change in nomenclature. Also, given the fact that it will be directed largely at women it is in all likelihood going to further strengthen the targetting of women for fertility reduction and again keep men outside the frame of responsibility for reproduction.

Further, it is said by many supporters of the family-planning program that if it were not for the agressive family planning program fertility would have been much higher in India. While one recognises the contribution of the family planning department in promoting contraception and increasing people's awareness about them it is too far fetched to give the credit of fertility reduction to the program. Fertility reduction has its own logic and worldwide it has come about only with change in people's objective reality, that is improved conditions of living, livelihood and social security. Conditions of poverty and large-scale inequities will normally not lead to the desired demographic transition. History bears witness to this!

SAYING NO TO A SEPARATE REPRODUCTIVE HEALTH APPROACH

While the elements defined in the package for reproductive and child health services are essential and must be provided it cannot by itself be an essential program. It must of necessity be part of a basic health and medical care program. Good quality basic health and medical care must be the starting point for meeting health care needs of a population and it must be made available universally and not linked in anyway to the ability to pay for it. One must also move away from the tendency of romanticising health care as was done with the community health approach (demystification, peoples health in peoples hand, non-medical model etc...). A basic medical model is essential and desireable (not over-medicalised as in the USA) and its social components must be constructed on such a base - doctors and nurses must form the base and paramedics and others must provide the support to give it a social and people-centred character, that is standing the classical community health model on its head ! I will come back to this later.

Thus, while recognising the importance of reproductive health, especially in a country like India which still has relatively high fertility, an overwhelming proportion of deliveries being conducted at home, often under unhygienic conditions, a supposed unconcern for gynaecological morbidities, an embarrasingly high proportion of abortions being done outside the legal framework, etc... it becomes even more important to emphasise the need for making available comprehensive health services to all, and especially to women as a group for their special needs. And as mentioned earlier the danger of beginning with reproductive health (as a separate or special program) is narrowing down the focus to the uterus, precisely what the women's health movement wants to avoid. Thus the demand must begin with provision of easily accessible and free of cost (at the point of care) comprehensive health care for all, with a clear recognition and provision for special needs of women, as well as of other vulnerable groups like children, the aged, tribals etc.

Thus, fitting the suggested reproductive health services, which have been well thought out, within a comprehensive basic health system should be the essential goal and not fitting it into the current family welfare framework. Hence one cannot but agree with the recommendations in the report about five specific actions to be taken - define a package of essential services; improve access to good quality services; make services more responsive to client needs; make sure that the frontline workers have the skills, support and supplies they need; and strengthen the referral system. But such a package, we emphasise again, must be one of comprehensive basic health care in which the package suggested by the report becomes an essential part.

It is important to emphasise a comprehensive package of total health and medical care because India's experience with separate programs for each major area of health problem has not only shown major failures but also resulted in wastage of the already small amount of resources which the public health sector is allocated from the state finances. Hence, its time that structural changes are made in provision and financing of health care and not by adding another set of special programs for a select group of population. We have done the latter for too long and wasted public money on programs which have been not only unable to fulfil their objectives but also have alienated people from the public health system, especially in the rural areas.

BASIC HEALTH CARE

While this is not the forum to discuss a detailed plan of action we can atleast define the provisions which should go into this comprehensive package in the context of the five specific actions stated in the Report under review. First, a list of services which comprehensives primary (or basic) care should include:

- general practitioner/family physician services for personal health care

- first level referral hospital care and basic specialist services - paediatrics, gynaecology and obstetrics, general medicine, general surgery, dental
- services and opthalmology, including special diagnostics
- immunisation services for vaccine preventable diseases
- maternity services for safe pregnancy, abortion, delivery and postnatal care
- pharmaceutical services - supply of only rational and essential drugs as per accepted standards
- epidemiological services, including laboratory services, surveillance and control of major diseases with the aid of continuous surveys, information management and public health measures
- contraceptive services
- health education and information
- ambulance services

The above must be viewed as a single package of minimum care which must be available universally and without any direct payment. They must be supported by secondary and tertiary levels of care, which are already quite well developed in India and only need to be reorganised in the new context. The provision of such care of necessity has to be a public-private mix (given the fact that India probably has the world's largest private health sector), with monopoly buyer/s, which need not be the state alone. This also means regulation, control and audit, none of which presently exist vis-a-vis the private health sector. And it goes without saying that special needs of women, including their reproductive health needs as discussed in the World Bank document will be an integral part of this package with each service available at the appropriate level.

THE PRIVATE HEALTH SECTOR

The private health sector as it exists today is not fit for collaboration in such a venture but its sheer size necessitates its planned and regulated involvement. The state has to start a process of planning for and involving the private health sector in the same manner in which it does with regard to many areas of economic activities. The myth of the private health sector being more efficient and of providing better quality care has already been adequately exploded in India and the time is ripe now to start the overdue need for its regulation, control and audit. In an organised public-private mix of health care services the private sector will play a dominant but regulated role at the first level of care, that is family physician services, as also participate in terms of its capacity at other levels.

FINANCING

With regard to financing it must be pointed out that vis-a-vis the overall budget the amount allocated to family welfare (over 17%, in 1994-95 Rs. 13.5 billion or $ 0.42 billion) is a substantial amount. And we must remember that with the current orientation of health services, resources from other sub-sectors of the public health system are also used for the family planning program, especially human resources. It is understandable that this amount is far less than what is required for the suggested reproductive health approach, but what is worse is that the overall health care budget is far more inadequate than what is needed to meet peoples' basic health care demands. We have to demand the overall increase of resources for the public health sector close to the WHO recommendation of 5% of the GDP. And we must remember that any provision within the limit of this ratio can in no way be termed as high cost. And we must also emphasise that presently all this cannot come from tax revenues and hence other avenues of financing, especially from the organised sector (employers and employees), farm incomes of the middle and rich peasntry etc. need to be tapped through insurance, social insurance, health care taxes and cesses etc. and not user charges which is by now an ancient concept. Thus the role of the state in organising the finances for such a system will be crucial and its responsibility of prime importance especially for the poor.

LABOUR WELFARE

Article 154 of the ROC Constitution stipulates that employer and employee should cooperate with each other in order to enhance business. Based on this principle, the Basic Labour Law was enacted, ensuring labour rights, establishing employer-employee ethics, increasing productivity, and promoting economic development.

LABOUR MOVEMENT

Labour movements are a natural phenomenon in developed nations. In addition to enforcing the Basic Labour Law, efforts have been made by the government to strengthen labour administration, upgrade labour service quality, guide and help union organizations, mediate between employer and employee, ensure stable production, strengthen guidance to contracting parties, implement bonus and dividend systems, and protect labour rights.

LABOUR WELFARE IMPROVEMENT

Labour welfare is the key to smooth employer-employee relations. In order to increase labour welfare, measures have been taken to assist working people obtain loans for purchasing and repairing housing to actively help solve their housing problems, build recreational facilities, upgrade labour education, assist enterprises and vocational welfare organizations to set up household necessity supply systems and nursery services, expand collective weddings and social get-togethers for unmarried workers, sponsor skill evaluation and competition, and establish a labour license policy.

There are now 6,826 labour welfare organizations in Taiwan, benefiting 958,770 people. In addition, for the purpose of better safety and sanitation conditions, the government has put emphasis on supervising and testing work conditions, especially safety devices, and appointed hospitals to accept workers' health insurance.

LABOUR INSURANCE

Labour insurance has been in force since 1950. It has succeeded in protecting the laborer and maintaining social stability.

Based on the labour insurance program, the government plans to establish an insurance program to cover all citizens by the year 1995. Through the end of 1993, a total of 8,144,183 workers had been insured under the labour insurance program. They paid US$7.46 billion but received US$23.33 billion in payment of claims, a ratio of 1:3.13 Medical insurance ranked highest, accounting for 59.45% of total payment.

Vocational Guidance

Rapid economic growth and population increase have made vocational guidance an urgent task for the government to undertake in order to fully utilize manpower resources. There are 22 vocational guidance centres dividing their operations into five different zones in Taiwan. With modern facilities and a complete network, these centres have successfully coordinated job opportunities and utilization of manpower. From Jan. to Dec. in 1994, 50,316 people found employment through these centres. These counselling centres have served to reduce the unemployment rate and the social problems and juvenile delinquency among unemployed youth. The unemployment rate in 1994 was 1.48%.

In order to meet the needs of the transforming social structure, to promote industrial improvement, and to accelerate economic development, the two vocational training centres in northern and southern Taiwan and regional employment service centres consult industry's needs and provide job training in, for example, lathe operation, furniture-making and plumbing, as well as other fields. Provincial Government owned banks have also been asked to provide starter loans to help young trainees open up their own business.

HARMONY BETWEEN EMPLOYER AND EMPLOYEE

In order to enhance the harmony between employer and employee, the Provincial Government has recently mapped out the five following points as a general guideline: (I) establish the idea of equality and respect between the two parties; (2) keep communication channels open between the two parties; (3) the employer should upgrade the benefits for the employee and the employee should fulfil his duties; (4) both parties should have a balanced rights and obligations recognition; and (5) resolve labour disputes in a spirit of fairness.

Labour Safety and Sanitation

In order to ensure labour safety and sanitation, the Provincial Government strictly supervises working conditions inspection, ordinary safety and sanitation inspection, vocational sanitation inspection, and dangerous machines or equipment inspection, as well as actively encouraging improvements in factory work environments, strengthening labour safety and sanitation services, expanding labour safety and sanitation regulations, prevention guidance and educational training. We are also actively promoting environmental monitoring of industry, promoting awareness of danger and pollution, implementing investigation and analysis of workplace hazards and studying preventive measures to forestall the occurrence of industrial accidents.

LABOUR WELFARE IN INDIA

"During the pre-independence period, industrial relations policy of the British Government was one of *laissez faire* and also of selective intervention. There were hardly any labour welfare schemes. After independence, labour legislations have formed the basis for industrial relations and social security. These legislations have also provided machinery for bipartite and tripartite consultations for settlement of disputes.

Soon after independence, the government at a tripartite conference in December 1947 adopted the industrial truce resolution. Several legislations, including the following, were enacted to maintain industrial peace and harmony: Factories Act, 1948, Employees State Insurance Act, 1948 and Minimum Wages Act, 1948. The payment of bonus act was passed in 1965.

In the early 1990s, the process of economic reforms was set in motion when the government introduced a series of measures to reduce control on industries, particularly large industries. The workers have opposed economic liberalisation policy for fear of unemployment while entrepreneurs have welcomed it in the hope of new opportunities to improve Indian industries. The new economic policy has directly affected industrial relations in the country, because the government has to play a dual role, one of protecting the interest of the workers, and second to allow a free interplay of the market forces. Economic reforms, by removing barriers to entry, have created competitive markets.

Fiscal stabilisation has resulted in drastic reduction in budgetary support to the public sector commercial enterprises while exposing these enterprises to increased competition from private sector.

Labour and Labour Welfare sub-sector consists of six main programmes viz. Labour Administration, Rehabilitation of bonded labour, Assistance to Labour Cooperatives, Craftsmen training programme, Apprenticeship training programme, Employment Services and Sanjay Gandhi Swavalamban Yojana.

Manpower, employment policy and labour welfare in India: post-independence developments:

Many researches has been done in the following themes, such as:

1. Manpower: trends and magnitude.
2. Employment policies and programmes.
3. Labour welfare: legal framework and initiatives.
4. Women workers: legislations and empowerment.
5. Industrial relations and labour laws.
6. Restructuring of labour laws: the great debate.
7. Labour laws and welfare: India and ILO.
8. Labour reforms: India and WTO. II. India's Five Year Plans at a glance. III. Edited extracts from India's Five Year Plans on employment and labour related matters (I plan to X plan including mid-term appraisal of the X Plan).

Strengthening of Medical wing of the Directorate of Industrial Safety and Health

There are different types of industries in Maharashtra like heavy and light engineering, heavy and light chemical industries, petrochemicals, pesticides, fertilizers, textile and Electronic Industries. All these pose their own potential hazards, which may cause acute and chronic side effects on the health of the workers. In Maharashtra, the chemical factories which include heavy chemical complexes or small chemical factories which may produce acute effects on the health of the workers to such an extent that it may result in death. Pesticides spilled on the body of the workers are equally dangerous.

IMPROVEMENT OF COMMUNICATIONS, MOBILITY OF FACTORY INSPECTORS

For the quick transmission of messages relating to factory accidents, gas leaks, fires and disasters in the area a broad network of office/residential telephones is an essential-requisite for the Factory Inspector, the concerned Dy.Chief Inspector of Factories, the Chief Inspector and from C.I.F.to higher authorities. Quick transmission of such messages to the area Factory Inspector and others not only facilitates a prompt inquiry into the mishap and its causes but also enables the concerned authorities to bring into action the various control measures in the case of disaster. An outlay for Tenth Five Year Plan 2002-2007 is Rs.150.00 lakh. Out of that an outlay Rs.5.00 lakh is provided for Annual Plan 2002-2003.

TRIBAL SUB-PLAN AREA

Labour and Labour Welfare

Labour sector addresses multi-dimensional socio-economic aspects affecting labour welfare, productivity, living standards of labour force and social security. To raise living standards of the work force and achieve higher productivity, skill up gradation through suitable training is of utmost importance. Manpower development to provide adequate labour force of appropriate skills and quality to different sectors is essential for rapid socioeconomic development. Employment generation in all the productive sectors is one of the basic objectives. In this context, efforts are being made for providing the environment for self-employment both in urban and rural areas. During the Ninth Plan period, elimination of undesirable practices such as child labour, bonded labour, and aspects such as ensuring workers' safety and social security, looking after labour welfare and providing of the necessary support measures for sorting out problems relating to employment of both men and women workers in different sectors has received priority attention.

The Central Board of Workers Education through its regional offices is striving to educate the workers to help to avoid wasteful expenditure, adopting cost effectiveness and by enhancing productivity of qualitative nature. They have been conducting the following programmes:

- Rural Awareness Programme.
- Functional Adult Literacy Classes.
- Short-term programmes for the unorganised sector to educate them on their rights, ethics and hygiene.

- Participative Management.
- Orientation Courses for Rural Educators.
- Leadership Development Programme for Rural Workers.

LABOUR RESEARCH AND TRAINING

V.V. Giri National Labour Institute, a fully funded autonomous body of the Ministry of Labour, conducts action-oriented research and provides training to grass root level workers in the trade union movement, both in the urban and rural areas, and also to officers dealing with industrial relations, personal management, labour welfare, etc. The Institute completed the following research projects during 1999-2000:

- Dynamics of Labour Market: Kerala.
- Women and labour Market.
- Labour laws, contractual parameters and conditions of construction workers.
- Adverse sex ratio and female labour force participation.
- Wage determination in rural labour force markets.
- Information on requirements for rural labour.

The following study was however of utmost significance "Study on payment of wages wholly in kind and perceptions regarding Mode of payment: A study in selected States". This Study was undertaken in pursuance of directions of the Committee of Secretaries at a meeting held on1.4.99 for the purpose of amendment to the Minimum Wages Act, 1948. The study was completed in four states, viz. Tamil Nadu, Maharashtra, Bihar and Punjab.

Bibliography

Banerjee, G. R. : *Papers on Social Work: An Indian Perspective,* Bombay, Tata Institute of Social Sciences, 1995.

Banks, S. : *Ethics and Values in Social Work: Practical Social Work Series,* London: Macmillan Press Ltd. 1995.

Bedi, M.S. : *Social Development and Social Work* , Himanshu, Delhi, 1994.

Bhalla, S.K. : *Social Work With Lawbreakers of Society,* MD Pub, Mumbai, 2008.

Borgatta, E. F.: *Encyclopedia of Sociology,* New York: Macmillan, 1992.

Chaturvedi, Pratima : *Social Work : Theories and Practices,* Book Enclave, Delhi, 2005.

Congress, E, P.: *Social Work Values and Ethics,* Chicago: Nelson-Hall Publishers, 1998 .

Das, D.K. Lal : *Practice of Social Research : Social Work* Perspective, Rawat, 2000.

Desai, M.: *Curriculum Development on History of Ideologies for Social Change and Social Work,* Mumbai: Social Work Education and Practice Cell, 2000.

Devi, Ranjna K. : *Social Work, Philosophy, Concepts and Dimensions*, Omega, Delhi, 2009.

Feibleman, J. K.: *Understanding Philosophy: A Popular History of Ideas,* New York: Souvenir Press, 1986.

Fink, A. E.: *The Field of Social Work,* New York, Henry Holt and Co., 1945.

Friedlander, Walter A.: *Introduction to Social Welfare,* New Delhi, Prentice-Hall, 1982.

Iqbal, Shaikh Azhar : *Problems of Social Welfare and Social Work*, Sublime, Delhi, 2005.

Katare, Prakash M : *Social Work and Folk Culture*, Arise Pub, Delhi, 2006.

Kumar, Hajira : *Social Work, Social Development and Sustainable Development*, Regency, Delhi, 1997.

Nagpaul, Hana: *Social Work in Urban India*, Rawat, Delhi, 1996.

Naqi, Mohammad : *Social Work for Weaker Sections*, Anmol, Delhi, 2005.

Parmar, P.M. : *Social Work and Social Welfare in India*, Sublime, Delhi, 2002.

Pascusal Gisbert, S.J.: *Fundamentals of Sociology*, Orient Longman Limited, 1973.

Ram Ahuja: *Indian Social System*, Rawat Publications, Jaipur and New Delhi, 1997.

Reamer, G. : *Social Work Values and Ethics,* Rawat, Delhi, 2005.

Rizwi, A K : *Social Policy and Social Work*, Mohit Pub, Delhi, 2008.

Sundar, I. : *Social Work Practices in Health and Medical Profession*, Sarup Book Pub, Delhi, 2009.

Index

A

Administrative Reform, 60, 61, 66.
Approach, 12, 39, 41, 42, 43, 45, 47, 51, 54, 57, 60, 63, 75, 80, 103, 105, 116, 134, 136, 140, 142, 144, 145, 147, 148, 149, 183, 203, 207, 235, 242, 250, 254, 255, 256, 257, 258, 260, 261, 262, 263, 279, 280, 281, 284.
Arya Samaj, 17, 57, 131, 140, 146, 147.

B

Backward Caste Movement, 22.
Brahmo Samaj, 17, 130, 140, 142, 143, 144, 145, 153, 157, 158, 159, 160, 161, 162, 163, 164.

C

Child Abuse, 51, 97, 273.
Child Labour, 224, 226, 270, 277, 289.
Child Marriage, 130, 143, 153, 231.
Child Welfare, 15, 95, 251, 261, 270.
Commissions, 63, 66, 206, 266, 270, 271, 272, 273.
Communication, 91, 134, 163, 180, 221, 236, 238, 248, 286.
Communist Movement, 170, 171, 175, 184.
Community, 1, 3, 7, 8, 12, 13, 14, 15, 24, 44, 67, 68, 69, 70, 74, 75, 91, 94, 96, 99, 100, 101, 103, 110, 115, 118, 122, 123, 124, 151, 168, 177, 189, 190, 198, 204, 226, 228, 231, 232, 234, 235, 236, 237, 238, 239, 242, 246, 247, 251, 258, 261, 262, 263, 266, 280, 281.
Contributions, 55, 59, 62, 80, 215, 244.
Criminal Justice, 15, 250, 251, 252, 254, 255, 256, 257, 258.
Criminal Law, 88.
Cultural Relations, 241.
Culture, 10, 12, 52, 106, 107, 108, 109, 111, 127, 143, 147, 148, 181, 185, 186, 188, 205, 214, 215, 216, 225, 238, 239, 240, 241, 242, 243, 244, 245, 246, 247, 255.

D

Dalit Movement, 23, 164, 165, 166, 170, 171, 172, 174, 175, 176, 177, 178, 180, 181, 182, 183, 184, 185.
Departments, 11, 13, 61, 71, 91, 184, 227, 231, 232, 266, 267, 268, 269, 273, 275, 277, 280.
Domestic Violence, 15, 52, 95, 273, 287.

E

Education Policy, 208, 210, 213, 214, 215, 221.
Empowerment, 69, 99, 173, 223, 226, 227, 228, 250, 253, 254, 255, 258, 259, 260, 261, 263, 269, 275, 277, 288.

F

Family Welfare, 282, 284.
Freedom, 4, 19, 20, 24, 29, 30, 54, 145, 158, 178, 196, 197, 198, 200, 205, 224, 239, 240, 242, 243, 244, 245, 246, 247, 248, 249, 251, 268, 269.

G

Gandhi, 19, 20, 23, 24, 25, 26, 27, 28, 29, 30, 31, 32, 34, 35, 36, 37, 38, 134, 139, 163, 186, 187, 188, 189, 190, 191, 192, 193, 194, 195, 196, 197, 198, 199, 200, 201, 202, 208, 214, 268, 274, 275, 278, 288.
Governments, 16, 48, 61, 66, 73, 91, 95, 96, 138, 152, 202, 206, 213, 217, 218, 219, 222, 248, 266, 267, 272, 273, 274.
Guidelines, 4, 246, 271.

H

Hindu Reform Movements, 138.
Human Development Strategy, 41, 43.

I

Indian Nationalism, 153, 157, 201.
Industry, 15, 218, 225, 258, 287.
International Federation, 2, 3, 68, 69, 70, 76, 99.

J

Justice, 1, 7, 14, 15, 16, 34, 66, 68, 69, 70, 81, 82, 88, 99, 100, 103, 158, 164, 179, 180, 193, 194, 228, 235, 250, 251, 252, 253, 254, 255, 256, 257, 258, 259, 260, 262, 265, 269, 270, 274, 275.

K

Kiran Bedi, 141.
Kothari Commission, 208, 210, 213, 218.

L

Labour Insurance, 285.
Labour Movement, 285.
Labour Welfare, 284, 285, 287, 288, 289.
Laws, 10, 11, 27, 55, 59, 60, 61, 65, 66, 78, 135, 136, 138, 150, 151, 152, 179, 188, 222, 253, 255, 264, 270, 271, 288, 290.
Leadership, 7, 19, 23, 110, 130, 133, 136, 143, 170, 171, 188, 200, 202, 278, 290.

M

Majority, 26, 28, 31, 33, 45, 46, 113, 152, 155, 170, 172, 174, 183, 186, 212, 248, 257.
Management, 3, 11, 12, 53, 54, 57, 72, 74, 94, 191, 204, 206, 210, 262, 283, 290.
Maternal Mortality, 267, 276.
Motivation, 128, 240, 241.

N

National Policy, 208, 211, 266.
Nationalist Movement, 128, 171, 176, 182.

O

Occupations, 22.
Organizations, 3, 7, 14, 15, 20, 23, 28, 54, 55, 56, 57, 58, 59, 61, 62, 63, 64, 65, 66, 74, 75, 91, 92, 105, 119, 133, 153, 204, 211, 213, 228, 229, 267, 270, 273, 276, 285.

P

Panchayati Raj, 229.
Peasant Movement, 18, 19.
Performance, 50, 64, 110, 111, 152, 213, 235, 248, 274.
Philosophy, 2, 10, 36, 37, 77, 78, 79, 80, 81, 82, 83, 91, 92, 93, 119, 136, 140, 153, 159, 170, 180, 185, 188, 190, 193, 194, 195, 196, 197, 198, 247, 258.
Policy, 1, 3, 7, 10, 15, 41, 42, 43, 48, 49, 61, 74, 75, 95, 98, 100, 102, 104, 136, 145, 174, 191, 206, 207, 208, 209, 210, 211, 213, 214, 215, 216, 218, 221, 226, 228, 234, 250, 251, 265, 266, 269, 271, 279, 280, 285, 287, 288.
Political Ideologies, 87, 88.
Political Organization, 109.
Political Participation, 243.
Politics, 2, 4, 37, 80, 81, 83, 84, 132, 133, 138, 167, 173, 174, 178, 183, 193, 200, 201.
Profession, 1, 2, 4, 7, 8, 9, 10, 11, 12, 13, 15, 16, 32, 69, 72, 74, 75, 76, 80, 98, 102, 103, 105, 107, 208, 220, 235, 248, 269, 273, 277, 288.
Professional Intervention, 74.
Projects, 8, 94, 197, 204, 237, 244, 268, 275, 290.
Prostitutes, 31, 41, 48.
Prostitution, 10, 31, 273.
Psychological Research, 90.
Punishment, 28, 194, 200, 250, 253, 256, 259, 260, 273.

R

Raja Ram Mohan Roy, 140, 153, 155, 157, 158, 160, 163.
Ramakrishna Paramhansa, 140.
Reform Movement, 128, 130, 131, 133, 134, 135, 136, 137, 140, 157, 158.
Rehabilitation, 96, 141, 228, 230, 250, 255, 258, 275, 288.
Relationship, 4, 5, 19, 28, 40, 53, 54, 75, 111, 128, 160, 171, 178, 200, 254, 255, 257, 262.
Relationships, 5, 14, 84, 89, 90, 95, 99, 150, 200, 232, 249, 263.
Research, 1, 2, 3, 7, 10, 14, 56, 57, 58, 62, 69, 70, 74, 80, 82, 90, 95, 97, 208, 214, 220, 221, 226, 229, 261, 262, 263, 271, 290.
Revolutionary Movements, 17, 135.
Rural Labour, 33, 290.

S

Sarojini Naidu, 20.
Sarvodaya, 190, 191, 196, 197.
Scientific Approach, 203.
Sexual Harassment, 50.
Social Control, 101, 102, 176, 260.
Social Development, 38, 39, 40, 41, 42, 43, 44, 82, 91, 225, 266.
Social Institutions, 17, 28, 37, 50, 53.
Social Movements, 45, 50, 51, 52, 135, 170.
Social Problems, 1, 7, 10, 11, 45, 46, 47, 49, 50, 51, 52,

53, 54, 71, 94, 97, 136, 286.
Social Reform Movements, 135.
Social Service, 7, 141, 199, 209, 241, 250.
Social Welfare, 1, 3, 8, 11, 23, 24, 26, 27, 33, 34, 35, 36, 37, 39, 40, 74, 88, 227.
Social Work, 1, 2, 3, 4, 6, 7, 8, 9, 10, 11, 12, 13, 14, 15, 16, 67, 68, 69, 70, 71, 72, 74, 75, 76, 94, 97, 98, 99, 100, 101, 102, 103, 104, 139, 203, 204, 227, 231, 232, 249, 250, 251, 253, 254, 255, 260, 261.
Social Work Goals, 7.
Social Work Mission, 7.
Social Workers, 1, 2, 3, 4, 6, 11, 12, 13, 15, 53, 67, 68, 69, 70, 71, 72, 74, 75, 76, 94, 95, 96, 97, 98, 99, 102, 104, 203, 232, 249, 250, 251, 273.
Society, 1, 2, 7, 9, 11, 15, 17, 18, 19, 20, 23, 24, 26, 27, 28, 29, 31, 32, 33, 35, 36, 38, 39, 40, 43, 44, 45, 46, 47, 49, 50, 51, 54, 55, 58, 60, 61, 63, 69, 71, 74, 77, 81, 83, 85, 86, 87, 88, 90, 91, 94, 98, 100, 101, 108, 109, 110, 111, 117, 118, 125, 126, 127, 128, 129, 130, 131, 133, 134, 135, 140, 141, 143, 145, 147, 148, 150, 151, 152, 153, 157, 161, 162, 166, 167, 168, 169, 171, 172, 175, 176, 177, 185, 188, 190, 191, 193, 194, 195, 196, 197, 199, 201, 203, 213, 226, 227, 235, 236, 239, 241, 243, 244, 245, 247, 248, 250, 251, 255, 261, 266, 271, 275.
Swami Vivekananda, 139, 140, 148.

T

Technology, 2, 180, 192, 206, 213, 218.

U

Untouchability, 23, 26, 32, 33, 146, 193, 199, 202.

V

Violence, 15, 20, 21, 22, 24, 25, 26, 27, 34, 35, 37, 45, 52, 95, 97, 163, 186, 189, 190, 191, 192, 193, 194, 195, 196, 199, 200, 201, 202, 203, 246, 248, 253, 258, 263, 273.
Voluntary Association, 216, 233.
Voluntary Organizations, 28, 54, 55, 57, 58, 61, 62, 66, 211, 229, 273.
Voluntary Sector, 60, 62, 227.

W

Welfare, 1, 3, 6, 8, 11, 15, 16, 23, 24, 26, 27, 33, 34, 35, 36, 37, 38, 39, 40, 55, 56, 61, 72, 74, 88, 94, 95, 133, 161, 163, 181, 183, 184, 190, 191, 194, 197, 226, 227, 228, 229, 250, 251, 252, 261, 264, 267, 268, 269, 270, 275, 278, 282, 284, 285, 287, 288, 289, 290.
Widows, 130, 133, 146, 150, 156, 157, 162.
Wisdom, 158, 216, 238, 240.

□□□